# Questions

# on

# Revelation

# Questions on Revelation
## Larry Wilson

Copyright©1993

**To Order:**
**Wake Up America Seminars, Inc.**
**P.O. Box 273**
**Bellbrook, Ohio 45305**
**(513) 848-3322**

First Edition, June 1989
Second Edition, September 1993

*Published by*

**TEACH Services, Inc.**
Donivan Road
Route 1, Box 182
Brushton, New York 12916

# Acknowledgements

This book is dedicated to those within the Seventh-day Adventist Church who search the Scriptures daily to find present truth. "Let no one come to the conclusion that there is no more truth to be revealed.... There is no excuse for anyone in taking the position that there is no more truth to be revealed, and that all our expositions of Scripture are without error. The fact that certain doctrines have been held as truth for many years by our people, is not proof that our ideas are infallible. Age will not make error into truth, and truth can afford to be fair. No true doctrine will lose anything by close investigation." (Ellen White, *Counsels to Writers and Editors*, p. 35.)

Special appreciation is due to Suzy and Sharon for their help on this edition. I am deeply indebted to a dedicated staff (paid and unpaid), generous volunteers and a rapidly growing number of wonderful people who support this unique ministry.

Wake Up America Seminars, Inc. is a non-profit religious organization. WUAS is not affiliated, endorsed nor sponsored by any religious denomination. Our mission is singular, we herald the salvation and imminent return of our Lord Jesus Christ through whatever means possible.

# Mine Eyes Have Seen the Glory

### Julia Ward-Howe, 1861

Mine eyes have seen the glory
of the coming of the Lord.
He is trampling out the vintage
where the grapes of wrath are stored.
He has loosed the faithful lightning
of His terrible swift sword,
His truth is marching on.

He has sounded forth the trumpet
that shall never call retreat.
He is sifting out the hearts of men
before His judgment seat.
O be swift my soul to answer Him
be jubilant my feet,
Our God is marching on.

In the beauty of the lilies
Christ was born across the sea.
With a glory in His bosom
that transfigures you and me.
As He died to make men holy
Let us live to make men free,
While God is marching on.

Glory, Glory Hallelujah!
Glory, Glory, Hallelujah!
Glory, Glory, Hallelujah!
His truth is marching on.

# Questions on Revelation
# Table of Contents

Chapter 1. Introduction ........................................................ 1

Chapter 2. Historical perspectives and comparisons ................ 21

Chapter 3. Prophets can make mistakes ............................... 47

Chapter 4. Problems with prophetic interpretation ................. 71

Chapter 5. A study on the close of two probations ................ 95

Chapter 6. The 144,000 will soon appear ........................... 123

Chapter 7. Jesus in the Most Holy Place in A.D. 64? .......... 141

Chapter 8. The coming wrath of God, the 1,335 days
and the shaking .............................................. 157

Chapter 9. Questions on Armageddon ................................ 175

Chapter 10. Questions on Christ's righteousness ................... 193

# Introduction

The first edition of this volume was published in 1989. It was written for the Seventh-day Adventist reader because Adventists have a unique set of considerations on Bible prophecy that goes beyond the concern of most Christians. My books, *Warning! Revelation is about to be fulfilled, The Revelation of Jesus* and *18 End-Time Bible Prophecies,* were written for people who base their faith on the Bible alone; therefore, those books do not specifically address Adventist issues or the Adventist mindset. Now that more than one hundred thousand books have been distributed, a number of Adventists have asked for a response to a number of questions. And often, the first two topics that come up are my variances with the historical claims of prophetic fulfillment taught by the Church and the writings of Ellen White.

When the first edition of this book was published, my views on prophecy were not widely known. Now that four years have passed and the reaches of this ministry have grown exponentially, I have noticed that many of the same questions keep surfacing again and again as people begin to understand the message that I share. Therefore, this edition of *Questions on Revelation* is expanded beyond the contents of the first edition. Also, this edition contains a few articles from past editions of our monthly publication, *Day Star,* that address key Adventist questions about prophecy in general, and Revelation in particular. Therefore, the reader should regard each chapter in this book as a stand-alone unit that contributes to the overall theme of *Questions on Revelation.* The Bible contains immense treasure, and those who search for it must be patient, willing to explore many hours before they find the beautiful threads of gold. Even then, it takes many threads, to produce a handsome cloth.

My hope is that Adventists and non-Adventists alike will find something in this book that will be helpful and meaningful. I recommend this book to non-Adventists for the same reason that I recommend the Old Testament to non-Jews. The better one understands the origin of ideas, the more likely he will appreciate the disputes or the improvements that follow.

## Early interest

I have had a special attraction for the Bible for many years and I continue to have a deep desire to know what the Bible contains. For more than 23 years, I have studied and investigated the Bible, especially the books of Daniel and Revelation. If I were to sum up my findings in a sentence it would be this: The contents of The Plan of Salvation can only be seen when one synthesizes the whole of Scripture. In other words, I approach the Bible as a book containing many clues about God and His plan to save man. As I become acquainted with various clues, I begin to see how they interconnect with each other to reveal God's grace, love, power, justice and mercy. I know the words "The Plan of Salvation" are often said, but few people really understand that salvation's process was *planned* from the very beginning. Who can surprise God? For many years I have been gathering all of the clues about the Plan that I could find. I continue to study them so I can *see* salvation's process for myself and I testify that my appreciation for God's plan is greater than ever.

My journey toward prophetic understanding can be divided into four phases: an investigative phase, a paradigm shift, the discovery of a predictable design and finally, the dissemination of my findings. (A paradigm shift is a total melt-down of previously held ideas and the reconstruction of a new view.)

From 1970 until 1976, I studied and examined my *inherited* position on prophecy. I use the word inherited to emphasize the idea that when one becomes part of a church, either through birth or rebirth, he doesn't necessarily understand *everything* the church teaches. He may understand enough to be a member, but it takes time and effort to fully examine everything any church teaches. And frankly, most people don't care enough about knowing *everything* to invest the time and effort that such research requires.

The paradigm shift began around 1976. By that time, I was convinced that my church, the Seventh-day Adventist Church, was putting some round pegs in square holes when it came to the interpretation of prophecy. I found that some of the Church's positions failed to maintain fidelity to Bible text, some conclusions lacked scriptural support and some claims of prophetic fulfillment lacked historical confirmation. As I studied the origin of the Church's prophetic framework, I discovered how many of the Church's positions came to be, but understanding how things came to be is no substitute for truth. As one Adventist pioneer once said, "One text is of more value than ten thousand words of explanation."

I could not offer an explanation for every verse in Daniel or Revelation in 1976, so I couldn't say much about the Church's positions that didn't seem accurate. I did conduct a number of Revelation Seminars between 1977 and 1980 using Revelation materials prepared by the Texas Conference of Seventh-day Adventists and these materials only raised more questions in my mind than they answered. But, keep in mind that prophecy is a broad subject and fellowship with "the Body of Christ" does not require agreement on *every* verse in the Bible. Therefore, I saw no reason to openly quibble about my uncertainties, but I continued to search for understanding.

After while, I began asking Adventist scholars, teachers and preachers about the properties of inspiration because I had reached a brick wall in my personal study. I could not resolve a number of passages in Daniel and Revelation with the views of Ellen White. Adventists hold that Ellen White was a prophetess, inspired by God just like Paul, John and Peter. And, by 1978 I began wondering if Ellen White's writings were a complete and inerrant exposition on the meaning of prophecy. Many pastors assured me that Ellen White was fallible, but none of them could identify one instance of prophetic error. They assured me that her prophetic views were in full agreement with the Bible. I found a certain irony in their admission that she was fallible because no one had ever proven from the Bible that she was. It seemed a lot like the Catholic position on the infallibility of the pope. Yes, Protestants deny the claim, but Catholics cannot find one instance where the pope has made a mistake when speaking *ex cathedra*.

Months passed and I could not resolve how inspiration worked. I began to examine Ellen White, specifically the Adventist mindset about her. I found that Adventists generally follow this logic: The Bible is the Word of God. The Bible was written by inspired men and women. Because human beings are finite, the Bible contains a few discrepancies, but in terms of the expressed will of God, the Bible is the infallible Word of God. Ellen White was inspired just like the writers of the Bible. Therefore, the writings of Ellen White are at a minimum, on par with the Bible.

Her writings are a modern-day infallible explanation of truth, revealing the expressed will of God.

I call this logic the "White Principle" because many Adventists use this logic to either exalt the writings of Ellen White *above* the Bible or they trust Ellen White's view of the Bible more than they trust their own. I italicized the word "above" because many Adventists unconsciously make Ellen White the final authority on truth. My claim can be proven by presenting Adventists with a prophetic challenge. Many Adventists will appeal to Ellen White, "the inspired servant of the Lord," for proof of their position rather than the Bible. Doesn't this practice reveal the higher authority? If this practice were to continue for a few more centuries, would her writings altogether shadow the importance and the authority of the Bible?

I don't find the writings of Ellen White to be on par with the Bible. And my rejection of the "White Principle" significantly reduces the number of Adventists willing to examine my prophetic position. For example, when I challenge Adventists with the contents of Revelation 11:13, they will often refuse to discuss the meaning of the verse. (For the reader's sake, the verse says: **"At that very hour there was a severe earthquake and a tenth of the city collapsed. Seven thousand people were killed in the earthquake, and the survivors were terrified and gave glory to the God of heaven."**) Adventists can't explain this verse even though they claim it has been fulfilled. They can't identify the location of the earthquake nor the date it took place. Neither can they identify the 7,000 people that perished in the earthquake. But, many Adventists will reject any explanation of Revelation 11:13 that is different than Ellen White's view of Revelation 11:1-13 which dates back to the French Revolution.

## Two different subjects

It's a difficult situation. How can one discuss the meaning of Revelation 11:13 with Adventists who insist that they can't discuss the Bible without including the writings of Ellen White? Devout Adventists read the writings of Ellen White very often and very closely. Therefore, prophetic ideas that run contrary to her writings are usually detected and rejected rather quickly. In April, 1993, I was holding a seminar in Sacramento, California, and the audience was two-thirds Adventists and one-third, non-Adventist. Our sponsors had rented a building on the grounds of a lovely park because the meeting was open to the public. I fully explained at the beginning of the seminar that the content of my seminar was based upon the Bible and the Bible only. (When conducting a seminar, I present this principle at the very beginning as well as the fact that Wake Up America Seminars is not endorsed nor sponsored by any religious organization.)

As the seminar progressed, a number of Adventists became very irate with me because I was presenting a view of prophecy that is quite different than the views of Ellen White. They interrupted the meeting several times with shouts from the back of the building that my views were wrong — contrary to the "servant of the Lord," Ellen White. At a break in the seminar, a rather agitated group of Adventists gathered around me, and among them was a hostile dentist who demanded to know if I believed that Ellen White was wrong in some of her views about end-time events. I answered, "Yes." My antagonist responded with an emotional burst and he angrily denounced me as a false prophet. (I have never claimed to be a prophet — either true or false!) He said that he was going to pray for me that I should stop leading people astray with these falsehoods. If words were stones, I would have been stoned right there! But, the most interesting point about such confrontations is this: Few of my adversaries will open the Bible and attempt to explain Revelation.

The non-Adventists in the Sacramento seminar saw the tension. They did not understand all of the issues behind the hostility, but they did gain a quick perspective on the power of new or different ideas. Non-Adventists are often repulsed when they see Adventists insisting that Ellen White's view of the Bible is infallible. I suspect Adventists are often called a religious cult, not because of doctrine, but because of the way they deal with the writings of Ellen White. (A religious cult is defined as a body of people having or appealing to external authority outside the Bible.) Many Adventists would rather defend the inerrancy of Ellen White than investigate the textual content of Daniel and Revelation. Therefore, it should not come as a surprise that a profitable conversation is impossible between those who insist on interpreting Bible prophecy using the Bible alone and those who insist on interpreting Bible prophecy using Ellen White's writings.

As I see it today, the root problem with the Adventist position on prophecy is this: Many Adventists find no distinction between the writings of Ellen White and the Bible. The line has become blurred. Many believe that her writings are a modern-day version of the Word of God. Specifically, many believe that Ellen White's book, *The Great Controversy,* is an accurate road-map of end-time events and they are enthusiastically distributing millions of copies. They believe that Ellen White and the Bible have equal authority and one is simply an extension of the other. If such a view were true, then prophetic understanding cannot develop any further. Ellen White is dead. Her understanding of prophecy was limited and it now remains unchangeable. Did she know everything about prophecy? Did God reveal everything there is know about prophecy to her? No. And, she clearly stated that more light on prophecy was forthcoming. Truth is ever unfolding and Paul clearly summed up the limitations of prophets when he said, **"For we know in part and we prophesy in part."** (1 Corinthians 13:9) Could it be that the Jews of old killed the prophets of God because greater truths than those written by Moses were revealed later on?

I know my observations and conclusions will not set well with many Adventists. I can't help that. I fully expect that adversaries will wrest certain statements from their context to make me look foolish. But, the compelling issue before all of us is not friendship, fellowship or even Ellen White. The issue facing all nations is God's soon coming actions. What does the Bible predict that God is going to do? What does the Bible say the next prophetic event will be? What should we be watching and waiting for?

I hope this book will cause everyone, Adventist and non-Adventist alike, to reconsider his prophetic positions. Even though I find Ellen White to be fallible (wrong on a few prophetic points), she remains a true prophetess to me. Ellen White did not know everything. She clearly said so. Paul didn't know everything and he said so. How could they know everything when the book of Daniel was sealed up until the end of time? (Daniel 12:4,9) Yes, I know some Adventists say that the end of time began in 1844. If that is the case, then how much longer does the end of time last?

Every Adventist knows that Ellen White said she was a lesser light leading people toward the greater light, the Bible. And Ellen White's writings are not to be treated as an extension of the Bible. We must continuously test and retest the views of all prophets as God continues to reveal more truth to us. If Seventh-day Adventists are truly Protestant, they should press the Protestant banner higher. They should be foremost in saying: "The Bible and the Bible *alone* as the rule of faith." But, this isn't happening today. Why?

## Keep the line distinctive

The Adventist Church should not treat Ellen White as an external authority to the Bible and neither should the Church disdain the writings of Ellen White. Both have their distinctive place and value. When I say that Ellen White's view of prophecy is wrong in some areas, this produces a lot of grief for some Adventists. Adventists often respond to such remarks by saying one of two things: Either she was a true prophet, or she was a false prophet. (These words really mean: Either she was God's infallible servant or she was a liar — there is no middle ground.) Or, Adventists will say: How can you pick and choose from her writings the things that are true and the things which are not? (These words really mean: How can *you, heretic Larry Wilson,* tell us what was inspired and thus infallible and what was not inspired?) The point here in both cases, is the assumption that inspired people are infallible. Because most human beings receive this assumption as a basic truth, this problem is most pervasive and very hard to detect. In fact, the only way to test for it is to either find error or more truth! I'll come back to this point in a moment. For now, just remember there can be a big difference between truth and that which is called truth.

The assumption that inspired people are infallible is not limited to Adventists. Roman Catholics believe the pope is inspired. Therefore, they add papal infallibility and Church traditions to the authority of the Bible. Christian Scientists believe that Mary Baker Eddy was inspired. Therefore, they add her writings to the Bible. Mormons believe that Joseph Smith was inspired. So, the Book of Mormon stands on par with Scripture. Jehovah's Witnesses have gone one step further. Rather than add the writings of Charles Russell to the Bible, they rewrote the Bible according to Charles Russell. Islam has displaced the Bible with its own authority — the Koran. I bring up these points because the word "cult," as defined earlier, actually includes a lot of people on this planet! And someday soon, I anticipate that the properties of inspiration will become a hotly debated subject among these religious bodies.

## Back to the paradigm shift

So, 1976 - 1982 was a period of confusion and reorganization for me. I went through a complete paradigm shift. What I once thought to be true became obsolete. My understanding of the properties of inspiration changed during that time. My understanding of the writings of Peter, John, Paul *and* Ellen White changed. Although I didn't recognize it back then, these changes opened an important door to a new perspective on the Bible. As a result, I became even more inquisitive about the Bible and I pressed on to understand the prophecies.

Around 1980, two things happened within the Adventist Church that were seen as threats, but I now believe they were clouds with silver linings. First, the apotelesmatic view of prophecy, offered by Dr. Desmond Ford from Pacific Union College, was reviewed by a large number of Adventist leaders and scholars at the Glacier View Summit in Colorado. In essence, Dr. Ford claimed that the apocalyptic prophecies of Daniel and Revelation can have multiple or partial fulfillments. Church leaders reviewed and rejected his claims on the basis that apocalyptic prophecy has one fulfillment. The Adventist Church correctly teaches that the fulfillment of prophecy occurs in a progressive, non-repeating pattern. The Church also concluded that prophecy behaves in a consistent way. Therefore, all interpretations must conform to valid rules of interpretation.

The second shock wave was Walter Rea's demonstration that considerable portions of Ellen White's writings were not her own. Using computers to scan and compare text, Rea found large sections of Ellen White's books were, in many cases, copied word for word from the writings of other religious authors. This revelation caused a strong stir among those who believed that Ellen White's writings were totally original, given to her by God.

Neither of these events influenced my study. After four or five hours of investigation, I rejected Dr. Ford's presupposition of multiple fulfillments on the grounds that multiple fulfillments reduce the intended meaning of prophecy to putty. In plain English, this means that prophecy in the hands of a skilful manipulator can mean one thing at this time and something else at another time. I also found Walter Rea's discovery to be consistent with my newly acquired understanding of inspiration, so I wasn't disappointed to learn that Ellen White had liberally copied from others.

My view of inspiration is that God shines a *spotlight* on some aspect of a subject and the inspired person *sees* that component of truth. Then, after the vision is finished, the seer attempts to explain in his own words what he has seen. In some cases, he may need to study the subject more fully on his own to more fully understand what he saw and how it fits into the body of existing truth. (In fact, Paul went to the desert for three years after receiving visions so that he could figure out the things he had been shown. See Galatians 1:16-18.) I know that after the Rea discovery was widely circulated, many Adventists either denounced Ellen White as a true prophet or they defended her inerrancy by saying, "Well, she was shown what to copy and what not to copy." As far as I was concerned, both responses were inappropriate. The response of both groups stems from an improper understanding of inspiration. (And, Adventists aren't the only people having this problem.) One should not condemn an inspired person because he recites or duplicates the words of others. Didn't Peter quote from Joel on the Day of Pentecost? Did Paul quote from sources outside the Old Testament? (1 Corinthians 14:34) Secondly, the claim that God showed Ellen White what to copy and what not to copy has no merit. Where is the evidence to support such a claim? Further, it has been shown that people other than Ellen White gathered and compiled materials for some of her books. Thus, she, in a number of cases, wasn't the one doing the copying even though she was the one who approved the contents of the books bearing her name. But, Ellen White did not think of herself as an infallible spokesperson for God. She did not think later generations would exalt her writings to the level of the Bible. Consequently, she saw nothing wrong or misleading with copying excellent passages from the studies of others. It was common practice in her days. But, we live at another time and we're the ones having the misunderstanding of inspiration — not Ellen White.

## Back to the story

Even though my enthusiasm was renewed for Bible study after gaining some insight on the properties of inspiration, I felt at times like I was going a circle. From 1982 to 1987, I faithfully studied the prophecies. I was fully convinced that every verse was important. I assumed that every verse made an important contribution toward the big picture of God's plan. And it dawned on me one day that I was approaching the subject of prophecy from the wrong direction. Instead of trying to synthesize or determine the meaning of every detail, I felt I should *first* look for a *predictable* design within the prophecies. Maybe God assembled the prophecies in a particular way and the key to understanding the prophecies was linked to identifying the way God put them together.

I have long believed that prophecy cannot be of private interpretation, nor can the interpretation of prophecy be the exclusive property of well-studied scholars. I also believe that God had the prophecies written in an obscure manner so that they would remain obscure until He wanted people to know what they mean. But, when the time came for understanding, I reasoned that their contents must be plainly obvious for all who "have ears to hear what the Spirit says to the churches." After all, why would God keep the meaning of prophecy from common people? There are billions of us. I was also convinced that God would not grant one person the understanding of truth about prophecy so that all other people must come to that person to hear the truth. Truth is self evident. It needs no defense or excuse. It stands on its own feet. And, whether a billion people agree or disagree with it, truth is not affected — it remains true. And, perhaps best of all, those who want to understand truth, can see it — regardless of the messenger's ability to explain it!

So, I concluded that there must be a common denominator to prophecy. Prophecy must conform to a set of rules so that any person, regardless of religious background, language or physical location on this planet, can understand it. (After all, the Second Coming is not a week-end event sponsored by a local church.) So, I began searching for predictable order, a specific design within the prophecies, and to my amazement, I found one! The books of Daniel and Revelation consistently behave in a clearly defined way! Why did it take so long to see this? I found a comprehensive, predictable design that respects the order and content of *all* texts in Revelation; even better, every verse fully contributes to the grand design which is both wonderful and elegant.

But, detecting a design and resolving all that the design offers are two different things. By 1987, the design was unfolding. Large prophetic pieces were fitting into predictable places — not according to my view of history, but according to God's design of prophecy. And, history was right there, confirming the design. I felt the joy of a person assembling a large picture-puzzle when the last "flat-sided" piece of the perimeter has just been snapped into place. Even though I knew that many unknown pieces remained, I sensed that I was on to something very wonderful and most important. The framework was coming together.

By 1988, three rules of interpretation were observed well enough that I could express them in three short paragraphs. As it turns out, these rules have proven to be more precious than fine gold because they explain the elegant and profound design of prophecy in just a few words. Even more, I have seen people from all faiths take these rules and arrive at essentially the same conclusions as I have. This is an important test to me because the fulfillment of prophecy affects every human being on earth. Therefore, the meaning of prophecy cannot be parochial. One does not have to be an Adventist, Catholic or Baptist to understand prophecy. The contents of prophecy belongs to all people because it affects all people. So, here are the first three rules that I have confirmed:

1. Apocalyptic prophecy is identified as a prophecy that spans a period of time. Apocalyptic prophecy has a beginning and ending point in time, and the elements within the prophecy occur in the order in which they are given.
2. A prophetic fulfillment only occurs when all of the specifications of the prophecy or its elements are met, including its chronological placement within the prophecy.

3.   If an element is not literal, the Bible will clearly identify the meaning of the symbol with relevant scripture.

Many Adventists believe that I just made up these rules. This is not the case. They often accuse me of making up the rules so I can present something new or sensational and cause trouble for the Church. But, this is not the case, either. I do not wish to cause or bring trouble to anyone. The truth is that most Adventists have not earnestly examined the prophecies and become acquainted with the contents of each verse in Daniel and Revelation. It is easier to place confidence in the traditions of the Church and the supposed infallibility of Ellen White than to faithfully search the Scriptures. Therefore, when a new or *foreign* view rises that is clearly contrary to long-standing tradition, it is only natural that many would rather reject the new view rather than give it due consideration. Church leaders also have two responsibilities that naturally militate against new views. First, Church leaders believe they are the *defenders* of the faith delivered to them. How can one be a "teacher of Israel," operating in the defensive mode, while being a student in the research mode? So, Church leaders, for the most part, see new ideas about truth as a threat to the stability and mission of the Church. Secondly, the Adventist Church is beset with all kinds of crazy ideas today, and it is administratively expedient to stand by the "tried and true" rather than to expend the resources necessary to deal with each new idea that comes along. Church leaders have lots of projects and programs to accomplish and any diversion of time and energy for "wild goose" chases is regarded as an impediment.

I understand these things. These issues are not unique to Adventists. All churches have this mindset because religion itself seriously limits the expansion and development of new ideas. Somehow, people think of religion as something that doesn't (or shouldn't) change. How ironic. Especially when one considers that God is ever revealing new things for people to understand.

### A few words about the rules

A rule is an expression of something that is observed to be constant. For example, the behavior of gravity is called the "law" of gravity because gravity behaves in a constant manner. If one weighs 150 pounds in Washington D.C., he will also weigh 150 pounds in Los Angeles because gravity on earth is constant.

I must emphasize the point that man *cannot* make up the rules of design; rather, man may only discover God's design through observation. For example, Sir Isaac Newton did not make up the law of gravity. But, after years of study, Newton observed that gravity behaves in a constant way and he formulated a rule that expresses the *constant* operation of gravity. Newton's rule is an expression of what Newton observed. Gravity does not behave according to Newton, rather gravity behaves in a constant way and Newton wrote down an expression that has been validated to be true in all cases. Newton's expression about gravity is called a rule (or law). The same is also true about electricity. Ohm's law came into existence through observation. If the physicist, Georg Ohm, (yes, it's spelled Georg) had not noticed the constant behavior of electricity during the last century, someone else would have eventually discovered and expressed the constant relationship that exists between voltage, amperage and resistance. Again, my point is that man does not make up the rules; rather, it is only his privilege to observe God's grand design (whether in natural science or prophetic science) and express the behavior of things in writing. But, consider this point. If one is not studying gravity, electricity or prophecy, what is the possibility that he should understand the importance or the operation of the rules?

If one doesn't carefully investigate the prophecies for himself, he is likely to conclude that any view of prophecy, other than what his church teaches, is wrong. After all, how many conflicting interpretations on Revelation are there? But, the question remains. Did God follow a clear design when He gave the prophecies to Daniel and John? I believe the answer is an unqualified yes. I find that God followed a very constant design in the apocalyptic prophecies of Daniel and Revelation and it is our privilege to identify and express the consistent operation of the prophecies into rules of interpretation. Once the rules of design are known, they can be tested and the unknown elements of prophecy can be solved with the same accuracy that we solve the unknown in algebra. In fact, I find that God sealed up the book of Daniel until the end of time because the detection of His apocalyptic design can only be seen or observed *at the end of time.*

The book of Daniel deals with many historical events in the past. So, today's student of Daniel can "observe" the grand design of Daniel by looking backward over 2,500 years. By closely comparing fulfilled prophecies of Daniel with historical events, we confirm that apocalyptic prophecy constantly behaves in a well defined, consistent manner. But, again, if one does not study the Bible, he cannot see the design nor have confidence in *any* rules. His confidence then is limited to a belief structure, a prophet or his religious system. I'm afraid this is the case with many Adventists. Many don't search the Scriptures. And, in the near future, their ignorance will produce a terrible surprise. I find that many Adventist expectations about the future are simply wrong. For example, the Church claims that seven trumpets are historical events in the past. Does it *really* matter if they are in the future or in the past? Yes. Especially if you understand what the trumpets are and how they are soon to affect every person on earth!

**Prophecy not that important?**

Having a false view of prophecy may not seem harmful right now; after all, this week should come and go with its usual round of cares. But, false knowledge becomes harmful when reality comes knocking. Here's an example. Many sincere Christians anticipate a pre-tribulation rapture. They believe that they shall escape the terrible things that are coming upon the world. So, believing in a pre-trib rapture today seems harmless enough — in fact, I wish the doctrine of the pre-trib rapture was true! But, suppose there is no rapture. Suppose the Great Tribulation breaks out upon the earth and millions of Christians, anticipating the pre-trib rapture, discover that their prophetic hopes will not be realized. What will be the net effect when reality arrives? Great disappointment. They will feel deceived. They will blame God, their churches and their preachers. And, many will abandon their faith in God because of bitter disappointment.

Adventists know about great disappointment. In fact, the Adventist Church arose out of the ashes of the great disappointment of 1844. In those days, some estimate that nearly 100,000 people believed in the message of William Miller, the Baptist evangelist, who proclaimed the return of Jesus to be on or about October, 1844. When October 22 came and went without the appearing of Jesus, the Millerite movement literally evaporated overnight. The residue was a handful of less than 100 people who went back to their Bibles to find their error. The point here is that a wrongful prophetic expectation in October, 1844, transformed a great multitude into a tiny remnant — all this in one day. Can a prophetic disappointment short circuit one's faith in God and His Word? History says yes. Therefore, the study of prophecy is a two-edged sword. To ignore it is to remain in darkness. To believe in it is to risk disappointment. Which side of this coin should faith seek?

### 1987 and onward

I began to publicly present my discoveries to small groups in Ohio in 1986. The following year, I began writing the first edition of the book, *Warning! Revelation is about to be fulfilled.* The task of writing was even more difficult than studying prophecy. (I failed English, both in high school and college.) But, writing is a valuable exercise. Good writing forces a clear and logical progression of thought. And, now that I have spent thousands of hours writing, I have come to even enjoy it although I still do not like to write personal letters. (Writing is a very slow and deliberate process for me.)

Toward the end of 1988, I felt the call of the Lord to resign from my employment of 17 years in the Adventist Church. I had served the Church as a pastor, a college staff administrator and a hospital department head. But, living by faith is the test of fellowship with Jesus. Jesus says His sheep hear His voice and the call of the Lord was very present within me. I was reluctant for obvious financial reasons to resign; after all, financial security is highly important. But, spreading the gospel of Jesus is even more important.

In 1989, my faith-full wife and I set out, not knowing how the call would work out. She was willing to work full time so that I could conduct seminars and continue writing. I knew that God had called us to tell others about the prophecies. So, we had to try it. If the Lord didn't bless our efforts after two years, I promised Shirley that I would get a job and then we could investigate where we went wrong.

When setting up the ministry, I made a covenant with the Lord concerning money. I told the Lord that I would go forward as long as He provided the financial means to do so. I would not ask for, nor solicit money to finance the ministry. I reasoned that if God wanted *this* message to go forward, He would meet the expenses as they came. By following this design, Wake Up America Seminars could be as big or as little as God wanted it to be. And, for four years, Wake Up America Seminars has met *every* financial obligation, since day one, without delay! We have seen God do things that are as wonderful as the parting of the Red Sea. It's a wonderful life learning how to rest upon the everlasting arms of Jesus.

Even after getting the ministry underway, one prophetic element still eluded me. I accepted the operation of the day/year principle in prophecy on the basis that history confirms its operation. But, I also understood, as a result of the three rules given above, that some near-future prophetic time-periods had to be reckoned in literal time. However, I did not know what principle governed the reckoning of prophetic time-periods. How could some time-periods use the day/year principle and others be literal time-periods? I wondered what principle or rule distinguished between the two?

I was looking through one of my many translations of the Bible one night for something and I happened to turn to Leviticus 25. This chapter discusses the origin of sabbatical and Jubilee years, and chapter 26 discusses the fact that if Israel didn't observe the sabbatical years, God would remove them from the land so that the land could receive its sabbath of rest anyway. This highly interested me because 2 Chronicles 36:21 says that the land enjoyed its sabbath rests during Israel's 70 years of Babylonian captivity. I wondered if the 70 years in Babylon was a "payment" or atonement for the violation of 70 sabbath years. And to my amazement, I discovered that there are exactly 70 sabbatical years in the 430 years of Israel's and Judah's apostasy. (Ezekiel 4:5,6) This explains why the Babylonian captivity lasted for 70 years! In other words, the 70 years of captivity was not an arbitrary "jail term" placed upon Israel. God removed Israel from the land, so *the land* could catch up on the sabbath rests that Judah and Israel had failed to give it during their 430 years of apostasy!

This data opened a new door. To make a long story short, the Jubilee calendar unfolded and grew into a subject of great interest, and importance. The more I examined God's method of reckoning time, the clearer I saw the purpose behind the Jubilee calendar. This is how the fourth prophetic rule of interpretation came to be:

4.  The operation of the Jubilee calendar explains when God reckons prophetic time as a day for a year and when He reckons time as literal time.

I don't have space enough to explain all that this rule has to offer, but I have found this rule to answer many questions involved with prophetic issues of time and timing.

**Today and beyond**

Thus far, I have found the presence of four rules within apocalyptic prophecy. Even though these rules are stated in my own words, one must keep in mind that prophecy does not behave according to Larry Wilson. Rather, prophecy behaves according to its Designer. I have tested these rules quite closely, and find them to be true. There may be more rules to come. However, if there are more, they cannot lessen the requirements of the four rules stated above any more than a new discovery about gravity can lessen the general truths discovered by Newton. If any of the four rules can be proven to be untrue, then it ceases to be a rule. Period.

So, I now find a distinct difference between prophetic truth (looking backward) and prophetic faith (looking forward). Prophetic truth is confirmed by history. We can easily compare the fulfillments of prophecy with history. On the other hand, prophetic faith looks to the future and our prophetic faith is only as secure as the rules we follow. The meaning of apocalyptic prophecy is not subject to, nor dependent upon, any man's opinion. In fact, differing opinions only cancel each other. This is why, for the most part, prophecy means nothing today. But, to those who understand God's design of prophecy, the meaning is both clear and sure.

Here is a profound statement (I rarely say anything profound): The correct understanding of apocalyptic prophecy was reserved by God until the end of time because apocalyptic prophecy reveals the truth about the order of events that were *planned* for salvation. I find that the sequence, order or placement of all prophetic events is subject to apocalyptic prophecy. This means that the visions of Bible writers and Ellen White are subject to the timing and order of events revealed in apocalyptic prophecy. In other words, God shined a spotlight on various elements within the plan of salvation to individual prophets down through the ages. And, their comments about their visions reflect what they saw. But, at the end of time, God turns on all of the lights in the room and the final generation can see the whole structure in complete form. The order and placement of all events then makes sense. The darkness is gone and the truth is seen. For this reason, I compare the unsealing of the book of Daniel to turning on all the lights. The rules that explain the meaning of Revelation were hidden in Daniel until the end — which is here.

## Multiple or partial fulfillments

A few comments need to be made about Desmond Ford's apotelesmatic principle of prophecy. Lately, some well-meaning Adventists have modified Ford's idea to lessen the confrontation between Adventism's historical views and the contemporary views of prophecy that are now rising. Some Adventists strongly insist that prophecies can be repeatedly fulfilled, applied or partially fulfilled. This concept, they claim, is demonstrated in Matthew 24, where Jesus merged the end of Jerusalem with the end of the world into *one* prophecy. This dual application of prophecy, they claim, means that prophecy can have more than one fulfillment. But, a close examination of Matthew 24 does not confirm the claim.

Matthew 24 contains information about the end of Jerusalem *and* the end of the world, but the two are not the *same* event. Everything predicted about the end of Jerusalem has been fulfilled. Period. And, everything predicted about the end of the world in Matthew 24 will be fulfilled. Period. No one denies that parallels exist, but the specifications about the end of the world and those about the end of Jerusalem are separate and distinct.

But, the unsaid purpose behind the concept of dual fulfillments is often this: Adventists are looking for a way to maintain the *inerrancy* of Ellen White and they also want a better, more thorough explanation of prophetic text. After all, large segments of Daniel and Revelation are never mentioned by Ellen White. So, after examining this matter, here are my observations:

1. A fulfillment is a full-fill-ment. God knows every detail about the future and He has predicted the details in advance. All that shall come to pass will come to pass just as God said. A prophecy doesn't reach full-fill-ment until all that God has said about the event takes place. For example, trumpet three can't be full-filled until everything described in trumpet three occurs. Furthermore, trumpet three has to occur *after* trumpet two. If the trumpets do not occur in their order, how can one tell which trumpet is next or even worse, where any trumpet occurred?

2. Suppose that trumpet two is a great asteroid impact upon a sea, how can a partial fulfillment of trumpet two occur? Or, how can trumpet two occur multiples of times unless trumpet one occurs multiples of time. Maybe the question should be asked, how many times do the seven trumpets sound *in their order?*

3. Suppose the fifth trumpet is the physical appearing of Satan. The Bible predicts that the devil will torment those not having the seal of God for five months. When does the five month time-period occur? Can it occur more than once? Can it partially occur?

The premise behind dual fulfillments, multiple applications or a partial fulfillment of prophecy is faulty from the start. For example, if one looks closely at the second trumpet, he will see that dual fulfillments, multiple applications or a partial fulfillment is nothing less than *multiples of interpretation* because there is no historical evidence to show that the event has taken place. In other words, trumpet two can't be different things at two different times. Whatever trumpet two represents can only be satisfied by the full-fill-ment of the specifications given in trumpet two and trumpet two must happen *before* trumpet three and *after* trumpet one. So, the use of dual, partial or multiple fulfillments to defend the infallibility or limited knowledge of Ellen White does not accomplish a desired end. The fact remains, she simply did not know everything. God did not show her everything there is to know about end-time events. Therefore, some of her prophetic conclusions can be proven wrong because her knowledge about the future was partial. But, this does not lessen her work as one inspired by God. She, as did all the writers of the Bible, gave the best she had. This is one of the limitations of being finite — yet God gently works within our limitations to reveal things higher than the highest human thought can reach. For this reason, later generations have the privilege of knowing more about God than previous generations. So, what privilege is ours today?

## Summary

I find the writings of Ellen White to be a most valuable asset. I have read most of her works and I find that she was inspired by God just like Paul, John and Peter. Many Adventists will also say the same words, but mean something entirely different. So, the dividing lines becomes the properties of inspiration and the meaning of Bible prophecy. If an inspired person becomes an infallible person, then no human being could ever qualify to remain a prophet.

I have included a chapter in this book showing that Ellen White's limitation was no different than other prophets. For example, Paul didn't know about the 1,260 years of Little Horn power. Peter didn't know about the 2,300 years of Daniel 8:14. Does this lessen their contribution to truth? No. A broad understanding of inspiration sets the stage for a better understanding of the contents of the Bible. Specifically, one needs such an understanding if he insists on studying the prophecies. After all, the Bible is the only book on earth that reveals the history of God during the existence of man. And, the Bible is the only book on earth that reveals what God is about to do to terminate the existence of sin.

Larry Wilson

September, 1993

# Historical perspectives and comparisons

To counteract the influence of my prophetic views, Adventist pastors and Church leaders are distributing warnings to the laity about my "deadly and highly deceptive views." One pastor in particular has been energized by the steady advancement of my views. He has written and distributed a number of documents to Church leaders refuting my works and recently, he published a denigrating article drawing a distinct parallel between David Koresh and me. (David Koresh was the infamous Branch Davidian who died in the Waco, Texas, calamity.) (*Adventists Affirm,* Spring 1993, "Guarding Against End-Time Deceptions.") I have been mildly surprised that Church leaders easily accepted, duplicated and distributed the writings of this pastor since most of them have not read any of my materials. I guess his comments are readily accepted by Church administrators because he defends "the good *old* Adventist faith" and they assume that the pastor *is one of them.*

Adventist leaders are fully convinced of the truth-full-ness of their positions on prophecy and as evangelicals, they strongly defend their prophetic positions. It would be fair to say that most Church leaders reached their position by demonstrating a high level of allegiance to the traditional views of the Church. So, when laymen began asking questions about prophecy, most leaders will affirm that they have investigated and verified the foundational truths of Adventism; therefore, "one does not have to drink a whole gallon of sour milk to know if the milk is bad." As a result, I have been publicly condemned before thousands at Adventist campmeetings by Church leaders who have not read one chapter of even one book.

After a meeting in Africa where I was publicly denounced, a man (who fully understands my prophetic positions) met with the speaker in private and asked how he could publicly condemn someone he had never met and even worse, misrepresent his prophetic positions before the people. (Usually, my accusers cannot explain what I am teaching except to say they know it is different than what they believe.) The speaker replied: "I don't have to read everything Larry Wilson has written to know if he has truth. The minute I saw one error, I closed his book. If he speaks contrary to the prophet (Ellen White), there is no light in him." My friend asked, "But, isn't truth advancing?" The speaker replied, "The prophet makes it clear that new light will not contradict the views of the pioneers."

A closed mind is truth's biggest obstacle. When Luther was brought before the Diet at Worms, Church leaders weren't interested in Luther's discoveries. They had not read his books. They didn't care to know what truth he may have found. No, they were anxious to condemn Luther because he was causing trouble within the Church. What makes this matter so ironic is that Adventists greatly admire the courage of those who, like Luther, received the Millerite message and were summarily evicted from their Churches because of their stand on advancing truth. Even Ellen White and her family were evicted from the Methodist Church because they were "walking contrary to Church rules." (*Life Sketches,* pp. 52-53) So, if Martin Luther and Ellen White and her family had submitted to Church rules, or stayed within established doctrine, where would the Adventist Church be today? But, the very thing that caused Martin Luther, Ellen White, James White, Joseph Bates and a host of others to be evicted from their Churches is the very same thing that propels the Revelation story forward; namely, a clearer understanding of the Bible.

As I analyze the problem, Church leaders and pastors are reacting from fear. They may put many faces on their arguments, they may disguise their complaint with a thousand quotes from Ellen White, but the real issue is fear. They fear that new prophetic ideas will bring division and cause dissension within the Church. They fear that members will lose confidence in the Church, its leaders and its teachings. They fear that members will be fascinated with something new and speculative, and as a result, they will redirect their financial support away from the Church. They fear that members will be deceived and in the end, lost because they turned from the doctrines they preach. They fear that some members of the Church will be harmed for years to come by teachings like mine. They fear that they will lose control of the laymen. It is easier to prey upon fear itself and scare Church members by saying that they could be deceived than it is to open up the Bible and give some clear answers. So, they promote fear.

The fears of Church leaders could be dispelled quickly if the leaders of the Church would do one simple thing: Tell the members of the Church what the truth is. For example, I told the pastor who wrote the article in *Adventists Affirm* that he has nothing to fear from my teaching if he would simply open his Bible and logically explain the meaning of Revelation *from the Bible*. After all, I said, Church members are giving consideration to my views on Revelation because they are dissatisfied with the illogical explanations of their pastors. But, he refuses to take the Scripture and explain Revelation, verse by verse. Rather, he resorts to predisposing people against my views by calling for loyalty to historic Adventism. Is his motto true: "Stay with the system because the system is safe."? Pastor X elevates the importance of complying with Church rule, and he exalts the "servant of the Lord," Ellen White, as though she had greater authority than the Bible. Will this prevent people from investigating the truth? It might stall some for a while. But, truth is not thwarted by bad publicity — even if all the pastors in the world oppose it, truth will go forward. The Apostle Paul wrote, **"For we cannot do anything against the truth, but only for the truth."** (2 Corinthians 13:8)

There is nothing more powerful than a truth whose time has come. And, truth can afford to fair and open. Truth has nothing to hide. Truth can withstand the closest scrutiny. Truth is precious to those who search for her and threatening to those who don't understand her. And when truth meets opposition, God gives truth greater power. I say these things about truth because Adventists claim that truth is progressive — ever unfolding. But, when it comes to 1993, Church leaders denounce those of us who *may* have discovered more light on a given topic without seriously investigating the claims. This is not unusual. History reveals this repetitive process. New ideas are denounced automatically and those having a new idea are called heretics without the benefit of understanding. Does this sound like an organization who believes in progressive truth?

Unfortunately, many Church members are satisfied with a superficial knowledge of God, lulled into deep spiritual sleep by dull and meaningless preaching. How many times would you watch the last sermon from your pastor on a video tape? I fear that many Adventists don't know what they believe or why they believe the things they do. And, I also find that many Adventist members are easy prey for vain and foolish ideas because their pastors have not re-established this generation upon the pillars of Adventist faith. I fear that the Adventist Church is in deeper trouble than it realizes. When leaders appeal to the laity to be loyal to the *institution* because it is THE institution, something is very wrong. Let the leaders appeal to the laity to be faithful to the truth for truth's sake while maintaining an open-minded position. The Bible says the Bereans were more noble than those in Thessalonica because they searched the Scriptures to see if the things Paul said were true! (They didn't trust Paul. Acts 17:11) When Church leaders use fear and denunciation to bias the laity against new ideas, good or bad, the Church is revealing a fundamental weakness. Such actions reveal that it doesn't have good solid answers to today's questions. One simple truth, rightly presented from the Bible, can destroy 10,000 wrong ideas.

Some time ago I received a letter from a Church administrator who made it quite clear that he did not appreciate nor did he believe that my prophetic conclusions were correct. He stated that my rules of interpretation were faulty, and therefore, my prophetic conclusions were wrong. His letter was written from the perspective that *my* views would soon be proven false by the passage of time. I responded to his letter by saying that in actuality, we were in the boat together on prophecy because both *his* views and *my* views about prophecy would be fully exposed by the passage of time. In other words, no one having a prophetic position shall escape the great revelation that is coming. Everyone is about to see what's what, and what's not. Everyone will also see how closely his understanding of the Bible aligns with reality! Watch for this process. It will prove to be most interesting.

### Independent ministries: cause or symptom?

According to a 1991 report published by the president of the Southwestern Union Conference, the Seventh-day Church has identified more than 800 "independent ministries or private organizations" within its ranks. What is propelling such a phenomenal development in a small Church with less than 8 million members world-wide? Why, in the last two or three decades, is Church membership fragmenting into so many pieces? Are independent ministries rising up because rank and file Seventh-day Adventist members are weak in their understanding of Bible truth and are therefore easily mislead? Are independent ministries springing up because some traditional Adventist views are weak and are not easily defended from the Bible? Or, are independent ministries rising up because the leadership of the Church has become stale and irrelevant? Has the prophetic main-spring of Adventism wound down? Has Adventism become over-institutionalized like so many other Protestant Churches? Has the Advent movement stopped moving and become stagnant because the Lord has delayed His coming? Has the Adventist Church lost sight of its prophetic purpose? Will misguided zealots rise up and lead the Church into embarrassment or will Church administrators produce a great plan that will rally the membership and renew the commitment of the saints to a prophetic destiny? These are important questions. Where are the answers?

### Revelation seminars

Perhaps one of the main reasons that many Adventists today are not interested in prophecy dates back to Church emphasis on Revelation Seminars during the 1970's and 1980's. During that time, tens of thousands of Adventist members attended Revelation Seminars conducted by their pastors. They came expecting to gain a clearer understanding of the book of Revelation, but many were disappointed. Members discovered that the so-called Revelation Seminar consisted of a series of 24 presentations designed to convert unsuspecting attendees to Adventism instead of answering serious questions about prophecy. In many cases, these church-sponsored seminars left more questions unanswered than answered. Significant portions of Daniel and Revelation were either omitted or the explanations given were logically deficient. As a result, members began to lose interest in Revelation Seminars and today, I've been told that the number of seminars conducted in the USA has dropped by more than 60%.

If this claim is true, this is a tragedy! The books of Daniel and Revelation are particularly relevant to those living in the last days. And, if the Church correctly understood these two books, a great Bible-based revival would occur! And just at the time when final events on earth are about to begin, it grieves me that the majority of Church members have lost interest in the study of prophecy!

Even though lay leaders have openly expressed disappointment with the content of the Revelation Seminars, they are grateful for the thousands of new people who attended and decided to join the Church. But, many questions about Daniel and Revelation remain unanswered. For example, here are eight issues which the Revelation Seminar raises, but it fails to offer logical answers that maintain fidelity to Bible text:

1.  The Revelation Seminar teaches that the Two Witnesses are the Old and New Testaments and that they were "killed" in 1793 during the French Revolution and resurrected in 1796 (3.5 years later). The Bible says that when the Two Witnesses are resurrected, there is a severe earthquake *at that very hour* and 7,000 people die as a result. (Revelation 11:13) When did that earthquake occur? Who are the 7,000 people who perished in that earthquake?

2.  The Revelation Seminar teaches that *the beast from the abyss* that killed the Two Witnesses was France (Revelation 11:7), but the Bible says that when the beast comes up out of the abyss, the wicked will be astonished when they *see* the beast *because* the beast once was, now is not, and yet will come. (Revelation 17:8) Three verses later, the Bible identifies this same beast from the abyss as the eighth king that belongs to the seven heads. (Revelation 17:11) How can France possibly meet these specifications?

3.  The Revelation Seminar teaches that the beast in Revelation 13:1 is the papacy which received a deadly wound in 1798. Further, the Seminar teaches that the deadly wound is almost healed (papal power almost restored). So, who are the seven heads? What did the angel mean when he told John that "five heads are fallen, one is, and one is yet to come?" How can the seven heads also be seven kings and seven mountains?

4.  The Bible says that the deadly wound *had been healed* when the leopard-like beast rises from sea. This suggests that the leopard-like beast rises from the sea after the wound was inflicted in 1798. The

Bible says this beast will have authority over the whole world and
it will make war upon the saints for 42 months. (Revelation 13:5,7)
Lastly, the Bible predicts that all inhabitants *will worship* the leopard-like beast except those whose names are written in the Book
of Life. (Revelation 13:8) But, two questions arise. The Revelation
Seminar teaches that the beast was wounded in 1798 (papal power
broken), but the Revelation Seminar places the 42 months *before*
the deadly wound is inflicted in 1798. How can this be? The Bible
places the 42 months *after* the deadly wound *had been healed*. Secondly, if the Revelation Seminar position on the 42 months is correct
(A.D. 538-1798) and the identity of the beast is correct, how can
the papacy have power and authority again? In other words, the
leopard-like beast is only granted power for 42 months — no more,
no less. So, how can the papacy have authority outside of its allotted
time-period?

5.  The Revelation Seminar teaches that the sun, moon and stars men-
    tioned in the sixth seal (Revelation 6:12) are literal. However, it
    says the sun, moon and stars in Revelation 8:12 are symbolic. What
    rule of interpretation produces this result? Who are the people that
    die from drinking bitter water in Revelation 8:11? Where are the
    ships that were sunk, and the sea creatures that died in Revelation
    8:9? And where are the great fires of Revelation 8:7 that burned
    up one-third of the trees and all of the green grass?

6.  The Revelation Seminar teaches that the fifth trumpet was fulfilled
    by the rise of Othman, a barbarian pirate, who founded the Ottoman
    Empire in 1299. But, the Bible says that a star, who had fallen to
    earth, specifically an angel king (Revelation 9:11), was released from
    the abyss during the fifth trumpet. Was Othman an angel king in
    heaven and then expelled? Was he put into the abyss and then
    allowed to come up out of abyss with a swarm of soldiers?

7.  The Revelation Seminar teaches that the fourth seal represents the
    time-period: A.D. 538 to 1500. It claims that sword, famine, plague
    and wild beasts represent the persecution and destruction of 25%

of the earth by the papacy during the Dark Ages. But, sword, famine, plague and wild beasts are repeatedly mentioned throughout the Bible as punitive judgments from God. (See Ezekiel 14; Leviticus 26 and Deuteronomy 32.) So, why would God punish *His own people* for a thousand years and allow the papacy to flourish?

8. Jesus is identified as THE LAMB nearly thirty times in the book of Revelation. The Revelation Seminar teaches that the "lamb-like" beast of Revelation 13:11 is the United States of America. This view originated in England around 1699 as prophetic expositors speculated on the rise of America. But, how can the USA satisfy the specifications of Revelation 13:11-18? According to the Bible, the lamb-like beast will perform signs and wonders, even calling fire down out of heaven *to deceive* the inhabitants of the world. How will the USA do this? Revelation 13 also indicates that the lamb-like beast will have dominion over the whole world, but Daniel 2 clearly teaches that no nation will rule as a universal empire on earth. So, how can the USA be the lamb-like beast? Doesn't it make sense that the lamb-like is an imposter of THE LAMB? Doesn't the devil *come up* out of the abyss (earth) masquerading as THE LAMB because the devil was first cast *into* the earth (abyss)? (Revelation 12:9)

## Historicism: prophecy in the past

There are other factors within the Church that contribute to the loss of interest in prophecy. I suspect that the vagaries of historical minutia contribute to the malaise with the Church. Since 1863, Adventists have claimed that 95% of the prophecies were fulfilled. Even though many laymen would like to understand the details of Revelation, most are ill-prepared to put forth the effort to investigate 2,000 years of history. After all, how relevant are two millenniums of history to one's spiritual need right now.

The Revelation Seminar basically predicts two things for the future: the implementation of the mark of the beast and the outpouring of the seven last plagues. And, because Adventists believe that the first beast of Revelation 13 is the papacy, and its mark of authority is Sunday worship, there is a growing amount of trepidation in quadrants of the Church about the rising popularity and power of Pope John Paul II. Adventists believe that the United States and the Catholic Church are going to unite to enforce Sunday observance upon our world of 5.6 billion people. The observance of Sunday, according to Adventists, is the mark of the beast.

To warn the world of the dangers of papal power, a number of SDA members are sacrificially distributing the book, *The Great Controversy*, written by Ellen White. This 100 year-old book is the most important book within Adventism when it comes to the Church's views on prophecy. Ellen White clearly identifies the papacy as the great antichrist beast of Revelation 13:1 (GC 439), the pope as the man of sin (GC 446) and the lamb-like beast of Revelation 13:11 as the United States of America (GC 441). Some members have gone so far as to rent highway billboards to denigrate the pope. But, such efforts by a few zealots will not stop the rising power of Catholicism. Why would Adventists do such things when they fully believe that the Bible predicts that the deadly wound will be healed anyway? Will these abrasive actions slow the healing of the deadly wound? No. Such actions in the United States will only serve to increase religious tensions between 0.6 million Adventists and 63 million Catholics.

## The beginning affects the ending

To appreciate the historical view of prophecy espoused by Adventists, one needs to know a little about the origin of Adventism. Adventists inherited a number of prophetic concepts from the Millerite movement which they embellished with the passage of time. William Miller, a Baptist farmer-turned-lay evangelist in New England, concluded in 1831 that Jesus was going to return to earth "about 1843." This conclusion was reached by his careful study of the prophecies, especially Daniel 8:14. When Miller began to share his views, only a few saw light in his conclusions. But, time passed and Miller's conclusions eventually made an impact on New England. One must realize that Miller eventually imposed a certain premise upon the prophecies of Daniel and Revelation. His premise was not new, but it was urgent. His premise was this: The proximity of 1843 appears to be the end of the world; therefore, *all* pre-Advent prophecies in Daniel and Revelation must be fulfilled by 1843.

Miller's ministry received an evangelical "jump start" on November 13, 1833. That night, nature showered New England with a dazzling meteoric shower of falling stars. Because Miller believed the end of the world was about ten years away, this phenomena provided the leverage he needed to gain public attention. He showed that the meteoric shower was a fulfillment of Revelation 6:13 indicating that the sixth seal of Revelation 6 was open and very soon, Jesus Himself would appear. (The sixth seal mentions the falling of stars, a dark day and an earthquake.) Looking backwards into recent history, Miller produced evidence of a dark day in a New England newspaper (May 19, 1780) and he found a killer earthquake in Lisbon, Portugal (November 1, 1755) where 60,000 people died. These three events, he claimed, clearly proved that the sixth seal was open and the next verse in Revelation describes the heavens opening up to reveal Jesus. His claim was made even more impressive because the 2,300 evenings and mornings of Daniel 8:14 would end in 1843.

My point for reviewing this bit of history is that the Millerites were convinced that *all* pre-Advent prophecies had to be fulfilled by late 1843. Their conviction included the seven last plagues. But, as 1843 neared its end, and Jesus didn't come, the Millerites began to review their calculations. They found a mistake. They had overlooked one year between 457 B.C. and 1843 because years are not counted according to mathematical scale in the transition from B.C. dating to A.D. dating. (There is no zero year.) This discovery made 1844 instead of 1843 the terminus of the 2,300 years. This renewed the hopes of the Millerites and more importantly, it gave the Millerite movement a needed window of time, more opportunity to spread their message and raise the excitement.

The historical record of the Millerite movement demonstrates a fundamental weakness that goes with the interpretation of prophecy. If one wishes to impose a certain view upon prophecy, he can find evidence enough to support his claim if he is willing to ignore or dismiss those prophetic elements that he can't explain. This explains why the Seventh-day Adventist Church, the remnant of the Millerite Movement, came into existence having a certain view or mindset about prophecy. And, the only concessions Adventists have made to the original Millerite position on Daniel and Revelation is that they believe portions of Revelation 13 - 16 are still future; namely, the mark of the beast, the close of probation and the seven last plagues. Most of the other prophetic elements, they claim, have been fulfilled.

**Still holding on...**

Early Adventists, especially Millerite-turned-Adventists were highly dedicated people. It takes courage and determination to stand up and defend prophetic ideas that others scoff at. But, persecution drives dedicated people toward understanding. The more they were ridiculed, the more early Adventists studied the Bible. And, in time, much of the opposition faded because Adventists could show some compelling answers for their faith from "the Book." As a result, the Church grew.

Ellen White's ministry served a most valuable function from 1844 to 1863, the time-period between the disappointment and Church organization. Bible conferences were periodically held to determine the content of Bible truth. During these conferences, presentations were made on various subjects by those who had studied out certain things. Then, the listeners would challenge the presenters to see if the Bible really supported the conclusions set forth. These conferences became the anvil where ideas *from the Bible* were hammered out. These ideas later become the bed-rock doctrines of Adventist theology. And, at these conferences, God sometimes revealed His approval upon certain conclusions *reached from Bible study* through Ellen White. Thus, those attending these conferences received special affirmation from God about the truthfulness of certain key doctrines distilled from the Bible. In those early days of Church formation, no doctrine of the Church was based on vision. Adventists were adamant about this point. They insisted on the Bible and the Bible alone. Ellen White was not regarded as an authority. She was regarded as a messenger. And it was clear in those days what truths God had affirmed and what God had not confirmed.

But, with the passage of time, the value of these early events has become dim. Even worse, details have become blurred as to the nature of what really took place. It is true that God affirmed certain key points through

Ellen White. It is not true that every prophetic conclusion held by the Church *today* was confirmed through her back *then*. Herein lies a problem.

Because the properties of inspiration have been misunderstood and because God did confirm certain conclusions about key points through Ellen White, a sweeping conclusion about the entirety of Adventist doctrine has been made, passed down and spread around, and the conclusion is wrong. This conclusion is that God has put His stamp of approval upon *all* of the prophetic conclusions of the Church through Ellen White. I've heard a number of Adventist pastors confidently assert that the doctrines of the Adventist Church have God's stamp of approval. They say, "The Seventh-day Adventist Church has THE truth" as though truth were in its final form by 1915 (the year of Ellen White's death). This concept is the logical end of the "White Principle" discussed in the previous chapter. Therefore many Adventists say that any deviation from the "historic" positions of early Adventism is wrong and unacceptable. Period.

The assumed infallibility of the Adventist position, believed to have been confirmed by Ellen White, is enthusiastically supported by a number of independent ministries within the Church. Most of these ministries claim to hold on to the historic faith as first delivered to the saints. For example, one independent minister recently wrote, "Those who set themselves up as teachers of the people, who teach contrary to our prophet, Ellen White, who reapply the prophecies of Daniel and Revelation without a "Thus saith the Lord," who insist that Ellen White made mistakes, have set themselves up as "better" prophets than the one chosen of the Lord." (*Our Firm Foundation,* September, 1993, p. 31) If a portion of this remark is directed at my work, then it reveals a misunderstanding of inspiration, the work and ministry of Ellen White, the origins of the Church and my efforts. I have never claimed to be a prophet. And, I certainly do not set myself up as better than Ellen White. And saying that Ellen White was wrong in certain places is not self-exaltation. Rather, it is an admission that she was fallible. She knew in part and prophesied in part. (1 Corinthians 13:9) But, the writer above believes in the infallibility of Ellen White. As far as he is concerned, she has told him what to believe about prophecy and there is no more discussion.

Many Adventists, especially the clergy, so confident of their prophetic position, overlook a most serious matter. Soon, all prophetic views are about to be exposed for what they are. This includes everyone: Adventists, Mormons, Catholics, Jehovah's Witnesses and all others. This takes me back to the letter from the Church administrator mentioned earlier. From his perspective, I am the one who will be embarrassed. But, from God's perspective, all conclusions on prophecy shall be tested and proven good or bad. Then, embarrassment will seek its owners. If it turns out that my conclusions are wrong, I'll publicly state my error. I have nothing to lose. In fact, I have published three corrections already. So, let our prophetic conclusions align with every verse in the Bible as closely as possible. Then, the light of day will confirm or deny our positions.

### Views contrasted

Adventist laymen, for the most part, don't have a working knowledge of the prophetic positions held by the Church, so the following is a brief comparison of our conclusions. Take a few moments and study the differences. At first, some differences will seem to be insignificant, but the conclusions significantly diverge toward the end of time. I am often called a "futurist" by those Adventists who claim to be "historic." Because they have not taken the prerequisite time to understand my teaching, the label "futurist" is applied. It is generally used to refer to someone who reapplies the prophecies to the future — often discounting the historical identity and 1,260 year reign of the little horn power of Daniel 7. But, the reader will notice that I not only stand firm on the 538-1798 reign of the little horn power (the papacy), I also stand firm on 1844 as the terminus of the 2,300 evenings and mornings. Neither do I find multiple applications of apocalyptic prophecy possible. There is one and only one fulfillment of each element of apocalyptic prophecy. So, if believing that some prophetic elements are yet to be fulfilled, then Adventists must be futurists, too.

I'm convinced that the books of Daniel and Revelation have more to say about end-time events than the Church is willing to allow. I say this, not because I want Daniel and Revelation to say more than they should, but on the basis of the rules of interpretation that I find to be valid. The rules must determine our conclusions — not the other way around.

(Note: The SDA Church does not have a unanimous position on every detail of prophecy. Therefore, the following SDA positions presented should be regarded as a general view of Adventist teachings. Adventists do vary on those portions of Scripture that Ellen White said nothing about. The Adventist reader may wish to examine the Church's position more closely by reading these books: *The Great Controversy, Early Writings,* by Ellen White; *Thoughts on Daniel and Revelation* by Uriah Smith; and *God Cares,* Volumes I & II, by C. Mervyn Maxwell.)

**Future expectations**

| SDA | LW |
|---|---|
| Protestants and Catholics unite | Appearing and empowerment of 144,000 prophets |
| Sunday laws enforced upon the whole world | Global earthquake, world-wide fires, two asteroid impacts, chain of volcano eruptions, collapse of global economic infrastructure |
| Close of probation | Friday/Saturday/Sunday laws implemented to appease God. Persecution for disobedience |
| Seven last plagues occur | Devil physically appears claiming to be God |
| | Tattoo of the devil implemented; universal day of worship set up |
| | Close of individual probation |
| | Seven last plagues occur |

| Dan 2 | Head | Chest | Thighs | Legs | Feet | Toes | Rock |
|---|---|---|---|---|---|---|---|
| SDA: | Babylon | Medo-Persia | Grecia | Rome | 10 kingdoms that rose out of Rome | | Jesus |
| LW: | Babylon | Medo-Persia | Grecia | Rome | Many kings | 10 last kings | Jesus |

| Dan 7 | Lion | Bear | Leopard | Terrible beast | Little Horn | Court seated | Judgment began |
|---|---|---|---|---|---|---|---|
| SDA: | Babylon | Medo-Persia | Grecia | Rome | Papacy | 1844 | 1844 |
| LW: | Babylon | Medo-Persia | Grecia | Rome | Papacy | 1798 | 1844 |

| Dan 8 | Ram | Goat | Horn Power |
|---|---|---|---|
| SDA: | Medo-Persia | Grecia | Papacy |
| LW: | Medo-Persia | Grecia | Future appearing of the devil in the flesh |

**Time Periods**

| Reference | SDA | LW | Reference | SDA | LW |
|---|---|---|---|---|---|
| Dan 7:25 | 538-1798 | 538-1798 | Rev 9:5 | 1299-1449 | Future |
| Dan 8:14 | 457-1844 | 457-1844 | Rev 11:2 | 538-1798 | Future |
| Dan 9:24 | 457-34 | 457-33 | Rev 11:3 | 538-1798 | Future |
| Calvary | A.D. 31 | A.D. 30 | Rev 11:13 | ? | Future |
| Dan 12:7 | 538-1798 | Future | Rev 12:6 | 538-1798 | 538-1798 |
| Dan 12:11 | 508-1798 | Future | Rev 12:14 | 538-1798 | 538-1798 |
| Dan 12:12 | 508-1843 | Future | Rev 13:5 | 538-1798 | Future |
| Rev 8:1 | Future | Future | Rev 20:2 | Future | Future |

**Daniel 9**

SDA: 70 weeks (490 literal years) began in the Autumn of 457 B.C., ends in the Autumn of A.D. 34.

LW: 70 weeks (490 literal years) began in the Spring of 457 B.C., ended in the Spring of A.D. 34.

**Daniel 11**

**SDA:** History of rulers through Medo-Persia, Grecia, pagan Rome then papal Rome. The ultimate king of the North: probably the papacy. The king of the South: not sure.

**LW:** Daniel 11:2-35 is a history of kings through Medo-Persia, Grecia and pagan Rome down through A.D. 70. The kings of the North and South are so named because Israel is located geographically between them. Daniel 11:36 through 12:3 is a prophecy that enlarges the specifications of the horn power in Daniel 8, the stern-faced king. The stern-faced king is the physical appearing of the devil. He is called the King of the North because he will cause great destruction.


**Daniel 12:1**

**SDA:** Close of probation

**LW:** Close of probation


**Revelation 2 and 3 - The Seven Churches**

**SDA:** The seven churches cover seven time-periods or church ages since Jesus was on earth. They are: Ephesus, Smyrna, Pergamum, Thyatira, Sardis, Philadelphia, Laodicea. The time-periods are A.D. 31, 100, 323, 538, 1798, 1840, 1844 — end.

**LW:** All seven churches co-existed at the time Revelation was written. They were the primary recipients of copies of the vision given to John on Patmos. The seven candlesticks are not chronological nor do they represent seven time-periods. This idea is externally imposed upon the text rather than found within the text.

The seven Churches represent the conditions or experiences of the universal body of Christ. The promises and threats of Jesus can be applied to any person at any given time since the vision was given. For example, there are some in the Church *today* who have lost their first love as those in Ephesus.

### Revelation 4 through 6 - The Seven Seals

**SDA:** The seven seals generally correspond to the seven time-periods of the seven churches. They represent religious milestones from the time of Christ to the end of the world:

Seal 1. White horse: the purity of truth during the apostolic age; A.D. 31 - 100

Seal 2. Red horse: the persecution and affliction of early Christians; A.D. 100 - 323

Seal 3. Black horse: the apostasy of Christianity; A.D. 323 - 538

Seal 4. Pale horse: the dominion of false doctrine (Dark Ages) papal supremacy; A.D. 538 - 1500

Seal 5. Souls beneath the altar: Persecution of the Protestants by the papacy; A.D. 1500 - 1755

Seal 6. Harbingers of Christ's return; Lisbon earthquake, 1755; Dark day, May, 1780; Falling of the stars, November, 1833; Islands and Mountains moved at Second Coming

Seal 7. Half hour of silence; Heaven empty for 15 days during the Second Coming

**Note:** Adventists are uncertain about the purpose, identity and contents of the book sealed with seven seals. They do however, distinguish the book with seven seals from the books of record.

**LW:** The seven seals were placed on the Book of Life before the world came to be. The Book of Life was written by the Father. Through His foreknowledge, the Father wrote a complete history of the world in advance and He blotted out the names of those who would choose to refuse His salvation. Then, He sealed the book with seven seals so that no one could know its contents until the right time. When the little horn power was brought down in 1798, Jesus was found worthy in Heaven to receive the Book of Life and He begin opening the seals. As each seal is broken, the exposure of the book's contents draws nearer and new truths about Jesus are unfolded, thus the opening of the seven seals is a process revealing all that Jesus is. The contents of the Book of Life will be seen when the seventh seal is broken open at the end of the millennium. Then, God will be fully exonerated from Lucifer's claim that God is manipulative because the books of record and the Book of Life will be shown, at that time, to be identical. The seals and their respective time-periods are:

Seal 1. White horse: The religious impediment to proclaiming the salvation of Jesus was finally removed in 1798 when Berthier took the pope captive. This process continues until the close of mercy. This beginning stands in marked contrast to a salvation controlled by clergy for more than a millennium.

Seal 2. Red horse: The promotion and distribution of the teachings of Jesus (The Bible) throughout the world; the establishment of Missionary and Bible Societies, both in Europe and America, at the turn of the 19th century marks the opening of this seal. This printing and distribution of the Bible continues until presses can print no more. This event stands in marked contrast to the limited access people had to the Bible during the rule of the Catholic Church.

Seal 3. Black horse: The proclamation of the ministry of Jesus as man's High Priest and judge in heaven's sanctuary includes the pre-Advent judgment. This "new light" was discovered in 1844 and its value reaches to the close of mercy.

Seal 4. Pale horse: This seal reveals the authority of Jesus. Specifically, the opening of this marks the beginning of the Great Tribulation. Under this seal, the seven trumpets sound. In Adventist terms, the opening of this seal marks the beginning of the early time of trouble.

Seal 5. Souls beneath the altar reveals the faith of Jesus. These are martyrs for Christ's sake. Martyrdom comes to an end at the close of mercy. Many will stand firm and lose their lives because of the testimony they maintain.

Seal 6. Global and cosmic signs mark Christ's return and the revealing of His glory.

Seal 7. The half hour of silence occurs at the end of millennium, when the seventh seal is broken and the Book of Life is opened and its contents revealed.

Timing of seven seals compared:

| | Seal 1 | Seal 2 | Seal 3 | Seal 4 | Seal 5 | Seal 6 | Seal 7 |
|---|---|---|---|---|---|---|---|
| **SDA** | A.D. 31 | 100 | 323 | 538 | 1500 | 1755 | 2nd Advent |
| **LW** | 1798 | 1800 | 1844 | 1994? | 1996? | 2nd Advent | End of 1,000 years |

**Note:** I find that the Lamb's Book of Life is the book sealed with seven seals because it is the only book in Revelation's story that the Lamb receives.

### Revelation 8 and 9 - The Seven Trumpets

**SDA:** The seven trumpets, the seven seals and the seven churches of Revelation cover the same time-period, but with different emphasis. The churches reveal the state of God's people at different times, the seals represent religious events and the trumpets represent political events. Adventists believe that the earthquake and the manifestations that accompany the casting down of the censer *before* the trumpets begin represents the close of mercy. (See Revelation 8:2-6.) The trumpet events and their respective dates have long been thought to be:

Trumpet 1.  A.D. 395; Alaric leads the Goths against Rome

Trumpet 2.  A.D. 428-465; Genseric leads the Vandals against Rome

Trumpet 3.  A.D. 460; Attila leads the Huns against Rome.

Trumpet 4.  A.D. 476; Odoacer forces the collapse of Rome.

Trumpet 5.  The rise of the barbarian Othman who became the founder of the great Ottoman Empire in 1299.

Trumpet 6.  The fall of the Ottoman Empire on August 11, 1840.

Trumpet 7.  1844 to the close of mercy.

**LW:** I believe the seven trumpets are yet future and the first four trumpets serve as awakening events to the whole world that Jesus is coming. Contrary to the Adventist position, I believe the casting down of the censer occurs before the first trumpet sounds. And, the accompanying earthquake marks the end of Christ's *daily* ministry in heaven on behalf of man. After the earthquake, the Great Tribulation begins.

Trumpet 1. Meteoric showers of burning hail / horrific world-wide fires

Trumpet 2. Asteroid impact on the sea / great tsunami, many ships and seaports destroyed / sea creatures die by the millions

Trumpet 3. Asteroid impact on a continent / contaminated water caused by ground waves sheering septic systems and water wells / many people die from drinking bad water

Trumpet 4. Series of great volcano eruptions / period of great darkness around the world follows

Trumpet 5. The devil is released from the spirit world so that he can physically appear at various places on earth. His demons torment the wicked and lay the blame upon the 144,000.

Trumpet 6. The devil sets up his one-world-church-state / the wearing of the tattoo (mark) of the beast implemented

Trumpet 7. The close of mercy / God's temple and the Ark of the Covenant literally seen in the heavens by man / Seven last plagues follow

In short, I find that the seven trumpets to be forthcoming "Acts of God" that are central to Revelation's story. In fact, it is the response of man to the first four trumpets (legislated attempts to appease God) that produces world-wide religious intolerance and religious persecution.

Timing of seven trumpets compared:

|      | Censer | T1    | T2    | T3    | T4    | T5    | T6    | T7    |
|------|--------|-------|-------|-------|-------|-------|-------|-------|
| SDA: | Future | 395   | 428   | 460   | 476   | 1299  | 1840  | 1844  |
| LW:  | 1994?  | 1994? | 1994? | 1994? | 1994? | 1996? | 1996? | 1997? |

**Note:** Adventists believe that the casting down of the censer and the seventh trumpet occurs at the close of probation. I believe the casting down of the censer marks the *beginning* of the seven trumpets (seven first plagues) and the seventh trumpet marks the close of probation. I anticipate the first four trumpets will sound at short intervals and could begin as early as late 1994 or early 1995.

### Revelation 10 and 11 - The little book, The Two Witnesses

**SDA:** Adventists teach that Revelation 10 applies to a time period beginning in 1840. In essence, the statement, "There is no more time," means that there are no more prophetic time-periods left to be fulfilled before the coming of Jesus. The little book that lies open in the hand of the angel, which John was required to eat, represents the prophecies of Daniel and Revelation which were believed to be understood about August, 1840. And, the prophetic conclusion that Jesus was coming in 1844 was sweet to tell....

But, the great disappointment of 1844 turned out to be very bitter to endure. Shortly after the bitter experience, Adventists came to understand the ministry of Jesus in heaven and the relevancy of 1844 to His work in heaven's sanctuary. By 1859 they had come to understand the Sabbath and its role in prophecy. A few years later, Adventists began to see that a world-wide work lay before them, and the responsibility of presenting the three angel's messages must be given *again,* this time, on a global scale. Today, Adventists consider the first presentation of the prophecies from 1840 to 1844 and the *giving again* of the prophecies of Daniel and Revelation as the time-period between 1844 and the close of probation. (See Revelation 10:11.)

Adventists teach that Revelation 11:1-13 applies to the French Revolution (1789-1798). The Two Witnesses are the Old and New Testaments. The beast from the abyss is France. The 1,260 days that the Two Witnesses prophesy in sackcloth occurred between A.D. 538 and 1798. The Two Witnesses were "killed" during the French Revolution for 3.5 day/years (1793-1796) when France outlawed ownership of the Bible and in legislative assembly joyfully declared there is no God. The resurrection of the Two

Witnesses is interpreted to be the rise and establishment of Bible Societies which translated and published millions of Bibles during the 19th century.

**LW:** Revelation 10 applies to events that are about to take place. The little book in the angel's hand represents a final and correct understanding of all the prophecies in Daniel and Revelation. The statement, "There shall be no more delay (or time of waiting)," is directed at the four angels in Revelation 7 who are holding back the four winds until the 144,000 are sealed.

In this chapter, John enters into the experience and work of the 144,000. He eats the book which is sweet to understand (digests the meaning), but telling the world the truth about God's salvation during the time-period of God's wrath will be very bitter because of intense persecution.

The work of Adventists since 1844 represents the first giving of the prophecies. But, there are portions of Daniel and Revelation which are incorrectly understood. But, when time arrives for the sealing and empowerment of the 144,000, the truth from Daniel and Revelation will be fully disclosed, and the gospel will be powerfully presented *again* all over the world in 1,260 literal days. This is the "prophesying again" mentioned in Revelation 10:11.

**Summary on Revelation 11:**

|  | 2 Witnesses: Candlesticks Olive Trees | 1,260 days | Beast from Abyss that kills them | 3.5 days |
|---|---|---|---|---|
| **SDA:** | 1. Old Test. 2. New Test. | 538-1798 | France | 1793-1796 |
| **LW:** | 1. Bible 2. Holy Spirit | 1994?-1997? | Lamb-like (the devil) | Future, death decree |

**Revelation 12 and 13**

**SDA:** Adventists have two rules about prophecy that force the following conclusions. First, a beast in Bible prophecy is *always* a nation or kingdom.

Secondly, prophetic time-periods are *always* reckoned in day/years. Therefore, the great red dragon of Chapter 12 is primarily the Roman Empire, first seen as pagan Rome and then later, as papal Rome. The dragon (papal Rome) persecutes the woman for 1,260 years. Then, the earth (the USA) helps the woman by providing refuge. At the end of the chapter, the dragon (papal Rome) prepares for war against the saints.

The leopard-like beast of Revelation 13 is believed to be the papacy. Soon, the papal head will be healed and the persecution of the saints will resume. But, the 42 months in verse 5 are reckoned as day/years, therefore the time period is A.D. 538 to 1798.

Adventists believe the lamb-like beast of Revelation 13 is the USA. This beast was gentle like a lamb at first (had a constitution granting religious freedom), but later in an apostate state (religious liberties revoked), the USA will become a powerful tool of Satan. The Church teaches that the United States and the papacy will unite for religious and political reasons and become very close allies. The result is that the world's super-power, the USA, will impose papal doctrine (Sunday worship) upon the inhabitants of earth. Sunday worship is the mark of the leopard-like beast's authority. Thus, this evil duo will someday kill those who refuse to worship on Sunday.

LW: The great red dragon in Chapter 12 is the devil who was cast out of heaven. The story in Chapter 12 is about the devil who persecutes the people of God. The devil chases the woman to the wilderness for 1,260 years because the Jubilee calendar is in effect and time is reckoned in day/years. The earth helped the woman to escape from the torment of the dragon. This refers to the refuge that became available to the saints when God opened up a new continent with a wonderful constitution; namely, the USA. Angered by the escape of the saints, the devil is preparing for a final assault upon the people of God.

The appearing of the leopard-like beast of Revelation 13 is yet future. It rises to power in response to God's wrath. This beast represents Babylon which will be a confused union of the world's religious systems. The deadly wound received by the papacy in 1798 will be healed with the establishment of Babylon. Babylon will have power for 42 literal months because the 42 months occur after the Jubilee calendar comes to an end in March, 1994. Babylon will have authority over all nations and the inhabitants of earth will obey the laws imposed by Babylon or suffer severe penalties.

The lamb-like beast is the physical appearing of the devil claiming to be God. He will prove his divinity by calling fire down out of heaven and by working great signs, miracles and wonders. He will deceive the people of earth. Eventually the devil will set up his government. He will consolidate the world's religious systems into a one world religion which will be an image or likeness of Babylon. He will require everyone to wear a tattoo on their forehead or right hand in order to buy or sell. This is the mark of the lamb-like beast, the devil.

**Summary on Revelation 12 and 13:**

|  | Dragon | Leopard-like beast | Lamb-like beast | Seven heads |
|---|---|---|---|---|
| **SDA:** | Rome | Papacy | USA | ? |
| **LW:** | The angel Lucifer | Future rise of Babylon | Physical appearing of devil | World's religions |

**Revelation 14 — Three angel's messages**

**SDA:** The first angel's message began in the late 1830's. This message was the announcement that Christ was coming. The second angel's message began around 1840. This message was the announcement that Protestant denominations were part of Babylon because they would not embrace the Millerite message. The third angel's message began in 1844 and continues to the close of mercy. This announcement is that if anyone worships on Sunday — when Sunday becomes a testing point, he will receive the wrath of God.

**LW:** The Adventist Church, by God's design, has carried a partial understanding of the three messages around the world since 1844. But, with the unsealing of Daniel, the three angel's messages have been improved and I believe they will be *fully delivered* by the 144,000. The first message begins with the announcement of the judgment of the living.

The second message announces the corruption of Babylon which rises in response to the seven trumpets. The third message is a strong warning not to submit to, or receive the mark of the glorious being (the devil) who claims to be God (the lamb-like beast).

## Revelation 15 and 16

SDA: The seven last plagues are literal and they occur after the close of mercy. They fall upon all who received the mark of the beast.

LW: The seven last plagues are literal and they occur after the close of mercy. These are punitive judgments that fall upon all who chose the mark of the beast.

## Revelation 17

SDA: The identity of the seven heads, the beast from the abyss in verse 8, the eighth king, the ten horns: explanations vary widely — no consensus view.

LW: The seven heads are the religious systems of the world: Atheism, Heathenism, Islam, Judaism, Eastern Mysticism, Catholicism and Protestantism. (Head number 6 is the head that was wounded, but the deadly wound was healed.) The beast from the abyss is the lamb-like beast, the physical appearing of the devil. He is the eighth king that will rule over the seven religions of the world. The ten horns who receive power for one hour to kill all the saints with a universal death decree are ten kings that the devil will appoint when he sets up his one world government.

## Revelation 18

SDA: The message: "Come out of her (the harlot) my people..." is called the Loud Cry, also called the fourth angel's message, and it adds greater power to the three angel's messages down to the close of mercy.

LW: The call to come out of Babylon is the final and most powerful message given throughout earth. It joins with the three angel's messages until the close of mercy. This message begins when the devil sets up his one-world government and implements the mark of the beast during the sixth trumpet.

## Summary

The essential difference between my views and those of the Church might be summed up in one sentence: I find more end-time details about coming events in prophecy than the Church is willing to accept. Contrary to the claims of my adversaries, I have not diminished the pillars of Adventism. I stand firm on the holiness of God's law and the Sabbath-rest test. I stand firm on the importance of 1844 and the ministry of Christ in heaven's sanctuary. I stand firm on the state of the dead and a pre-Advent judgment. I stand firm on salvation by faith alone. And, I stand firm on the imminent return of Jesus. These are the pillars of Adventism, and as far as I can see, they have become brighter and more important as a result of following the rules of interpretation that I have found.

But, the reader should not lose sight of this point in matters pertaining to the future fulfillment of prophecy. Time will fully expose a great chasm between truth and error. Time will tell. Then, the wise will be separated from the foolish.

# Prophets can make mistakes

Prophets, in this study, are defined as people that God speaks to through a process known as inspiration. Prophets usually receive information from God in a dream or a vision and after the dream or vision is concluded, the prophet then tells what he saw or heard in his own words. This view of inspiration is called "plenary" because God allows the prophet to express his thoughts in his own words.

The plenary concept of inspiration stands in contrast to "verbal" inspiration. Verbal inspiration is defined as the process where God speaks to a person and the person either writes or says what God told them to say. Thus, those believing in verbal inspiration take the words of prophets to be inerrant and the infallible Word of God.

These two views on inspiration determine, to a great extent, how one interprets the writings of prophets.

### A parable

Here is a parable explaining inspiration as I have come to understand it: Suppose you, an ordinary person, are blindfolded and taken by the hand onto the stage of a totally dark auditorium filled with hundreds of silent people. The blindfold is then removed, but you can't see or hear anything because of the darkness and the silence. Your guide shines a narrow beam of light to your left and you see three people in the light. Then, he shines the spotlight toward the back of the auditorium and you see two people. Lastly, he shines the spotlight toward the right of the auditorium and you see one person. The blindfold is then replaced, and as you exit the room, your guide says that you should tell others everything you experienced and saw. When you begin to tell others of your experience, you will become known as a prophet because you speak about the things *revealed by God*.

Here's the meaning of the parable. God chooses very common people to become His servants. And, the vision experience is so life-like that Paul could not tell whether he remained "in the body" or whether he was taken "out of the body." (See 2 Corinthians 12:2.) On the other hand, John concluded he was taken "out of the body" during his vision on Patmos. (Revelation 4:2) The point here is that God reveals wonderful things to common people. He shines a *spotlight* on some aspect of truth. Then, the vision ends and the same common person begins to tell what he saw and heard. Even more, the prophet integrates the *revealed* information with what he already knows about God's truth (he conceptually connects what he saw with what he knows).

But, every prophet's view of truth is limited. (In the parable, the prophet only saw six people, but remember, the auditorium was full of people.) A hundred years pass and God does the same thing again, except this time, he shines the spotlight in places *not seen* before. Thus, more truth about the contents of the room is revealed. Centuries go by, and God continues this process — ever revealing more about the contents of the room. Thus, the truth about the contents of the room continues to unfold at God's discretion.

At the very end of time, God will fully reveal the contents of the room. The 144,000 will be taken into the room and God will flip on the ceiling lights so that they might behold the WHOLE truth about the contents of the room. The 144,000 will quickly see the contents of the room and they will powerfully proclaim the WHOLE truth.

### Five points

This crude parable teaches five important things about God, truth, inspiration and man. First, man cannot see more truth than God wants seen at any given time. Secondly, each prophet receives a partial view of God's truths. So, the testimony of any one prophet is incomplete until the 144,000 appear. Thirdly, truth is additive. Therefore, one must take into account all that has been written about truth, line upon line and precept upon precept, to understand what has been revealed and what was not revealed. Fourthly, the final generation on earth hears the whole truth (as it relates to the fulfillment of the Plan of Salvation) because God will reveal the contents of truth to His servants, the 144,000. They will powerfully announce the *everlasting* gospel to the world. Lastly, this parable teaches that new light is not inconsistent with previous light.

However, this parable demonstrates how more light opposes ideas that were thought to be light.

This last point needs some explanation. For example, the first prophet only saw six people in the room. And, many people believed his testimony and formed a church called, "The Church of Six People." But, later on, another prophet testifies that he saw 12 people in the room. Some students of the prophets combine the two reports and conclude that there must be 18 people in the room. They form a church called, "The Church of 18 People." But, other students of the prophets conclude that there are 12 people in the room because they believe the second prophet saw the *same* six people revealed to the first prophet, so the second prophet was shown six new people. This last group forms a church called, "The Church of 12 People." So, there is some diversity over the sightings of the prophets because the information from both prophets is incomplete and is therefore subject to a certain amount of ambiguity. (But, each church is certain that *they* have the truth on the contents in the room.)

But, when the 144,000 see the entire room lighted up, they will report that 1,000 people were in the room! Now, their report will anger those churches who insist that "their inerrant prophet" said there were fewer people in the room. But, a few people in each church, those who understood from the beginning that each prophet's report was incomplete, will rejoice to learn that the room is full of people. Whereupon, these will be thrown out of their churches for believing such foolishness.

So, a proper understanding of inspiration is most important to the study of the Bible. And, the contents of truth, revealed by later light is always consistent with the contents seen by previous light if one is willing to sort through the details and find the harmony. This is the point where so many people get confused: One must work hard to distinguish between what is light and what is called light.

### Inconsistencies not a stumbling stone

The plenary concept of inspiration helps to explain a number of inconsistencies found in the Bible. For example, in Matthew 8:28, Jesus met two men possessed by demons when they sailed across the lake to the region of the Gadarenes. Jesus commanded the demons to come out of the two men and enter a large herd of pigs. Whereupon, the pigs ran into the sea and drown themselves. But, a textual point about this incident rises. Two other gospel writers say that there was only one man and not two! (See Mark 5:2 and Luke 8:27.) So, what difference does it make if there are two men or one man? Very little as far as the story goes. But, this tiny point demonstrates that Bible writers had the freedom to say what they thought. Any student of the four gospels knows that there are a number of discrepancies between the gospels. But, such is not a problem if one correctly understands the properties of inspiration. Rather, the discrepancies make Bible study interesting. What a delight to solve a mystery and find the truth!

Bible writers demonstrate a large latitude in writing. Some express their own opinions and clearly say so. (See 1 Corinthians 7:12.) In other places, Bible writers express their opinions and they don't say that it is their opinion! (Examples provided later.) So, how can one distinguish between truth and that which is called truth? Before addressing this question, one more comment is needed.

Any discussion on the subject of inspiration is likely to generate a dispute for two *human* reasons. First, some humans fear that if every word written by prophets is not inspired, then non-inspired people cannot distinguish between that which was revealed and that which was not. In short, they claim that if the concept of plenary inspiration is true, then no one can *absolutely* separate truth from error. But, how can God expect us to absolutely separate truth from error when truth is ever growing? At any given time, we only have partial truth. Be warned: Plenary inspiration militates against those who enjoy thinking that they have intellectually surrounded and therefore understand, the WHOLE truth. Some people see everything in black and white terms. So, be careful. The plenary process undermines "the proof-text" or sound-bite approach to truth.

Secondly, the subject of inspiration often brings a dispute because *very few* people honestly try to reconcile *all* that has been written on any given topic by inspired people. For instance, I have observed people talking about some specific Bible topic and one will turn to *his* texts and offer them as evidence supporting his position. Then, the other person will dismiss those texts and offer *his* texts as proof supporting his position. Think about this observation: Texts from the *same* book militating against each other. How can this be when both sets of texts come from the Bible? Perhaps the better question should be, "How can one person ignore some texts and emphasize others when all texts have equal authority?" So, the next time you get into a discussion on some Bible topic, make sure you have considered the contribution of all relevant texts before you do.

## The $64,000 question

So, how can one tell when prophets are expressing their opinion and/or determine when they are expressing a direct revelation from God? Answer: By the harmony that comes from the sum of all the parts. For example, look at this text: **"In a similar way, Sodom and Gomorrah and the surrounding towns gave themselves up to sexual immorality and perversion. They serve as an example of those who suffer the punishment (vengeance KJV) of eternal fire."** (Jude 1:7) I fully understand how people can read this text and conclude, *on the authority of Jude alone,* that the Sodomites and the Gomorrahites are burning in an eternal (endless) fire right now. And, if this were the only text in the Bible commenting on punishment and eternal fire, I would agree that Jude's comment about God's punishment could be used to support an eternal burning fire.

But, if one is thorough about his study of the Bible, he realizes there are some 40 authors — all having the same experience called, "inspiration." So, why not examine all that has been said about God's punishment and eternal fire before reaching a conclusion? Notice this text: **"They (the wicked) marched across the breadth of the earth and surrounded the camp of God's people, the city he loves. But fire came down from heaven and devoured them."** (Revelation 20:9) Does Revelation conflict with Jude? Not if you place them side by side. John says that fire comes down from heaven at the end of the 1,000 years and it *devours* the wicked. Because of this, I take Jude's comment to mean that God rained fire down upon Sodom and Gomorrah and burned them up and this event serves as an *example* of what He is going to do again. Those who receive the punishment of the final fire will be devoured and the results are eternal. So, the proof of truth has to be found in the harmony of the sum of its parts. And sometimes, the harmony is difficult to find, but the contents of truth always align.

## Moral law and inspiration

Religion always distorts the truth about God. Because human beings are damaged by sin, it becomes inevitable that all religious structures become corrupt. God is far more generous with the diversity of man than religion allows. Religion by its nature, takes a set of beliefs and creates an exclusive God. Then people use their view of God to elevate *their* religion above all others and in the process, only separate themselves from each other. Some people claim there is only one God and that there are many different religions that serve Him. This is both true and not true. Yes, there is one God. But, every religion has its own God. For example, the God of the Baptist commands different things than the God of the Catholic. The God of the Moslem commands different things than the God of the Jew, etc.

When it comes to right and wrong, there are various commands from God that apply at various times. For example, at one time God commanded Noah to get on the ark, but in our day, such is not possible. At one time God commanded the Jews to offer a lamb on the altar of burnt offering, but in our time, such is not necessary. But, there are universal, timeless commands from God for all of humanity. These commands are called moral (basic) laws. In one sentence the commands say, "Love the Lord with all your heart, mind and soul and your neighbor as yourself." And, to prevent degenerate man from distorting the meaning of love, God defined the *results* of love so that human beings can test themselves to see if they are in compliance with His law of love. The test was written on two enduring tablets of stone. They are called the Ten Commandments. And, a life of love produces actions that are in harmony with God's law.

If righteous principles are applied to one's life, a noble and generous character comes forth. God made sure that the Ten Commandments are not hard to understand. They define moral truth in a profound way and in elegant form. And those willing to express these ten principles *through love*, glorify God.

These things have been said because the subject of inspiration is connected to the principles of right and wrong. When I say that prophets can make mistakes, the subject of moral law is one of the first to be raised, because many people think that moral law came through the prophets. But, consider this point: Moral law *was not* revealed through inspiration. God Himself came to earth and spoke the words from Sinai. (Exodus 20:1) I find no room for quibbling over the content of moral law. God Himself has spoken and what can any human being, inspired or non-inspired, change? Prophets are not God, they are *observers* of God. Prophets cannot alter what God has determined to be truth and herein lies a problem.

When Jesus walked upon the earth, He was Truth Incarnate. He came to reveal more about God's character and God's will. But, the Jews would not receive Christ as the Promised One nor did they believe His testimony for at least two reasons: Jesus said, **"This is the verdict: Light has come into the world, but men loved darkness instead of light because their deeds were evil. Everyone who does evil hates the light, and will not come into the light for fear that his deeds will be exposed."** (John 3:19,20) Secondly, Jesus told the Jews, **"If you believed Moses, you would believe me, for he wrote about me."** (John 5:46)

The first text above is self explanatory. But, the second text reveals something about human beings, religion and prophets. The Jews had exalted Moses to the place of God. They worshiped Moses. Of course, they would have denied such a statement and said that such a claim was blasphemous, but look at their actions. God, in the form of Jesus, stood right before them and they didn't recognize Him or the truth He presented. The Jews had taken the writings of Moses, shrouded them with false ideas, and the result was closed minds and self-righteousness. A terrible duo.

This brings us back to the point. Truth is always larger than any one prophet. Truth is larger than all prophets combined for God and His truths are infinite. And, He has not yet confirmed the details necessary for salvation in the end-time! But, when God chooses the 144,000, He will reveal the truth necessary for salvation in the end-time to them, and you can count on two things: First, the new truth from God will be consistent with moral law. Secondly, like the prophets of old, the 144,000 will greatly suffer the consequences of revealing more light. The 144,000 will greatly suffer because they will say things contrary to the beliefs of religious people. One must understand that prophets are always regarded as mere human beings in their day. They are not highly exalted until they are killed or die. Prophets suffer much because there is a big difference between truth and that which is called truth, and this revelation often makes people angry.

Notice the endless cycle. The devil leads religious people to corrupt the teachings of a dead prophet so that God's truth becomes highly corrupted. Later, God sends another prophet *to correct* the degenerate ideas people believe to be truth. The second prophet makes people angry and they kill him. Then, the second dead prophet becomes highly exalted. The devil leads people to corrupt the teachings of the second prophet so that God's truth is highly corrupted again. Then, God sends a third prophet... Do you get the picture?

**History and chronology**

There is one topic in the Bible where we can fully distinguish between a prophet's personal opinion and those truths he saw in vision. The test is simple. We simply compare his statements about timing with recorded history and notice the results. As a result of doing this, I find that many Old and New Testament writers alike thought they were living at or near the end of time. Notice the bold words in the following texts:

1.  (Obadiah 1:15) "The day of the Lord **is near** for all nations."
2.  (Joel 2:1) "Let all who live in the land tremble, for the day of the Lord is coming. It **is close** at hand."
3.  (Isaiah 13:6) "Wail, for the day of the Lord **is near**; it will come like destruction from the Almighty."
4.  (Ezekiel 30:3) "For the day **is near**, the day of the Lord **is near**—a day of clouds, a time of doom for the nations."
5.  (Zephaniah 1:14) "The great day of the Lord **is near—near and coming quickly.**"
6.  (1 Corinthians 7:29) "What I mean, brothers, is that the **time is short**. From now on those who have wives should live as if they had none."
7.  (1 Peter 4:7) "The end of all things **is near**. Therefore be clear minded and self-controlled so that you can pray."
8.  (James 5:8) "You too, be patient and stand firm, because the Lord's coming **is near**."

9.    (1 John 2:18) "Dear children, this is the last hour; and as you have heard that the antichrist is coming, even now many antichrists have come. This is how we know **it is the last hour**."

A host of scholars have used clever and fanciful footwork to show that "soon" or "near" in these texts means something other than "close at hand." But, a jury of ordinary people would have to say on the basis of textual evidence that all of the writers listed above used near and soon to mean "close at hand."

We shouldn't lose faith in the prophets nor should we throw out the Bible because they didn't know that thousands of years would come and go before Jesus would return to earth. In fairness to them we must remember that their understanding of truth was partial and thus faulty. It should not come as a surprise to learn that God revealed a number of things to the prophets which they *merged* into an opinion of what they thought was a soon coming reality. Look at the nine texts above again and read the previous sentence three times — this is a crucial point.

With respect to time and chronology, there are two tests that must be applied to the writings of prophets.  They are:

   1. Historical record
   2. Apocalyptic prophecy

History clearly shows that almost 1,900 years have come and gone since the prophet John wrote, "This is the last hour." (1 John 2:18) Did John make a mistake in calculating his chronological position within God's timing? Yes. Did God show John that he was living in the last hour? No. God does not lie. Does John's mistake lessen his work as a prophet? No. It simply reveals that John did not know about God's timing even though he was acquainted with the 1,260 days time-period in Revelation 12:6. (John wrote the book of Revelation.) What John didn't know is that God reckoned those days as 1,260 years! God did not tell John he was living in the last days nor did God tell John the meaning of the time-periods in Revelation. So, John was free to say that he *thought* he was living in the last hour.

There is another test we can apply to the truth-full-ness of a prophet's claim on chronology. The test is apocalyptic prophecy. Apocalyptic prophecy is defined as those prophecies in Daniel and Revelation having chronological structure. This means, apocalyptic prophecy lays out the chronology of time and marks its passage through the fulfillment of events as they occur. Daniel 2 is an excellent example of apocalyptic prophecy showing the passage of time. But, John didn't understand the prophecies of Daniel. If he had, he would have known that the little horn power of Daniel 7 would persecute the saints for 1,260 years. He would have known that the 2,300 year prophecy ended in 1844. But, it wasn't time for anyone to understand that part of God's truth in John's day. So, one cannot make an accurate statement about the nearness of Christ's return without first having knowledge of apocalyptic prophecies. This includes the prophets.

My point is that prophets can say whatever they want to say about the things they are shown. This is the meaning of plenary inspiration. But, their claims about the nearness of Christ's return must be tested by history and apocalyptic prophecy. And, on both counts, they all made a mistake.

Keep in mind, the mistake is not a moral issue. The mistake exists because, as Paul said, **"For we know in part and we prophesy in part."** (1 Corinthians 13:9)

## Comments about Hebrews

Paul makes certain claims about chronology in the book of Hebrews that Adventists need to resolve. Notice the highlighted portions of the following verses:

"We have this hope as an anchor for the soul, firm and secure. **It enters the inner sanctuary behind the curtain, where Jesus, who went before us,** *has entered* **on our behalf....**" (Hebrews 6:19,20)

**"When Christ came as high priest of the good things that are already here, he went through the greater and more perfect tabernacle that is**

not man-made, that is to say, not a part of this creation. He did not enter by means of the blood of goats and calves; but *he entered* the *Most Holy Place* once for all by his own blood." (Hebrews 9:11,12)

"Therefore, brothers, since we have confidence *to enter the Most Holy Place* by the blood of Jesus... let us draw near to God...." (Hebrews 10:19-22)

It is widely believed that Paul wrote the book of Hebrews about A.D. 64. And, from the above, it appears that Paul thought that Christ had entered the Most Holy Place as of A.D. 64 to officiate on behalf of God's people. This claim runs contrary to the Adventist position which says that Jesus entered the Most Holy Place in 1844.

Some Adventist scholars will argue that translations of the Greek text above is faulty. They argue that according to the Greek text, Paul does not place Jesus in the Most Holy Place at all, but only in the Holy Place. (Paul A. Gordon, *The Sanctuary, 1844, and the Pioneers*, pp. 43-56)

The Adventist argument has no merit for three reasons. First, the central point in Hebrews is that Jesus *recently* became man's High Priest on the basis of His sacrifice, and as such, He alone can enter into the very presence of the Father on our behalf. This theme runs parallel to the services of the High Priest in the Old Testament sanctuary because the *only person* who could enter into the "inner room" on the Day of Atonement was the High Priest. (1 Kings 6:16,19; Leviticus 16) Secondly, Paul clearly says that Jesus has gone into the "inner sanctuary," and he identifies the second or inner room as behind the veil, the Holiest Place. (Hebrews 6:19,20; 9:7) Lastly, Paul knew the High Priest could only enter the Most Holy Place at a specific time each year. (Hebrews 9:7) And, since Paul thought he was living at the end of the world, the appointed time for Christ to enter the Most Holy had arrived. (Compare Hebrews 9:26; Acts 17:31; 1 Corinthians 7:29 and 2 Corinthians 5:10.)

The Adventist Bible Commentary ignores the textual evidence in Hebrews on Paul's sense of timing on the ministry of Jesus. Adventists keep Jesus in the Holy Place until 1844. But, other Christians read the book of Hebrews and clearly see that Paul puts Jesus in the Most Holy Place in A.D. 64. Adventists resist their claim because they understand the importance of 1844. Therefore, they believe Jesus entered the Most Holy

Place in 1844, at the end of the 2,300 days. But, when asked for a Bible text that explicitly places Christ in the Most Holy Place in 1844, Adventists can't produce one. They *assume* that Jesus entered the Most Holy Place on the basis that the High Priest only entered the Most Holy Place on the Day of Atonement (Leviticus 16) which began at the end of 2,300 years (Daniel 8:14). This assumption is also underscored by the fact, they claim, that the seven trumpets of Revelation have been fulfilled.

**Paul saw Jesus without knowing the timing**

This writer believes that Paul intended to convey the idea that Jesus was in the Most Holy Place in A.D. 64. Here's why:

1.   The apostle Paul did not anticipate the second coming to be two thousand years away. In fact, Paul expected to be among the translated! "...Then *we* which are alive and remain...." (1 Thessalonians 4:15) He also begins Hebrews by claiming that God has spoken "in these last days." (Hebrews 1:2) And Paul identifies his sense of time as being the end of the age. (Hebrews 9:26)

2.   The central theme of Hebrews is the ministry of Jesus, "Our High Priest." The unique service of the High Priest's occurred once each year in the Most Holy Place on the Day of Atonement — in the presence of God. And, as far as Paul knew, Jesus had gone before the Father as man's High Priest to conclude the plan of salvation, "Once for all, at the end of the age."

3.   These is no evidence in any of Paul's writings showing that he understood the 2,300 day prophecy would terminate in 1844.

4.   It is consistent to say that God reveals information to prophets but rarely associates a chronological date with the event. The understanding of chronology is left to affected generations — thus all of the New Testament apostles thought the second coming was imminent.

5.   The importance of Christ's ministry in the Most Holy Place as described by Paul in Hebrews is enhanced when we apply the

2,300 day prophecy. If we understand that a prophet's
knowledge of chronology is subject to the tests of history and
apocalyptic structure, no problem exists concerning Paul's
mistaken opinion on the matter of timing.

Paul didn't understand the apocalyptic timing of the events in Hebrews!
God did not reveal the meaning of Daniel 8:14 to him. So, what was
Paul to think about the scenes presented before him?

Here's a simple solution to the problem. Paul was taken into vision and
zoomed forward to 1844 to behold the ministry of Jesus in the Most
Holy Place. When Paul came out of vision, he assumed that the ministry
of Jesus was taking place at the time of the vision and he writes accordingly.
What Paul saw was true. What Paul thought concerning the chronology
of Christ's ministry was wrong. He didn't know about 1844.

Adventists have had a difficult time with the timing in Hebrews when
dealing with other denominations that place a lot of emphasis on taking
the Bible *just as it reads*. Most of these denominations interpret the
timing of Hebrews just like Paul because they don't understand the
importance of 1844 either. Even a number of Adventist preachers are
beginning to deny the importance of 1844. They read Hebrews and say
that Jesus began His ministry as man's High Priest at the cross. But,
don't forget the tests of history and apocalyptic prophecy.

The solution to chronology becomes simple when we understand that a
prophet's statements involving chronology is subject to historical and
apocalyptic confirmation. Paul did see Jesus ministering as our High
Priest. He didn't know the timing — he assumed it was on-going at the
time of his vision. Again, history and apocalyptic prophecy combine to
clear up the problem. I think Paul would be quite happy to know what
we know now!


**Ellen White**

As said earlier in this book, this writer believes that Ellen White was
an inspired person, inspired in the same sense as John, Peter and Paul.
And, as the reader may guess, this writer believes that Ellen White must

be subjected to the same two tests regarding chronology, history and apocalyptic prophecy, as all Bible writers must be. And, applying these two tests to Ellen White and finding she is wrong on some chronology does not diminish her works any more than learning that Paul was wrong about the timing of the ministry of Jesus in heaven.

Ellen Harmon-White was born in 1827. She grew up during an era of great religious interest that swept both North America and Europe. William Miller came to Ellen's hometown with his "end of the world" message in 1839 and Ellen's parents accepted and endorsed the Millerite message. As every Adventist knows, William Miller taught that Jesus was returning to earth in 1843 (later corrected to 1844).

As the Millerite movement grew in momentum and size, men of various backgrounds joined Miller in preaching "the end of all things has come." Because the Millerites believed that 1844 marked the end of the world, they necessarily took the position that essentially all of Revelation's prophecies had been fulfilled (or were imminently being fulfilled). Below are six prophetic components from Revelation which the Millerites believed were fulfilled prior to 1843:

1.  The sixth seal opened in 1755, marked by the Lisbon earthquake.
2.  The fifth trumpet sounded in 1299 and the sixth trumpet sounded on August 11, 1840.
3.  The beast that kills the Two Witnesses is France.
4.  The Two Witnesses of Revelation 11 are the Old and New Testaments.
5.  The beast with seven heads ten horns in Revelation 13 is the papacy in various forms.
6.  The lamb-like beast of Revelation 13 is the United States of America.

These six items are presented for two reasons. First, the reader needs to appreciate that these six conclusions are still defended by the Adventist Church today. And secondly, all of these concepts predate the ministry of Ellen White. In other words, Ellen White grew *into* these views. They were widely accepted around the time her ministry began because it was believed in those days that the world was going to end on or about October 22, 1844. And this belief naturally required that all pre-Advent prophecies be fulfilled before 1844.

Those Adventists who endured the great disappointment of 1844 went back to their Bibles to find their error. In the years that followed, they made some important discoveries about God's truth and God confirmed the accuracy of some of their discoveries through Ellen White. But, the Advent group did not let go of the prophetic base established by the Millerite movement. They clung to certain "fulfillments" as proof that Jesus was imminently coming and Ellen White was no exception. Notice the surety of her convictions and the consistent use of strong language on the following points:

a.  Speaking about the opening of the sixth seal in Revelation 12:6, Mrs. White says, "In fulfillment of this prophecy there occurred, in the year 1755, the most terrible earthquake that has ever been recorded." (GC 304)

b.  Speaking about the sixth trumpet she says, "At the very time specified, Turkey, through her ambassadors, accepted the protection of the allied powers of Europe, and thus placed herself under the control of Christian nations. The event exactly fulfilled the prediction." (GC 335)

c.  Speaking about the beast that comes up out of the Abyss and kills the Two Witnesses she says, "As they were approaching the termination of their work in obscurity, war was to be made upon them by the power represented as the 'beast that ascendeth out of the bottomless pit....' This prophecy has received a most exact and striking fulfillment in the history of France." (GC 268,269)

d.  "The Two Witnesses represent the Scriptures of the Old and the New Testament." (GC 267)

e.  Speaking on the beast with seven heads and ten horns in Revelation 13, she says, "This prophecy, which is nearly identical with the description of the little horn of Daniel 7, unquestionably points to the papacy." (GC 439)

f.   Speaking on the identity of the lamb-like beast in Revelation 13, she says, "One nation, and only one, meets the specifications of this prophecy; it points unmistakably to the United States of America." (GC 440)

g.   Speaking about the concluding scenes of the seventh trumpet (Revelation 11:19) she says, "Therefore the announcement that the temple of God was opened in heaven and the ark of His testament was seen points to the opening of the most holy place of the heavenly sanctuary in 1844 as Christ entered there to perform the closing work of the atonement." (GC 433)

I find that Ellen White was fully convinced of the fulfillment of each one of these items and her consistent use of language clearly indicates so. She was *as certain* of the fulfillments presented above as she was about the appearing of Jesus in the middle of the 70th week. Notice her words: "...and Christ's baptism and anointing by the Holy Spirit, A.D. 27, *exactly fulfilled* the specification [of the prophecy]." (GC 410)

Now, two things must be said. First, I find items *a-g* to be faulty because they cannot be validated using the tests of historical confirmation or compliance with known rules of apocalyptic prophecy. Secondly, even though I find her conclusions to be wrong, this does not lessen her work as a prophetess. These prophetic conclusions did not originate with Ellen White and neither have they been explicitly confirmed by a vision. Rather, these prophetic conclusions were in vogue *before* her ministry began and she saw no reason to question them.

Apparently, God did not impress Ellen White with the necessity of validating these things; therefore, she says nothing about large segments of Daniel and Revelation. When challenged on these points, Adventists feel that they must defend the inerrancy and good name of Ellen White. But, when asked about texts that she said nothing about, they often shrug them off as unimportant. So, how can one discuss the contents of the Bible with those who will only discuss the writings of Ellen White?

I believe God reserved a complete and correct understanding of prophetic truth for the last generation. After all, the final generation is THE generation that will experience the Great Tribulation and the mark of the beast.

**The question rises again**

After reviewing items a-g, I ask, "Did Ellen White present her own opinions in these matters, or is she confirming the truth through inspiration?" We have to apply the tests of history and apocalyptic prophecy to confirm or deny the accuracy of her claims. And, one of the easiest places to challenge the claims of Ellen White with history is her view of the sixth trumpet. Ellen White was convinced that August 11, 1840 brought "an exact fulfillment" to the sixth trumpet. (See item b above.) What does history say?

1.  According to history, the Turkish empire *did not fall* on August 11, 1840 as the Millerites claimed. In fact, from 1783 to 1914, the boundaries of the Ottoman empire were reduced by a series of defeats. The war waged against the Sultan of Turkey in 1840 ended in 1841 without significant change. Today, the August 11, 1840 date set by the Millerites is not regarded by historians as an important date in Turkish history. In World War I, Turkey allied with Germany and lost even more territory. In 1923, the Grand National Assembly of Turkey proclaimed Turkey to be a republic and Turkey remains a sovereign nation to this day.

2.  The August 11, 1840 date is reached through a faulty King James translation of scripture that says: **"And the four angels were loosed, which were prepared for an hour, and a day, and a month, and a year, for to slay the third part of men."** (Revelation 9:15)

    Dr. Josiah Litch, the man that first concluded that the sixth trumpet must occur on the August 11, 1840 date, applied the day/year principle to this verse and derived 391 years and 15 days out of the hour, day, month and year mentioned.

    However, the King James translation of this verse is incorrect! The translation should read: **"And the four angels who had been kept ready for this very hour and day and month and year were released to kill a third of mankind."**

    Greek scholars around the world widely agree that the syntax of Revelation 9:15 points to a specific point in time and is therefore punctiliar and not the sum of chronological units of time. (See the NIV, NEB, NEV, RSV and ASV.) In short, this verse does not contain 391 years and 15 days. Rather, this verse points to a specific moment in time!

3.  Dr. Litch failed to adjust his 391 year, 15 day prophecy with the change of the calendar in October, 1582, when ten days were dropped from the calendar to correct for errors in the Julian calendar. Thus the August 11, 1840 date should be August 21, 1840. And *nothing* of historical consequence occurred on that date.

When presented with this evidence, many Adventist pastors and leaders will blindly insist on the fulfillment of the sixth trumpet. I suspect they do so for two reasons: First, they don't have an answer. Secondly, they believe Ellen White is infallible.

### The Historical Test

When the historical evidence of Turkish history is considered, when the Greek text is considered, and when the adjustment of the calendar is considered, Mrs. White's position on the sixth trumpet is simply wrong and if she were alive, she would clearly say so. She would update her position and remind all of us that she was not infallible. But, from her vantage point at the time, the sixth trumpet as interpreted by Dr. Litch, looked reasonable. However, just like statements from apostles John, Peter, and Paul, it can't be backed up with historical proof — nor by rules of interpretation that govern the meaning of apocalyptic prophecy.

Ellen White was aware of the potential problem that people would consider everything she said to be "the Word of God." She writes: "I find myself frequently placed where I dare give neither assent nor dissent to propositions that are submitted to me; for there is danger that any words I may speak shall be reported as something that the Lord has given me. It is not always safe for me to express my own judgment." (3SM 60)

God did not reveal much to Ellen White concerning chronology. In fact, she had to study the works of historians and others to understand the timing of most of her visions or dreams! Ellen White's son, W.C. White, says of his mother's visions concerning *The Great Controversy* and *The Desire of Ages*: "In a few of these scenes, chronology and geography were clearly presented, but in the greater part of the revelation of the flashlight scenes, which were exceedingly vivid... (they) were not marked geographically or chronologically, and she was left to study the Bible and history, and the writings of men... to get the chronological and geographical connection." (3SM 459)

According to W.C. White, most of his mother's visions and dreams on the great controversy between Christ and Satan were short segments or "flashlight scenes" of conversations or events that transpired. These scenes did not appear in chronological order, thus Ellen White had to study and search for herself to find the proper chronological place for these things. Given the comments of W.C. White, it is this writer's observation that most of her statements regarding chronology are her own opinion and were not confirmed by vision.

## She borrowed extensively from others

It is no secret that Ellen White's books contain the thoughts and writings of others. It is also no secret that people assisted Ellen White in the preparation of her books. Some, who have closely investigated these matters and seen the evidence, have been devastated. Walter Rea, a former Adventist pastor claims that Ellen White's *Conflict of the Ages Series,* is about 60% her work and 40% the works of others. His discovery, apparently validated by trustees of the White Estate, has raised some serious questions about Ellen White because many Adventists have come to believe that everything she wrote was original — right from God.

But, it's a repetition of history. Many Adventists have exalted Ellen White to the place of God. Of course, they would deny such a statement, but the Jews would have denied the same about Moses. And when Adventists find that Ellen White's writings are not entirely original, or that a considerable portion of her books are not entirely her own creation, they abandon their faith as if they have been deceived. But, this shouldn't be the case. True, they were deceived, but the deception was over the properties of inspiration.

Looking at the references taken from *The Great Controversy* above, we find that Mrs. White was very firmly convinced that most of Revelation was fulfilled. As mentioned before, her position on these points remained identical with the Millerite position which was the forerunner of Adventism. And I find that Mrs. White's endorsement of the Millerite position has literally stopped prophetic investigation within the Seventh-day Adventist Church since her death in 1915.

For more than ten years, a number of scholars and officials of the Church (including the White estate) have been aware of the historical problem with the sixth trumpet. They are fully aware of her use of the writings of others. So, what have they done to help the Church understand these matters? Nothing.

The longer nothing is done, the worse the problem. The Church faces a difficult choice. Either it openly admits that it has been wrong (and that Ellen White was wrong also) about the seven trumpets or eventually, as more people learn about the discrepancy, it must create some kind of mechanism to avoid such a confession. Some pastors have taken the latter course. They defend the error in *The Great Controversy* saying, "Ellen White was presenting Litch's position in the *Great Controversy* and not what John would have us understand about the trumpets." Such reasoning is unfair to Ellen White and even worse, creates a host of new problems.

We must be equitable. First, her language regarding the fulfillment of the sixth trumpet on page 335 is essentially the same language as her statements on the sixth seal, the Two Witnesses and the other points listed earlier. (Review items a-g and notice her use of language.) Secondly, to say that she was presenting Litch's position and not what John would have us believe places suspicion on her integrity. If she knew Litch's view was wrong, she would have said so. It is certainly out of character for Ellen White to present something as truth if she believed otherwise.

The heart of the problem is how do we continue to demonstrate confidence in Ellen White and yet recognize her limits as well as the limits of all prophets? What would be the reaction of Church members if the General Conference issued a statement saying, "We have investigated the claims of Ellen White on the sixth trumpet and find her to be wrong."? If they did, many in the church would abandon faith. Some would yawn and some would try to understand. But, sooner or later, discussions on this subject, Ellen White, the process of inspiration and historical records will cause a considerable stir within the church. Watch for it.

## Other problems with the trumpets

A historical view of the seven trumpets causes other problems. For example, why have we treated the seven trumpets as symbolic and the seven last plagues as literal? Why do we rely upon historical events for the first five trumpets that cannot be reconciled with the rules of interpretation used to eject Dr. Ford and his apotelesmatic view of prophecy from the Church in 1980? Truth is, the Adventist Church cannot show a historical fulfillment of the first five trumpets and maintain textual fidelity.

It is this writer's opinion that most people within the Church are indifferent about the trumpets (and the other five prophetic portions of Revelation mentioned earlier) because Ellen White thought these things were *fulfilled*. Some have said to me, "It is not necessary to understand what the first five trumpets were because the sixth one was fulfilled in 1840." Because the Church accepts her writings as inspired, many students of prophecy have been unwilling to consider any other explanation of Revelation than the views set forth in *The Great Controversy*. Since Adventists can't use Ellen White's writings to prove their prophetic positions, why should they build their prophetic understanding upon her? Adventists and all other Christians must stand solidly upon Scripture, the confirmation of history and the harmony of apocalyptic rules. There is no other ground from which to present a prophetic case.

## Fundamental Point

Historical records and apocalyptic prophecy agree because God Himself declares the end from the beginning. The apocalyptic prophecies of Daniel and Revelation are unconditional and inerrant. Neither Daniel or John understood what they saw in the visions that form the content of these books. Thus, both books contain very little (if any) personal opinion about chronology by their authors. These two books are uniquely designated as apocalyptic for they lay out the chronological structure of events culminating with the end of the world.

Unfortunately, many Adventists have a false sense of "prophetic security" in Ellen White. "We, the identified remnant of Revelation, having the Spirit of Prophecy (Ellen White's writings), know what is going to happen," they say. Such a position prevents further investigation of the prophecies and a faulty understanding of inspiration automatically condemns any who disagree with Ellen White. Herein lies a deadly peril. Like Israel of old, Adventists believe their favored status with God will ever remain unchanged — but look what is happening to the Church. Is it better prepared today to face the things before it than it was in Ellen White's day?

## When do the Trumpets sound?

It is this writer's opinion that all of the seven trumpets will sound in the near future. (This is presented more fully in the chapter on the seven trumpets.) The purpose of the seven trumpets is to awaken and arouse the people of earth that Jesus is about to close the door to mercy in heaven. This awakening will break open every mind and cause 5+ billion men and women to seriously consider the three angel's messages. Thus, the everlasting gospel will go rapidly to every nation, kindred, tongue and people.

There are a number of reasons why this writer believes the trumpets are yet to sound and will occur before probation closes. For now, a couple are listed:

1. The four angels that hold back the four winds in Revelation 7:1-4 have power to harm the earth, land and sea. After the sealing of the 144,000 is finished, the four angels loose the winds that harm the earth, land and sea. The predicted harm of Revelation 7:1-4 is clearly described in Revelation 8. The earth, sea and trees are seriously harmed during the first two trumpets. (Revelation 8:6-9)

2. The *purpose* of the seven trumpets in Revelation is similar to the Feast of Trumpets in the Old Testament. According to Jewish literature, trumpets began sounding on the first day of the seventh month to *warn* of the coming Day of Atonement (Yom Kippur) which occurred on the tenth day. The Day of Atonement in ancient Israel marked the annual close of God's mercy, and the trumpets warned everyone to get ready, get ready! If any Israelite was found with sins unconfessed and unforgiven on the Day of Atonement, he was cut off from the camp. In like fashion, the trumpets of Revelation begin blowing to arouse and awaken the people of earth to get ready, get ready! Jesus is about to close the door of mercy. The trumpets will open the minds of people on earth to hear the three angel's messages so that no one needs to be cut off from salvation. God has carefully designed the close of mercy so that anyone desiring to be saved, may be saved.

**Summary**

Ellen White wrote: "The Bible is written by inspired men, but it is not God's mode of thought and expression. It is that of humanity. God, as a writer, is not represented. Men will often say such an expression is not like God. But God has not put himself in words, in logic, in rhetoric, on trial in the Bible. The writers of the Bible were God's penmen, not His pen. Look at the different writers. It is not the words of the Bible that are inspired, but the men that were inspired." (1SM 21)

True prophets are ordinary people that receive revelations from God. They are free to express what they saw in their own words and free to exercise their own opinions regarding what they saw. Given the nature of dreams and visions, prophets of God can and do express opinions regarding chronology that have been shown to be wrong. The only way we can prove or disprove the chronological views of a prophet is through a harmony of historical records and by following rules of apocalyptic prophecy distilled from the Bible. Since Seventh-day Adventists claim that truth is ever unfolding, shouldn't it call for a no-holds barred Church-wide investigation of prophecy so that it can validate the claim?

# Problems with prophetic interpretation

After studying the prophecies of Daniel and Revelation for more than two decades, I have a few observations about the study of prophecy that might be helpful to those interested in studying prophecy. My purpose in this chapter is not to convince the reader of my views or my conclusions, but to alert the reader to some of the problems that are inseparable from prophetic study. My hope is that the reader can avoid some of the confusion that I have encountered in my study.

### Five Types of Prophecy

The student should be aware from the start that the Bible contains five different types of prophecy and each type of prophecy is distinct and separate from the others. They are:

### 1. Messianic Prophecies

These prophecies relate to the person of Jesus in either His first or second coming. These prophecies are usually regarded as statements concerning the ministry and/or experiences of Jesus. Two examples of Messianic prophecy are found in Isaiah 53 and Psalm 22.

### 2. Judaic Prophecies

These prophecies were given to the descendants of Abraham. Promises of blessings and curses are alike included. These prophecies have conditional elements in them most of the time. A good example of this type of prophecy is found in Deuteronomy 28. These prophecies also contain important object lessons for all generations for God's beneficent relationship with man is clearly revealed.

### 3. Day of the Lord Prophecies

These prophecies are scattered throughout scripture and relate to the vindication of God and/or His people. These prophecies often have parallel applications for they either demonstrate the wrath of God and/or the vindication of His people in contemporary settings. For example, Isaiah 24 and Ezekiel 7 can be viewed as parallels of the final days of Israel's history and the earth's history. Sometimes, these types of prophecies have conditional elements within them. Matthew 24 is also considered to be a Day of the Lord prophecy. The end of Jerusalem in A.D. 70 and the end of the world are mingled together in one prophecy because there are ominous parallels.

### 4. Local Prophecies

Local prophecies apply to specific people, places and times. For example, the prophecy concerning Nineveh is a local prophecy. Local prophecies usually require a "local prophet" or messenger to explain or proclaim the prophecy. In the case of Nineveh, Jonah was the local prophet. In the days before the flood, Noah was the local prophet.

### 5. Apocalyptic Prophecies

Apocalyptic prophecy is defined as structural prophecy; that is, prophecy that outlines a specific sequence of events that relates to or culminates with the end of the world. Fulfillment of apocalyptic prophecy is unconditional. A clear example of this prophecy can be found in Daniel 2. Apocalyptic prophecies may have conditional elements within their structure relating to the time of fulfillment. For example, the winds of destruction are held back in Revelation 7:3 until the servants of God are sealed. That the winds will blow is unconditional; *when* they blow is conditional.

### Distinctive Treatment Necessary

I mention these five classifications because a great deal of confusion results if one tries to interpret all types of prophecy using the same methods (hermeneutics). I have found that each type of prophecy operates under unique parameters and the rules governing the interpretation of each type of prophecy must be respected in order to correctly understand the meaning of that type of prophecy. In other words, when one approaches the study of prophecy, he should first identify the *type* of prophecy and the rules it follows before he proceeds to conclude what the prophecy might mean.

Apocalyptic prophecy was not added to the Bible for the purpose of "future telling" alone. Rather, apocalyptic prophecy was included in the Bible so that man can connect events *on earth* with events *in heaven*. Notice what this means: Before the world began, the Father determined by His own authority, that a number of events on earth would align with events in heaven so that man could determine his chronological position within "The Plan of Salvation." Since man cannot look up into heaven and observe events taking place there, God *connected* the timing of certain events in heaven with events on earth so that human beings could discover the order, the process and purpose of The Plan of Salvation as it unfolded. The synchronism of events in heaven and on earth is only revealed in apocalyptic prophecy.

Knowledge of apocalyptic events, their sequence and timing, uniquely provides a chronological framework, a panoramic view of God's time-line for the restoration of man. And, this knowledge is man's *only means* of determining where our present day falls within God's agenda for earth.

I have found four rules that govern the operation and interpretation of apocalyptic prophecy. When God gave the prophecies to Daniel and John long ago, He followed a specific design and the understanding of this design unseals the correct meaning of the prophecies. Understand that I have not make up the rules of interpretation; rather, I have observed four consistent behaviors in prophecy, and since these four behaviors are always consistent, I call these behaviors, "rules." Here are the rules in my words:

1.    Apocalyptic prophecy is identified as a prophecy that spans a specific period of time. Each apocalyptic prophecy has a

beginning and ending point in time, and the elements within the prophecy occur in the order in which they are given.

2. A prophetic full-fill-ment only occurs when all of the specifications of the prophecy or its elements are met, including its chronological placement within the prophecy.

3. If an element is not to be taken literally, the Bible will clearly identify the meaning of the symbol with relevant text.

4. The operation of the Jubilee calendar explains when God reckons time as a day for a year and when He reckons time as literal.

I mention these four rules because prophetic conclusions are directly connected to the rules or methods of interpretation used. The concept of interpreting prophecy by well defined rules is a critical matter. If God did not follow a constant design in the giving of apocalyptic prophecy, no one could be sure of any interpretation. One person says prophecy means this and another says it means that. And, who can determine which view is better or worse?

So, if our process of interpretation is harmonious with the design that God used in revealing the prophecies, we should be able to reach a correct understanding of prophecy before predicted events occur. I disdain the idea that one should interpret the Bible by the headlines of the newspaper. Rather, we should be able to interpret the prophecies *today* and anticipate the events that will be printed in the newspaper *tomorrow*.

### Trust in God

The study of prophecy is as large and broad a study as is the love of God. The study of prophecy reveals things about the character of God that could not be otherwise known. Unfortunately, most Christians don't know this. They frequently dismiss the importance of prophecy because (1) few actually search the Bible for the purpose of understanding prophecy and (2), most pastors have little or no knowledge of prophecy; therefore, they can't reveal the beauty and importance of prophecy. As a result, Christians believe that prophecy has little or no value.

But, a growing number of Christians want to know what Daniel and Revelation mean. That's why I'm writing this book. I hope my findings will enable the reader to quickly understand the Bible for himself. Don't let my conclusions be your conclusions. Think for yourself. Read the Bible for yourself and reach your own conclusions. Use this book to help you think about the properties of prophecy, but don't rely on me as your infallible guide. Put your faith in the Almighty.

### Five truths

The prophecies of Daniel and Revelation are intimately based on five truths. These five truths must be understood rather well *before* one can harmonize all that has been written in apocalyptic prophecy. The five truths are:

> a. The Salvation of God
> b. The Return of God
> c. The Ministry of God
> d. The Worship of God
> e. The Soul of man

These five truths are intimately connected to each other and they corporately form the foundation of The Plan of Salvation.

### Presuppositions

I find that the study of Bible prophecy always begins with a certain amount of "religious" baggage. This baggage is called, "presuppositions." A presupposition is a mental framework or point of reference that one has *before* he begins to study apocalyptic prophecy. Presuppositions are acquired through life's experiences, education, social values, parental influences, etc. And, presuppositions, more often than not, cause most people to prematurely terminate their investigation of the Bible. Here's why. When a student stumbles into information that is plainly contrary to what he already believes, he faces a dilemma. Psychologists call this process, "cognitive dissonance" (intelligent confusion). And psychologists confirm that cognitive dissonance doesn't last long. One of two things always happens. Either the student abandons what he first believed and incorporates the new-found data into his belief structure or he abandons the investigation because he cannot resolve the new-found data with his cherished beliefs. Truth can be hard to accept at times. But, the rule of truth is this: The seeker must receive all of it or he shall not be able to keep it.

Of course, the discovery and receipt of new truth causes social problems. Suppose a husband and wife are studying the Bible together and he becomes convinced of something that she doesn't want to believe. Suppose his new-found belief changes his behavior. What would be the social consequence? Carry this analogy into a larger sphere. Suppose a pastor becomes convinced of something that his church does not believe? What would the social or career consequences be? What would be the financial consequences? What should he do?

I find that is almost impossible for a person (myself included) to lay aside all presuppositions when studying the Bible. For this reason, few students of the Bible really discover what the Bible says. Rather, it is much easier to find texts in the Bible that confirm what we already believe to be true. For example, the Baptist finds that the Bible confirms his beliefs. The Church of Christ member finds that the Bible confirms his beliefs. The Mormon finds that the Bible confirms his beliefs. Thus, it is often said that the Bible can be made to say anything and Bible-based religious diversity proves this claim to be true.

But, truth is not subject to the presuppositions of any denomination or any man. Truth stands on its own. What one may believe or deny about the future has no bearing on what will happen. Therefore, when we approach the study of prophecy, one has to be willing to give up all he has believed so that he might be willing to receive everything that is true. And, this is too difficult for most people to do. Few people honestly search for more truth. Most of us live by this rule: "Either confirm what I already know is true, or tell me those things that I like to hear."

### In God's time

Looking back over the past 2,000 years, I have found a repetitive mechanism at work. It is this: Essential aspects of apocalyptic prophecy cannot be understood until God wants them known. In other words, God hides the meaning of prophetic passages with obscure language until the time for fulfillment arrives. Then, *at just the right time,* God allows the *affected* generation to understand the prophetic language. In fact, the language of the Bible becomes easy to understand when the time for understanding arrives. The cumulative result of this process is that later generations know more about the Plan of Salvation than earlier generations. Taking this observation to its logical conclusion, I can say that the final generation has the privilege of knowing more about God than any previous generation! But, so few today want to know more about God and His ways.

So, if I had to condense my observations into a sentence, I would say that the study of prophecy is difficult on two levels. There are textual difficulties in understanding the meaning of each verse and there are social difficulties when it comes to telling others about your findings. The discovery of truth is awe filling. It changes your life. It renews your confidence in God and it puts a sense of purpose and destiny within you. In fact, I have found that the pursuit of truth synthesizes the sixty-six books of the Bible into *one* living unit. The whole Bible has come alive for me! The Word of God has never meant more and said so much — in so few words. Nothing brings the five essential truths mentioned above into sharper focus than the study of prophecy.

### The five truths summarized

Since I have found the study of apocalyptic prophecy inseparable from five doctrinal truths, a brief survey of each truth is included in this chapter. Keep in mind, this is only a *brief* summary of the five truths.

### Truth # 1 - The Salvation of God

The first truth about God is this: God extended undeserved grace to human beings by providing complete atonement for all sinners. That atonement was made through the life and death of Jesus. Jesus came to earth, lived in complete harmony with God's laws (a sinless life), and died the second death so that sinners could be saved from the second death. And, God reckons the death of Jesus as "payment in full" for every sinner who will live by faith. Living by faith means this: One must be willing to go where God would have him go, willing to be all that God asks, and willing to do all that God says. The life of faith is summed up in this coined word: "GOBEDO."

## Truth #2 - The Return of God

The second truth about God is this: The Father has set a limit for the duration of sin upon earth. At an appointed time, Jesus will return to earth and gather to Himself all who have lived by faith (this includes the dead and as well as the living). The remainder of the living (the wicked) will be destroyed by Christ's glory at the time of the Second Coming.

One thousand years after the Second Advent, Jesus will return to earth for a third time. At that time, the wicked of all ages will be resurrected for two reasons. First, Jesus wants every wicked person to see why He could not save them. He wants the condemned to behold His fairness and justice in each case. And, He will fully respond to any question about His determination. Secondly, the wicked are raised so that they can provide atonement for their own sins. In God's economy, every sin will be atoned for. The final atonement is called the second death.

## Truth #3 - The Ministry of God

The third truth about God is this: Man has a direct connection to the Father through the intercessory ministry of Jesus in Heaven's temple. The importance of this truth is not widely appreciated on earth at this time because man's desperate, day-by-day need of God's bounty is not realized by most human beings. But, our ignorance will be revealed when the four winds of God's wrath are released.

The Bible teaches that every person shall stand before the judgment seat of Christ so that each of us can receive our just due. This "standing before the judgment seat of Christ" takes place *before* the second coming. The pre-Advent judgment of man serves three purposes. First, when Jesus returns to earth, He brings man's reward with Him. He does not convene court and conduct an investigation at the time of the Second Advent to see who should be rewarded with eternal life and who should be rewarded with the second death. That work will have already been done. His decision about the eternal destiny of each person is made *before* He arrives. Consequently, the dead which were judged righteous *before* the Second Coming are resurrected from their graves at the Second Coming and the living judged righteous *before* the Second Coming are called up into the clouds to meet the Lord in the air. The wicked that are not called up into the clouds will be killed by the brightness of His appearing.

Secondly, the timing of the pre-Advent judgment reveals that we are now chronologically close to the Second Advent. Just as the Day of Atonement in ancient Israel marked the end of the religious year, the commencement of the pre-Advent judgment in Heaven in 1844 indicates that we are living close to the end of the allotted time for sin.

Lastly, the understanding of the ministry of Jesus in Heaven's temple reveals the purpose and process of a number of events described in Revelation. In fact, this third truth bonds the other four truths together so that the dimensions of The Plan of Salvation can be seen. It is a most glorious, timely schematic revealing God's love.

### Truth # 4 - The Worship of God

The fourth truth about God is this: Those who worship God must worship Him in spirit and truth. This means that God will only accept the worship of a man if (1) he comes before God according to the terms and conditions God has set forth for His worship and (2), he must come before God with an attitude willing to accept and incorporate greater truths in his life.

The truth affirms the exalted position of God and the submissive attitude that God requires of human beings. For example, God did not accept Cain's worship because Cain refused to submit to God's command about worship. (Cain offered fruit instead of the prerequisite lamb.) If a human being can dictate how God is to be worshiped, then the human being has greater authority than God. For example, the Ten Commandments require that we worship God on *His* holy day, the seventh-day of the week. At this time, many people are either ignorant or negligent of this commandment. Further, many deny that worshiping God on the seventh-day is even a valid command. So, this is where the willing attitude of faith comes into focus.

During the Great Tribulation, God will demonstrate His awesome powers so that people will give due consideration to His sovereign authority and His Ten Commandments. The 144,000 will powerfully tell the whole world of God's requirements and the results will be most revealing. Who, upon learning the truth about the true worship of God, will submit to the terms and conditions that God has set forth in His law? Time will fully reveal those who truly love God.

God requires people to be open minded so that they can learn more about Him and accept greater truths as He reveals them. The more we know about God, the more meaningful our fellowship with God and the more inspiring our worship of God. God will not have a race of intellectual dwarfs in Heaven. Rather, He will have a class of human beings that enjoy learning, developing and appreciating His never ending mysteries throughout eternity.

### Truth # 5 - The Soul of Man

The fifth truth is the truth about the soul of man. This truth makes the study of prophecy complete: Man's soul (man's intelligence or persona) is the result of the union of the body with the "breath of life."  Man was created by God — he did not evolve from a single cell on some primordial sea. Man is the property of God and is therefore accountable to God for all his actions. When man dies, he ceases to exist. He does not go to heaven or hell *at that time.* When the body is separated from the breath of life, man ceases to be. Man has no awareness, intelligence or persona during death. Rather, it is as though man sleeps, awaiting one of two resurrections. (The pre-Advent judgment mentioned earlier determines which resurrection each man will participate in.) At the second coming, the righteous dead will be resurrected and granted immortality and those people found evil will be "put to sleep" for 1,000 years. The truth about the soul of man reveals something very important: There is no burning hell that continues throughout eternity. God is not a evil kidnapper. He does not torment the wicked in the fires of hell for millions and millions of years. Man either spends eternity rejoicing in the presence of God or, after providing his own final atonement, he won't exist at all. This is the truth about the soul of man and God's authority over it.

## Integral to prophecy

These five truths are integral to the resolution of all that is written in apocalyptic prophecy. In fact, the *events* described in apocalyptic prophecy contribute to the implementation and consummation of these five truths. If the student will validate these five truths, he can take a giant step toward understanding the 18 apocalyptic prophecies of Daniel and Revelation. They make sense just as they read.

## Can you answer this question?

Look through some old *National Geographic* and think about the enormous diversity on our planet: economic, educational, religious, ethnic, cultural, language and gender. Now, consider the number of people who live on this tiny orb: 5,600,000,000. Consider the vast oceans between continents and the concentrations of people in mega-cities. Now, review the words of Jesus, **"And this gospel of the kingdom will be preached in the whole world as a testimony to all nations, and then the end will come."** (Matthew 24:14) After reflecting for a few moments on these things, think about this question: What will cause billions of people to give due consideration to a gospel that runs contrary to their religious beliefs?

I believe the answer is found in Revelation. But, in order to understand the contents of Revelation, the Adventist student, who has an advantage because he already understands the essential contents of the five doctrines listed above, faces four more problems. The first problem concerns rules of interpretation. What rules (hermeneutics) or methodology of interpretation should be followed? How should the rules be applied? The second problem is language. How should symbolic terms be distinguished from literal terms? How should symbolic terms be defined? Thirdly, there is the problem of timing. Where do the prophecies fit chronologically? And lastly, what about the writings of Ellen White. How should her writings be used to determine the meaning of prophecy?

## 1. Rules of Interpretation

Rules of interpretation are necessary for two reasons. First, rules allow other people to explore your methods of interpretation to see *how* you arrived at your conclusions. Was your process consistent? Are your conclusions reproducible? Can others reach your conclusions without you telling them what they should find? Secondly, since prophecy involves the future, good rules keep us from widely missing the mark. After all, no human can see beyond today without the aid of divine revelation. Therefore, we must adhere to rules that can be shown to be trustworthy across ages past. History and those parts of prophecy that have been fulfilled validate each other. And by doing so, we gain assurance about the meaning of unfulfilled prophecy. If we apply rules that have been shown to be true with those portions of prophecy that have become history, we should be able to reach conclusions about the future that are close to the mark.

### Can two people reach the same conclusion?

Two people cannot have a meaningful discussion on prophecy if both parties use different rules (or, no rules) of interpretation. One can't compare apples to oranges. If one person is describing apples and the other person can only see oranges, how can anything beneficial occur? So, the definition of rules is the beginning line. Any change in the rules naturally means a change in the conclusions. Therefore, all discussions of prophecy should *begin* with a statement about the rules of interpretation. This is where corporate understanding has to start and Church scholars know it.

When Church scholars and leaders met in 1980 to deal with Dr. Ford's view of multiple or partial fulfillments of prophecy, the Church rejected Dr. Ford's concept on the basis of "self-evident" rules. These were presented by the Sanctuary Review Committee at the Glacier View summit in 1980 (and later published in a book titled *Daniel & Revelation's Committee Series*, Volume 3, p. 290). They were thought, in 1980, to be sufficient for the study of prophecy and indeed, Dr. Ford's view was dismissed as having no merit on the basis of these rules. They are:

1.   "The context is a sound an indispensable guide. Each aspect within the prophecy must be weighted and evaluated carefully."
2.   "A literal fulfillment is to be expected, unless there is clear inspired evidence that it should be non-literal."
3.   "Every detail must be met in the fulfillment. It is not a genuine fulfillment if only some specifications are met, but not others; nor can it be a genuine fulfillment if it is such only in principle and not in detail. All aspects of an apocalyptic prophecy must be met in order to have a true fulfillment of the prophecy."
4.   "Apocalyptic prophecies have neither dual nor multiple fulfillments. On the contrary each symbol has but one fulfillment."

A most fascinating thing has happened. The Church denounced Dr. Ford's apotelesmatic principle of interpretation in 1980, but it never got around to validating its own conclusions with the *same* rules it used to denounce Dr. Ford's views! I first learned that the Church had published these rules about 1987 and have been surprised to observe that it has not published a comprehensive document explaining the traditional views of the Church using its own rules. Shouldn't the Church test its beliefs with its own rules?

## 2. Language

The second problem facing the student of prophecy is this: language. Revelation uses three types of language:

1.   Symbolic / Spiritual
2.   Literal
3.   Analogous

The following examples are provided to demonstrate these types of language and that these types are freely mingled within the story of Revelation (sometimes in the same sentence!). Students must be very careful to avoid improper typing of the language. Making a sentence symbolic when it should be literal or analogous can only frustrate the intended meaning of a passage.

### Example 1 — "The Great City"

Revelation 11:7,8 says, "Now when they (the Two Witnesses) have finished their testimony, the beast that comes up from the Abyss will attack them, and overpower and kill them. Their bodies will lie in the street *of the great city,* which is figuratively called Sodom and Egypt, where also their Lord was crucified."

**Q.** What is *the great city* where the bodies of the Two Witnesses lie?

**LW.** "The *woman* you saw is *the great city* that rules over the kings of the earth."** (Revelation 17:18)

**Q.** Who is the woman?

**LW.** Revelation 17:5 says she is the great *prostitute* wearing the title of Mystery, *Babylon The Great*, The Mother of Prostitutes and of the Abominations of the Earth.

**Q.** What happens to *Babylon The Great* during the seventh plague?

**LW.** Revelation 16:19 says, **"The great city split into three parts, and the cities of the nations collapsed."**

The purpose of this first example is to show two things: First, the term, "the great city" is symbolic and refers to the great prostitute, Babylon. The scripture clearly explains the symbol. Secondly, in the last text above, the symbolic term "The great city" is mingled with the literal phrase "the cities of the nations" in the same sentence. The term "the cities of the nations" must be taken as literal because there is no relevant text saying it is otherwise. Review both the Church's rule # 2 (page 83) and my rule # 3 on page 74.

**Example 2**

Sometimes, Revelation will use identical words as literal in one place and symbolic in another. The distinction between literal and symbolic requires some investigation. Notice these verses and the word, "stars":

Revelation 1:20 **"The mystery of the seven *stars* that you saw in my right hand and of the seven golden lampstands is this: The *seven stars* are the angels of the seven churches, and the seven lampstands are the seven churches."**

Revelation 12:4 **"His tail swept a third of the *stars* out of the sky and flung them to the earth. The dragon stood in front of the woman who was about to give birth, so that he might devour her child the moment it was born."**

Revelation 6:12,13 **"I watched as he opened the sixth seal. There was a great earthquake. The sun turned black like sackcloth made of goat hair, the whole moon turned blood red, and *the stars* in the sky fell to earth, as late figs drop from a fig tree when shaken by a strong wind."**

Revelation 8:12 **"The fourth angel sounded his trumpet, and a third of the sun was struck, a third of the moon, and a third of the *stars*, so that a third of them turned dark. A third of the day was without light, and also a third of the night."**

When are "stars" used symbolically and when are "stars" used literally in the verses above? It is not hard to see the confusion of mixing language types from these examples. According to the rules, we first apply the language in literal terms. If the result appears harmonious within the context, then continue. But, if not, then consider the matter as symbolic and look for an interpretation of the symbol. Then apply the language as symbolic and see if the result is harmonious within the context.

### 3. The placement of time-periods

Bible prophecy contains a number of specific time-periods. And, the reader should be aware that each time-period not only affects those who live through its duration, each time-period contributes something to the larger time-period allotted for the existence of sin. God doesn't say that sin shall exist for 7,000 years on earth. But, if one puts all the time-periods together, the sum of all the parts appears to be 7,000 years.

When studying the issue of time-periods, remember the fourth rule. The Jubilee calendar determines when God reckons time-periods as day/years and when He reckons them as literal time.

### Large difference between application and fulfillment

Each element in apocalyptic prophecy has one fulfillment. There is only one group of 144,000 servants. The seven trumpets sound in their order only once. The seven seals are opened in their order only once. The beast with seven heads and ten horns persecutes the saints of God for one 42 month period and the mark of the beast is forced upon the inhabitants of earth only once.

By definition, a fulfillment occurs when all the specifications of a prophecy are full-filled. An *application* of prophecy, on the other hand, is an apologetic way of saying that the pioneers of the Church, using all the light that they had to work with, did the best they could, but their views weren't right. To defend the pioneers of the SDA Church, some Adventists will insist that *apocalyptic* prophecies can have multiple or partial fulfillments. They say the pioneers of the Church simply made an application of prophecy, but admit there is more to come from the *same* prophecies. Such a position is illogical.

For example, if the fifth trumpet is the release of the devil from the abyss to physically appear on earth, how many times can this happen? What about the five months of torment that occur during the fifth trumpet? How many times can they occur? Even more, how can the fifth trumpet be one thing in times past and something else in the future? This isn't multiple fulfillments, this is multiples of interpretation. Can the lamb-like beast have several identities depending upon the time one wishes to apply the prophecy of Revelation 13? Desmond Ford said, "Yes." The Church in 1980 said, "No."

The bottom line is this: If one allows for multiple fulfillments of apocalyptic prophecy, then no one can know how many times things can or will be fulfilled. Can you imagine the sixth seal (Second Coming of Jesus) taking place more than once?

### 4. The role of Ellen White

"The historicist method accepts the assumption that the prophecies of Daniel and Revelation are intended to unfold and to find fulfillment in historical time - in the span between the prophets Daniel and John respectively and the final establishment of God's eternal kingdom. The year-day principle is an integral part of this method inasmuch as it functions to unroll the symbolic time periods so that we are able to locate the predicted events along the highway of history." (*Ellen G. White and the Interpretation of Daniel and Revelation,* p. 1. A pamphlet defending the traditional position of the SDA Church, produced by the Biblical Research Institute Committee (BRICOM) of the General Conference, dated February, 1989. Note: In this statement, BRICOM presents the year-day principle as fundamentally necessary to the interpretation of Daniel and Revelation. BRICOM holds that *all* prophetic time-periods in Daniel and Revelation must be reckoned by the day/year principle. This assumption produces some very strange results which will be addressed later.)

The BRICOM document goes on to emphasize that the historicist method of reckoning time using the year-day principle is beyond dispute *because Ellen White confirmed* this concept.   "[Ellen White's] views fully endorse the historicist method and the main conclusions and positions arrived at by our pioneers who employed this system. Her divinely guided writings confirm the prophetic foundation (derived from Daniel and Revelation) on which the Seventh-Day Adventist Church rests today." (Ibid., p. 7)

Although this BRICOM document was produced to denounce multiple fulfillments of apocalyptic prophecy, the basic message of the 16 page pamphlet is that views other than those expressed by Mrs. White are unacceptable. "In the light of this survey we may be sure that if Ellen White were alive today, she would deplore the strained interpretations being urged upon the church as a result of employing the dual fulfillment concept. Furthermore, we may be sure she would request that her writings not be used to support such an error." (Ibid., p. 16)

The Adventist student now faces a dilemma. If he remains consistent with the explanations of Revelation as written by Ellen White, can he satisfactorily explain Revelation's story?

## Brief review of Revelation 11 and Ellen White

John was told, "...Go and measure the temple of God... and count the worshipers there. But exclude the outer court; do not measure it, because it has been given to the Gentiles. They will trample on the holy city for 42 months. And I will give power to my two witnesses, and they will prophesy for 1,260 days, clothed in sackcloth." (Revelation 11:1-3)

Ellen White adds, "The periods here mentioned - '42 months' and '1,260 days' - are the same, alike representing the time in which the church of Christ was to suffer oppression from Rome. The 1,260 years began in A.D. 538 and would therefore terminate in 1798." (GC 266)

John was told, "Now when they (the Two Witnesses) have finished their testimony, the beast that comes up from the Abyss will attack them, and overpower and kill them. Their bodies will lie in the street of the great city.... For three and a half days men from every people, tribe, language and nation will gaze on their bodies and refuse them burial.... But after the three and a half days a breath of life from God entered them, and they stood on their feet, and terror struck those who saw them.... And they went up to heaven in a cloud, while their enemies looked on.... At that very hour there was a severe earthquake." (Revelation 11:7-13)

Ellen White adds, "The period when the two witnesses were to prophesy clothed in sackcloth, ended in 1798. As they were approaching the termination of their work in obscurity, war was to be made upon them by the power represented as 'the beast that ascendeth out of the bottomless pit'.... This prophecy has received a most exact and striking fulfillment in the history of France." (GC 268, 269)

**Ellen White's view of Revelation 11's chronology**

1. Persecution of saints begins in A.D. 538
2. Death of Two Witnesses occurs between 1793-1796
3. End of persecution in 1798
4. Victims of earthquake or location unknown

**The chronology of Revelation 11**

We now face a chronological question. Notice the order of events:

1. The Two Witnesses prophesy for 1,260 days—
2. At the end of the 1,260 days they are killed—
3. Men from every nation, people, tribe and language gaze on their bodies for 3.5 days—
4. The Two Witnesses receive life—
5. They are taken up to heaven in a cloud in the presence of their enemies—
6. At that hour, there is a severe earthquake and 7,000 people perish.

Ellen White accepted the view of her day that the Two Witnesses were the Old and New Testaments. Accordingly, she believed the Two Witnesses were killed by France (the beast from the bottomless pit) during the French Revolution: 1793-1796. She recognized the chronological problem with the French Revolution since it occurred *before* the end of the 1,260 days (or 1798). She skirts this detail by saying, "The persecution of the church did not continue throughout the entire period of the 1260 years.... In foretelling the 'great tribulation' to befall the church, the Savior said 'Except those days should be shortened, there should no flesh be saved: but for the elect's sake those days shall be shortened.' Matthew 24:22" (GC 266, 267)

Ellen White concludes her explanation of Revelation 11 with the Two Witnesses going up into heaven while their enemies look on. She says, "Since France made war upon God's Two Witnesses, they have been honored as never before. In 1804 the British and Foreign Bible Society was organized.... (The Bible) has since been translated into many hundreds of languages." (GC 287) Here is a mystery. She does not mention the severe earthquake in verse 13 that causes a tenth of the great city to collapse at the time the Two Witnesses are taken to heaven nor the 7,000 people who perish in it. But, historically speaking, there was no earthquake and no bodies of the slain.

Does Mrs. White's use of Matthew 24:22 resolve the issue of chronology? She clearly recognized the problem, for according to her explanation, the Two Witnesses were killed *before* the end of the 1,260 days. If the reader agrees, then a very important issue is raised. The context of Revelation 11 does not predict the death of the Two Witnesses *before* the end of 1,260 days. The Greek verb used in Revelation 11:7 is "telesosin" which means "fully accomplished." In other words, this writer understands the prophecy to say that the Two Witnesses would prophesy 1,260 days and after they have *fully accomplished* their testimony at the end of days, they would be killed. Was the testimony of the Old and New Testaments to the world fully accomplished by 1793? This writer believes the Old and New Testaments were just beginning to get started in their global work by 1793 - which work is still going on!

**Which days are shortened?**

Is the reduction of days mentioned in Matthew 24:22 directly related to the 1,260 years of persecution as Ellen White indicates? The preceding verse in Matthew (verse 21) says, **"For then there shall be great distress, unequaled from the beginning of the world until now - and never to be equaled again."** Many people apply these verses to the Great Tribulation at the *end of the world* because Matthew 24:21,22 directly supports the language of Daniel 12:1, **"At that time, Michael, the great prince who protects your people, will arise. There will be a time of distress such as *has not happened from the beginning of nations until then.* But at that time your people - everyone whose name is found written in the book - will be delivered."** The language of these two references clearly relates to the coming, *unequaled* tribulation that occurs at the end of the world. Ellen White's use of Matthew 24:22 to avoid the chronological outline in Revelation 11 is, in this writers opinion, a mistake.

**The beast from the bottomless pit**

We also face an interpretative problem. Ellen White clearly identifies the "beast from the bottomless pit" as France. (GC 268, 269)

Can we take her interpretation and explain the rest of Revelation's story concerning the beast from the bottomless pit? For example, in Revelation 17:8, John says, "The beast, which you saw, once was, now is not, and will come up out of the Abyss and go to his destruction. The inhabitants of the earth whose names have not been written in the book of life from the creation of the world will be astonished when they see the beast, because he once was, now is not, and yet will come." John also says concerning this beast, "The beast (from the Abyss) is an eighth king. He belongs to the seven (heads) and is going to his destruction." (Revelation 17:11)

Can France satisfy these additional specifications belonging to the beast from the bottomless pit? Most Adventist writers studying these matters say, "No." The underlying problem with chronology and interpretation of Revelation through Ellen White is that she merged information from visions with commonly held reformation views on prophecy to explain Revelation. The result is an assortment of conclusions that cannot be justified historically as fulfillments, and neither can these interpretations be derived from Scripture by use of any known rules of interpretation. Thus Adventists, prophetically speaking, cannot say, "The Bible and the Bible alone" is the rule of faith. They need Ellen White's confirmation to validate things that cannot otherwise be known. Some within BRICOM would have the Church accept Ellen White's writings as a divine confirmation of the way prophetic things are and will be. Period. Consequently laymen can no longer look for new applications of prophetic matters within the Bible. In some ways, this is like the Catholic and Mormon faiths. The Catholics trust in the Pope for external authority on the Bible to declare what is truth through his "infallible" interpretations, and the Mormons use Joseph Smith to defend views that are completely contrary to Scripture.

**No need to abandon faith!**

One does not need to abandon the faith, Ellen White, or the Church in order to understand Revelation's story. Consider the following:

This writer takes the position that BRICOM's use of the term "historicist" is too narrowly defined. BRICOM states: "Futurism defers the fulfillment of the bulk of Revelation to a future point at the end of the world after an alleged secret rapture.... Other Adventist Bible students (ministers and laity alike) are taking a more futurist-oriented approach. They commonly claim loyalty to the historicist interpretations of Daniel and Revelation which we hold as a people.... The only way in which to retain the church's historicist positions, they believe, and at the same time to make certain prophecies relevant, is to employ the dual fulfillment device. But there is no consistency." (Ibid., pp. 3,4)

This writer, like BRICOM, rejects the dual fulfillment concept for reasons presented earlier. The dual fulfillment school of thought distorts the intended meaning of prophecy. On the other hand, a "futuristic" alternative does remain for the historicist. For want of a new label, this writer calls his view of prophecy the "sanctuarial view." In effect, this view is primarily concerned with the closing scenes of Christ's work in the Most Holy Place of the heavenly sanctuary. One cannot appreciate either the dimension of the Plan of Salvation or its economy without having all of the details in Daniel and Revelation working together.

Daniel and John harmoniously provide sufficient information through which the passing of events can be marked. Some of these are in the past, and some are in the future. Like BRICOM and traditional Adventism, this writer believes that Daniel's book provides the historical footings needed to reach 1844, and unlike BRICOM and traditional Adventism, I believe that John provides much more detail about the end of the world than previously thought. Given this is 1993 such a view has to incorporate an understanding of the future as well as a solid historical base. The sanctuarial view incorporates both views because it looks forward to the Second Coming and historical because it is intimately built upon the historical timing of the past.

This writer claims, in the previous chapter, that Ellen White merged information given in vision with pre-existing prophetic ideas. As a result, some of her conclusions are defective. The visions aren't defective, the pre-existing prophetic ideas are defective. Prophets don't always understand what they see in vision. Daniel clearly indicates this. (Daniel 8:27) Even more, as previously demonstrated, prophets don't always recognize where in chronological time their visions apply!

Most historical writers of the Reformation assume that Revelation's story began with the ascension of Jesus. This is quite understandable since they had no other post ascension dates upon which to peg Revelation 5:7. (This is the point in time where Jesus receives the book sealed with seven seals and begins to open them.) However, the consistent lack of any scriptural evidence to support A.D. 31 is glaring. Even Uriah Smith, considered to be the Adventist's best defender of the historical view of Revelation, does not produce *one* scripture to support Revelation 5:7 as taking place in A.D. 31. He just assumes that date to be true.

This is why Mrs. White's writings must be looked at carefully. Many Adventists assume that because she thought A.D. 31 marked the beginning of the seals, this confirms the validity of the assumption. *NOT SO!* There is no scripture, no record of a vision by Ellen White confirming this date, nor is there historical evidence to support it. In fact, this writer is convinced that apocalyptic structure indicates the date of the first seal is 1798!

It is this writer's opinion that God did not reveal all that occurred in heaven in 1844 to the pioneers. He granted knowledge necessary for their moment in time. He implemented a great disappointment because He wanted a people who would search the Scriptures and build their faith upon His Word. He wanted a people anxious for His coming. He wanted a people to begin a work upon the earth that would climax with the second coming. If God had allowed our pioneers to know that they would all die longing for the second coming, His goal of establishing a world-wide system to spread the gospel would not have been realized. But, in mercy He shielded our forefathers from this understanding much like Jesus shielded His disciples from the same understanding. Jesus said, **"I have much more to say to you, more than you can now bear."** (John 16:12)

**Summary**

The study of apocalyptic prophecy is deep. The matter is so broad and encompassing that many despair of sustained study. Faithful endurance and humbleness before God is the key to understanding. Rules of interpretation are our tools, hope in the soon return of Jesus is our motivation, and doing our part to hasten the return of the King of Kings is our privilege.

Adventists have all the elements of the everlasting gospel. What we're missing is an understanding of the prophetic setting of coming events. This misunderstanding has produced a generation of poorly prepared people. But we should not be discouraged. Prophecy is only understood on or about the time of fulfillment. In other words, when God is about to act, He "allows" understanding.

The gospel contained in the three angel's messages will be clearly and powerfully presented from the Bible as a witness to all nations. Apocalyptic conclusions, properly knit together, produces a fabric of incredible strength. There is nothing more powerful than a truth whose time has come and those seeking truth will rejoice upon finding it.

The issue of prophetic understanding will be central to the shaking of Adventism. Many will reject the opportunity to reexamine Revelation's story. Ellen White wrote: "The church may appear as about to fall, but it does not fall. It remains, while the sinners in Zion will be sifted out - the chaff separated from the precious wheat. This is a terrible ordeal, but nevertheless it must take place." (7BC 911)

# A study on the close of two probations

By definition, probation is a period of time granted by God to human beings for the purpose of salvation. Probation for Earth as a planet and for Adam and Eve as human beings, began with sin. Earth's *corporate* probation ends just before the Great Tribulation begins and probation for *individuals* ends just before the seven last plagues are poured out. The closing of both probations plays a prominent role in Revelation's story and the reader should understand the differences between them. The first and higher level of probation, corporate probation, is directed at Earth as a unit. God looks upon the human race as a group of people. For example, the *world* became corrupt, but Noah found grace in the eyes of the Lord. God's limit of patience with the *world* was fully reached in Noah's day when, in a corporate sense, an intolerable level of violence was reached. There are several examples of corporate probation coming to an end in the Bible. For example, God's patience with the sins of *cities* like Sodom, Gomorrah, Jericho and Jerusalem came to an end and they were destroyed. God's patience with *nations* like the Ammorites, the Hittites and the Babylonians came to an end and He destroyed them. In each of these cases, even though God's corporate patience came to an end, some individuals were saved! Remember Rahab from Jericho?

The second level of probation is directed at individuals. God grants every person a measure of grace. If a person rejects the promptings of the Holy Spirit, he commits the unpardonable sin and he terminates his own probation. (Matthew 12:31) For example, King Saul, Israel's first king, continued in a path of rebellion against God and ultimately committed the unpardonable sin. His probation came to an end the day he passed the point of no return.

One should carefully observe the distinction between corporate probation and individual probation because Revelation deals with both. There is a lot of confusion within the Seventh-day Adventist Church about the subject of probation because the properties of both probations are ill-defined. The reader should also know that God's patience with Earth, in a corporate sense, ends before God's patience with individuals comes to an end. In other words, God's patience with the world comes to an end before probation closes for individuals.

The close of corporate probation is not hard to understand if the reader will view the world as a unit. John 3:16 says, **"For God so loved the world that he gave his one and only Son, that whoever believes in him shall not perish but have eternal life."** God also deals with individuals. 1 John 5:12 says, **"He who has the Son has life; he who does not have the Son of God does not have life."** These two texts stand in contrast to each other. John 3:16 is a corporate text. Jesus died on the cross for the sins of the whole world, but His death does not necessarily save the whole world. Rather, it saves those who receive Him as Lord and Master. This is the underlying point in the second text. He that surrenders his life to Jesus has life!

Many Adventists are frightened about the close of individual probation. Yes, the sealing of human beings is an awesome event. But, a proper understanding of how it works, and of God's great mercy changes our fear into wonderment and praise for our God. Even if the rest of this article is hard to understand, you should know two things. First, the end of probation for individuals does not come without warning. Secondly, the end of probation is a period of time, 1,260 days to be exact. During this time-period, people will hear the gospel and make a decision for it or against it. After they are tested on their decision, they end their probation and God seals them. By the time the seventh trumpet is reached, the sealing is finished and Jesus says, **"It is finished. He that is filthy, let him be filthy *still*. He that is holy, let him be holy *still*...."**

### Corporate probation ends

Notice the five-step sequence of events described in Revelation 8:2-7:

1. And I saw the seven angels who stand before God, and to them were given seven trumpets.
2. Another angel, who had a golden censer, came and stood at the altar. He was given much incense to offer, with the prayers of all the saints, on the golden altar before the throne. The smoke of the incense, together with the prayers of the saints, went up before God from the angel's hand.

3.    Then the angel took the censer, filled it with fire from the altar, and hurled it on the earth; and there came peals of thunder, rumblings, flashes of lightning and an earthquake.
4.    Then the seven angels who had the seven trumpets prepared to sound them.
5.    Then, the first angel sounds his trumpet, etc.

The Adventist Church does not see a sequence of events in this selection of texts. The Church teaches that the casting down of the censer is the close of probation. Uriah Smith wrote in 1870, "This symbolic act can have its application only at the time when the ministration of Christ in the sanctuary in behalf of mankind has forever ceased." (D&R 474, 1944 version) But, two pages later, Smith says the first trumpet sounded about 1,600 years ago, around A.D. 400. (Ibid., p. 476)

But, *look* at the five-step sequence again. There is an unmistakable order of events. How can the casting down of the censer be a future close of probation and the first trumpet occur in the past? Was Revelation written in random order? Do adjacent verses in Revelation skip forward and backward hundreds of years? If adjacent verses skip forward and backward in time, how can one tell if a verse belongs in the future or in the past? If verses skip around in random order, then an inherent flaw exists: Prophecy defies logic. Did God design prophecy in an illogical manner? No.

**Defenses and responses to random order**

I suspect that many Adventists have accepted Uriah Smith's view of Revelation because they have been led to believe that Ellen White *confirmed* his prophetic conclusions. And, if Smith's view has been confirmed by God Himself, how can one disagree even if the conclusions are not logical? This is the crux of a most important matter. Is God logical? Can an ordinary person, with the help of the Holy Spirit, understand the Bible for himself without the aid of external authority? The Catholic Church says, "No." "That a person with no other equipment than a knowledge of the English language and a seventeenth century English translation of the Bible in his hands is qualified to decide all matters of eternal consequence for himself and the rest of mankind, is the ridiculous conclusion to which the principle of private judgment can finally be brought.... The centuries of thought and prayer that have gone into the interpretation of the Bible for all these generations likewise count for nothing." (*Some Bible Beliefs Have To Be Wrong,* Pamphlet #68, by Knights of Columbus, p. 5)

Some Adventist pastors stand side by side with the Catholic position on this matter — they only differ on the authorities. For example, one Adventist pastor recently urged Adventist readers to reject my explanations of prophecy because they are contrary to Ellen White's view of prophecy. He wrote, "Genuine 'new light' will always harmonize with Scripture (Isa. 8:20) and, for Seventh-day Adventists, with explanations such as those found in *The Great Controversy*." (*Adventists Affirm,* Spring 1993, p. 34)

So, here's the problem. If Revelation's text jumps forward and backward in random order, defying logical explanation, then the only way to know where each text chronologically belongs is by looking to someone or something that has authority *outside* the Bible. Indeed, if one cannot logically explain the prophecies, he either has to set himself up as the authority or he must appeal to external authority.

**Makes sense to me**

I do not find that Revelation was written in random order. On the contrary, I find that Daniel and Revelation follow a very clear, well defined behavior. Neither do I find that Ellen White confirmed very much of the content in Uriah Smith's *Thoughts on Daniel and Revelation.* If she did, where is the evidence to support the claim? It should be easy to produce because there is written evidence specifically confirming the validity of the seventh-day Sabbath and the termination of the 2,300 days in 1844. (*Early Writings,* p. 63) But, where is Ellen White's confirmation of Smith's view on the seven trumpets? Where is Ellen White's view confirming Smith's view of the seven seals? In fact, Ellen White says nothing about the first five trumpets or the first four seals in all of her writings. She says nothing about large segments of Daniel and Revelation.

But, when pressed to harmonize their prophetic views with Bible text, (such as the angel casting down the censer), many Adventists will say it describes the close of probation and dismiss the sequence of events described in the context. This position is often defended with the following:

1.  Some Adventist scholars claim that Oriental (as in Middle East) stories begin with the conclusion. In other words, they claim the Bible presents the conclusion first and then tells the story from the beginning. In this case, the casting down of the censer is the final event and the sounding of the first trumpet is the first event. If this is true, how should one consistently apply this rule of interpretation to *all* chapters in Daniel and Revelation? Do all stories follow this rule? If the "Oriental rule" cannot be consistently applied, then who has the authority to say which chapters in the Bible operate by this rule and which ones do not?

2.  Adventists recognize that the casting down of the censer indicates a sudden termination of something. And, many claim that Ellen White saw this scene in a vision. (See *Early Writings,* pp. 279-280.) But, Ellen White *did not* see the scene described in Revelation 8:3-5. If one will read her comments given in the reference above, she clearly says that she saw *Jesus* standing before the Ark of the Covenant, not an angel standing before the Altar of Incense. Ellen White's view says nothing about the seven angels receiving seven trumpets (the first event in the sequence), neither does she say anything about the sounding of the trumpets in this reference. I have no doubt that Ellen White beheld the close of individual probation when Jesus casts down His censer before the Ark of the Covenant. But she did not see the scene described in Revelation 8:3-5. In fact, I find that she did not know about the close of corporate probation, the termination of the daily, or the sounding of the seven trumpets. (More about this later.)

3.  Many seventeenth and eighteenth century Reformation writers believed the seven trumpets began with the fall of the Roman Empire around A.D. 400. This view was adapted by Miller for two reasons. First, he believed that the end of the world was

imminent, so placing the fulfillment of the trumpets in the past was not only commonly believed, it also supported his claim for the nearness of Christ's return. Secondly, the fifth trumpet contains a time-period of five months, which according to Miller's use of the day/year principle, represented a time-period of 150 literal years. Adventists still hold to the idea that the trumpets were fulfilled in the past. Even though they dispute the events that mark their fulfillment, they keep them in the past because they insist that *all* prophetic time-periods must be reckoned as day/years. So, the dilemma is this: If Adventists put the trumpets in the future, their day/year rule has to be set aside. They fear that once this is done, the eschatological beliefs of the Church would collapse.

## Distinct order

The order and arrangement of Revelation is not difficult to behold once a person understands the rule that determines the beginning and ending of each prophetic story. For example, Revelation 4:1-6:17 is one story that progresses in a chronological manner. Then, Revelation 7:1-8:1 is another story that progresses in a chronological manner. Then, Revelation 8:2-9:21 is another story that is presented in chronological order. In short, I find that there are 18 stories (prophecies) in Daniel and Revelation — each having a beginning and ending point in time, and the events within each story occur in the chronological order in which they are given. When all of the stories are aligned time-wise, they interlock with each other to form a matrix. This matrix reveals a panoramic view of God from ages past and it also reveals what God is going to do in the imminent future.

In graphic form, the book of Revelation was written in a serpentine fashion that looks like this:

**Individual probation**

The "end of individual probation" refers to a point in time when salvation is no longer available to human beings. This point occurs just before the seventh trumpet sounds. A parallel to this can be seen in Noah's day when the door of the ark was closed *before* it began to rain. For the sake of discussion, the events associated with the closing of probation for individuals is presented below:

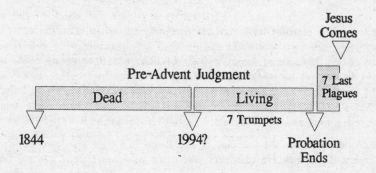

Obviously, certain assumptions outside the scope of this article, relate to the sequence above. However, a brief explanation of each item is given:

**1. 1844**   At the time appointed, Jesus began an investigative phase of the pre-Advent judgment in Heaven's sanctuary that concerns the dead. During this phase, Jesus makes a determination on those who have lived upon the earth. He reviews the books of records where the details of every person's life was recorded and He determines who shall receive life and who shall receive death. (Daniel 7:10; 2 Corinthians 5:10)

**2. Judgment of the living**   At the time appointed, the judgment of the living begins. This point in time is marked by an earthquake that accompanies the casting down of the censer. Jesus does not judge the living as He judged the dead. Rather, the living judge themselves. They either choose to live by faith during the Great Tribulation and stand firm in their faith, or they capitulate and receive the mark of the beast. The judgment of the living includes four steps:

a. Each person must hear the offer of salvation
b. Each person will have to make a decision
c. Each person is tested on their decision
d. Each person is sealed in their decision

The point is made that probation closes for people as they go through the four steps above. Obviously, people in different lands hear the warning message at different times and they are sealed in their decisions as their testing occurs.

**3. Close of probation for individuals** By the time the seventh trumpet is reached, all inhabitants of earth will have made their decision and Jesus closes the door of mercy saying, **"Let him who does wrong continue to do wrong, let him who is vile continue to be vile, let him who does right continue to do right; and let him who is holy continue to be holy."** (Revelation 22:11) Then, seven plagues follow and afflict those who received the mark of the beast.

**4. Second Coming** At the end of the seven *last* plagues, Jesus returns to gather the saints. He resurrects the dead who will receive eternal life and He gathers the living righteous to Himself. The rest of the dead are not aware of the Second Coming, and the remainder of the living are slain by the destructions attending the Second Coming.

**The sum of all the parts**

The following statement is the most important statement in this book: *The better one maintains textual fidelity with the Bible, the better the conclusions.* This means that the closer our views align with all that the Bible says on a matter, the more accurate and trustworthy the conclusion. Good conclusions require textual fidelity. Good conclusions are only as good as the supporting evidences. And, a study on the close of both probations requires that we gather as many pieces of related information as possible, assemble the parts and see what they produce. A good conclusion allows the evidence to speak for itself, and it reveals the harmony that is always present in truth.

For example, if the throwing down of the censer and the trumpets are intimately related, and the throwing down of the censer marks the beginning of the trumpets, we should be able to find clues within the Bible that help us understand the significance of throwing down the censer. Since there is no specific reference in the Bible of throwing down a censer, we must rely upon a collection of scriptures to understand the meaning of this action. Is it possible that the casting down of the censer in Revelation is something like Moses casting down the Ten Commandments in Exodus?

### The outline considered

An outline on the close of both probations is presented below. Then, each item is explained more fully on the pages that follow. The outline helps to see the big picture quickly, and the details that follow may help to explain it more fully:

1. John saw four angels holding back the four winds of God's wrath. The angels were told to "hurt not" the land, sea or trees until the sealing of the 144,000 is completed. (Revelation 7:1-4) This process obviously precedes the throwing down of the censer because the first two angels of the seven trumpets are the ones who harm the land, sea and trees! (Revelation 8:7,8)

2. The next prophetic event is the appearing of the 144,000. Their first work will be to reveal to the Church the testimony of Jesus. This coming revelation will cause a great shaking. John describes the shaking in Revelation 11:1-2 as a process of seeing who, in the inner court, measures up to the faith of Jesus. The Church is called the inner court because it is nearer to God; it represents those who have been favored with the opportunity to have a deeper understanding of God's prophetic purposes. But, don't overlook the grand purpose of the trumpets. During the trumpets, the Gentiles will be invited in to the banquet.

3. According to the rules of interpretation that I follow (listed on page 11,12 and 17), I find that the throwing down of the

censer and associated physical signs on earth (thunderings, lightnings and an earthquake) mark the end of corporate probation and the beginning of the seven trumpets. The first four trumpets inflict a mortal blow to earth by causing extensive devastation (world-wide fires caused by meteoric showers of burning hail, asteroid impacts and volcano eruptions). And, the last three trumpets bring great suffering to the people of earth as they kill and torment one another. I believe the seven trumpets cover a time-period of approximately 1,080 days.

4. Satan personally appears on earth claiming to be God during the fifth trumpet. Jesus allows him to appear by unlocking the Abyss. (Revelation 9:1-11) At the Second Coming, Satan is put back in the Abyss for 1,000 literal years. (Revelation 20:2,3) Satan's scheme, while "in the flesh," is deception at first and dominion over earth at last. He will implement the wearing of his mark (a tattoo showing "666" or the devil's name) during the sixth trumpet war which all must wear to buy or sell. (Revelation 13:11-18)

5. The third angel's message will become present truth after Satan physically appears on earth. (Revelation 14:9-12; 13:11-18) The warning in the third angel's message is specifically directed at those submitting to the lamb-like beast: the physical devil, Satan.

6. The mystery of God is fully accomplished by the ministry of the 144,000 by the time of the seventh trumpet. (Revelation 10:7) This mystery is that God will save any sinner by granting him undeserved grace. (Colossians 1:27; Ephesians 2:8)

7. The sounding of the seventh trumpet is directly connected to a special service in heaven. It reveals seven highly important matters:

   a. A loud announcement is made saying, **"The kingdom of the world *has become* the kingdom of our Lord and His Christ and He will reign for ever and ever."** (Revelation 11:15)

   b. The 24 Elders get up from their thrones and fall on their faces before God and say, **"We give thanks... because you have taken your great power and begun to reign."** (Revelation 11:17)

c. The Elders state that the time for God's wrath [as promised under the third angel's message] has come. (Revelation 11:18)

d. The Elders state that time has come to *avenge* the blood of the dead [martyrs who died from persecution during the fifth seal]. (Revelation 11:18)

e. The Elders state that time has come for rewarding God's servants, the [144,000] prophets [by doing the things they predicted]. (Revelation 11:18)

f. The Elders state that time has come for rewarding the [numberless multitude of] saints, and those who reverence His name [by hiding them from His wrath]. (Revelation 11:18)

g. The Elders conclude by saying that time has come to destroy those [wicked rulers and people] who destroy the earth. (Revelation 11:18)

8. John saw the close of probation for individuals. The context of Revelation 14:14-20 describes a scene where Jesus is instructed by an angel to wave His sickle over the earth to signify that the door of mercy has been closed. This sequentially follows the giving of the third angel's message. Then, the wicked are gathered and punished (crushed) in the winepress of God's wrath (the seven last plagues).

9. John saw how Jesus will tell the world that His mercy is ended. Revelation 11:19 describes a scene at the end of the seventh trumpet when the heavenly sanctuary in heaven is opened and the Ark of the Covenant is seen *in the sky* by all of the people on earth. This event will be far more remarkable than the angel tearing the veil at Christ's death and exposing the empty contents of the Most Holy Place to the Jews. A fearful foreboding will settle upon the wicked.

10. Revelation 15:8 adds to the scene of the seventh trumpet which occurs just *before* the first plague begins. John saw the heavenly sanctuary vacated and the empty room is filled with God's exceeding glory and smoke. Just as Moses saw the goodness of God as a bright glory (Exodus 33:19), John saw the wrath of God as a bright glory.

11. From the time the "daily" is terminated in heaven (the close of corporate probation — marked by the casting down of the censer) to the abomination that causes desolation (universal death decree for the saints) is 1,290 days. Those who endure the remaining 45 days will be especially blessed at the end of the 1,335 days. (Daniel 12:11,12)

**A bird's eye view**

Hundreds of pages could be devoted to discussion on the items above and their relationship to the big picture. You may agree or disagree with the statements given above; nevertheless, the texts given above must be included in any study of prophecy. Assembling a puzzle with pieces missing means at best, an incomplete and unfinished picture. So, the following diagram is offered to show how the elements above combine to reveal a simple but profound story.

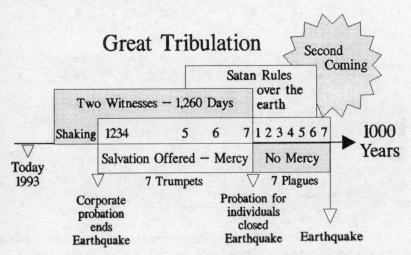

## 1. Today - 1993

God is stirring the minds of people with prophetic matters; drawing them into an interest for understanding and preparation because of the work that lies ahead.

## 2. Sealing of the 144,000 and the Latter Rain

Shortly before the first trumpet sounds, God completes His selection and sealing of the 144,000 (a selected group of individuals positioned all over the earth). These servants will be prepared for a grueling, formidable task. Some of the qualifications of these people include a broad knowledge of Scripture, a clear prophetic understanding, a deep sense of humility and unworthiness, and most of all, a heavy burden for the salvation of souls and spiritual discernment. These will be the "spark plugs" of the Loud Cry.

I believe the 144,000 will come from within the Seventh-day Adventist Church. In fact, I believe the SDA Church was brought into existence for the express purpose of producing the 144,000. I don't make these assertions on the basis that Seventh-day Adventists are any better than anyone else. On the contrary, I believe that the label, "Seventh-day Adventist" carries a somewhat less than positive influence in many circles. But, the basis of my claim about the origin of the 144,000 comes from this: People in the SDA Church are the only people that know about the five truths that are essential to proclaiming the end-time message. These five truths are: salvation by faith, the importance of God's law and the role of the Sabbath during end-time events, the state of the dead, the prophetic sequence leading up to the Second Coming and the sanctuary ministry of Jesus in heaven's temple. Just as the disciples of Jesus came through the Jewish economy, I believe the 144,000 will come through the SDA Church or, at least, they will understand the five pillars of Adventism.

The first work of the 144,00 will be to proclaim the testimony of Jesus. This will cause a great stir within the Church and lead to controversy. The 144,000 will prophesy things that will make some people rejoice and others tremble with rage. The shaking of Adventism will occur in response to the ministry of the 144,000. The shaking ultimately ends with the separation of the wise from the foolish.

The Latter Rain is a term that refers to the fullest outpouring of the Holy Spirit for the purpose of a great harvest. Pentecost is an "early rain" sample of both the harvest and the means used to obtain it. The 144,000 will have the Spirit of Prophecy within them for they will be possessed by the Holy Spirit.

### 3. Throwing down the censer

When the selection and sealing of the 144,000 is finished, the angel ministering before the Altar of Incense, throws down the censer indicating that Christ's "daily" mediation or intercession for the world has ended. With Jesus "out of the way" (see 2 Thessalonians 2:7), the wrath of God will begin to fall upon the earth. (For a discussion on this point, see chapter eight.) The angels having the seven trumpets will begin their harmful works. The sudden conclusion of the daily — symbolized by the throwing down of the censer, is not the close of probation for individuals; rather, it is a point in time when Jesus no longer corporately intercedes on behalf of the world as a planet.

With the corporate intercession of Jesus removed, the four angels who were holding back the winds of God's wrath commence their work. These judgments awaken and alarm the world. The 144,000 servants explain that God's patience with earth has ended and His patience with individuals is fast coming to an end. It is interesting to me that God connects the end of corporate probation and the beginning of the Great Tribulation with a political environment on earth that is calling for "Peace and safety." (1 Thessalonians 5:3)

Keep this point in mind. Corporate probation applies to groups of people. At one time, the Jews were God's chosen people. In A.D. 33, their corporate or national probation of 490 years ended with the final and full rejection of the testimony of Jesus. Revelation mentions a body of people called Babylon and there is a specific point in time when Babylon's probation is ended! (See Revelation 18:2.)

## The Daily

The significance of the throwing down of the censer, is connected to a service in the Old Testament sanctuary called the "daily." The "daily" is a term that refers to a round of services that were performed each day. These services included the evening and morning sacrifices of a year old lamb on the Alter of Burnt Offering and the burning of special incense on the coals of the Altar of Incense. Priests conducted the "daily" service on behalf of the *nation* of Israel. God designed the daily services to help Israel understand that it was only through the merits of the "daily" intercession on behalf of their nation that He could continually dwell in their presence without destroying them. (See Exodus 29:38-46; 30:7,8; Hebrews 7:25.) Keep in mind, the daily provided corporate atonement for the whole nation of Israel and was not directed towards any one individual. Corporate offerings were put on the horns of the Altar of Incense whereas individual offerings were put on the horns of the Altar of Burnt Offering. (Leviticus 4)

## The Sin Offering

If a person in the camp committed some sin, then a sin offering was required of the sinner at the Altar of Burnt Offering. This sacrifice provided atonement for the individual and/or his family. This service, unlike the daily, was designed to teach Israel that God was a *personal* Savior to any individual that would accept the terms of His covenant. Most of the Jews missed this point. They made their religion their God. As a result, they came to ignore the individual accountability for sin that God requires. The Jews came to believe they were special because they were the biological offspring of Abraham. True, the offspring of Abraham had the advantage of God's special attention, but God wanted Abraham's offspring to walk with Him in faith as Abraham had walked with Him. Such was God's reason for making Abraham the father of many nations.

The sin offering stands in contrast to the daily offering. The first was for individuals, the second for daily benefit of the nation.

## The censer's function

The censer was a small bowl (or literally, a skillet) in which coals off the Altar of Incense were placed. When the high priest entered the Most Holy Place on the Day of Atonement, he stood before God. The censer was a means of offering or conducting atonement. (Numbers 16:46) The smoke from the censer was all that separated the high priest from the consuming glory of God. (Leviticus 16:13) The point is made that the high priest conducted his business and left the Most Holy before the smoke cleared! In like manner, before the censer is thrown down in Revelation 8:5, much incense is placed on the altar. The final days of salvation will be short and that which separates the world from the wrath of God is disappearing fast.

## The Loud Cry

The throwing down of the censer in heaven is connected to physical manifestations on earth. There will be thunder, rumblings, flashes of lightning and an earthquake. These signs mark the end of the "daily" service or corporate mediation of Jesus in heaven whereupon the judgment (the testing) of the living commences. The casting down of the censer is important in this context because Daniel 12:11 indicates that 1,290 days later, something awful will happen. This is addressed below.

The purpose of the trumpets is to awaken and arouse the world that there is a living God requiring accountability. The first angel's message begins with "Fear God." That term means exactly what it says just as it did in Israel's day. (Exodus 19:20-22)

The 144,000 will be armed with a comprehensive knowledge of Scripture, filled with the gift of prophecy, and enabled by the power of the Spirit to give the Loud Cry: "Behold Jesus Comes." With God's servants ready and prepared, all that remains to be done is to awaken the earth to hear what His servants have to say. A global awakening begins with the first trumpet and ends with the seventh. During this time-period, every nation, kindred, tongue and people will hear the three angel's messages (Revelation 14) in very short time! Think of it! More than 5.6 billion people hearing the three angel's messages in a very short time-frame.

(For example, if the time-period is 36 months in length, 155 million *new* people will hear the gospel each month!)

### 4. Probation for individuals in the Church closes first

**"For it is time for judgment to begin with the family of God; and if it begins with us, what will the outcome be for those who do not obey the gospel of God?"** (1 Peter 4:17) Earlier, it was said that probation's closing for individuals involves four steps. They are listed again:

- a. Hearing the three angel's messages
- b. Each person making a decision
- c. Being tested on the decision
- d. Being sealed in the decision

The SDA Church was brought into existence for the express purpose of giving the three angel's messages. But alas, many within the Church do not have a clear understanding of the purpose or mission of the Church. Even though all human beings are daily tested and educated in the school of Christ, Seventh-day Adventists, like everyone else, face a very specific hour of test and trial. (Revelation 3:10) The Church's testing time *precedes* the sounding of the trumpets because the Church must be ready to fulfill its destiny during the time-period of the trumpets!

The Church's testing time comes in the form of revival and reformation. The revival will be based on the Bible prophecy. Prophetic messages will be presented showing the position and scope of work that God wants done. The power of the Holy Spirit will attend these messages and calls will be given for means to spread the message because the end has come! Those following the Spirit will respond and begin disposing of their possessions to further the final message while the foolish will only see this as another rise of fanaticism. The Church will fragment over the prophetic preaching of the 144,000. Many will balk on the very doorstep to heaven.

This is the testing time for the Church. It might be called the "Rich Young Ruler Test." The call to sell what we have and give so that the poor, the uninformed souls of the world, can know Jesus is no small test to North American Adventists. When it comes to material prosperity, no other nation is our equal. Our testing time period is short and the call for volunteers to dispose of their possessions for a specific work will produce a great controversy within the Church. Many of the leaders of the Church will oppose the work of God just as they did when Jesus walked upon the earth.

When the censer is thrown down and the corresponding earthquake on earth takes place, THEN reality will cause the ten virgins to awake. The wise and the foolish will be clearly identified. But, the tragedy of the ten virgins parable is that when they were awakened, the foolish could not get oil for their lamps and enter into the banquet. So it will be. When awakened by the blast of the first trumpet, the foolish virgins will seek to appease God for fear of those things coming upon the earth. But, fear is not the basis of faith. The foolish virgins had an opportunity to know truth, but they rejected it. The foolish virgins are so called because they did not discern between the important and the vain during the shaking. Therefore, the awakening (the shaking) comes as a test from God. Faith has to be tested to see if it will stand loyal to God.

As the trumpets sound, the wise virgins will press forward to accomplish their global work. Daniel 12:3 says, **"Those who are wise (margin: teachers) will shine like the brightness of the heavens, and those who lead many to righteousness, like the stars for ever and ever."** The probation of the Adventist Church closes first because it was first to hear the gospel. This is confirmed in Revelation 11:1,2 where John was told to count the worshipers of God in the *inner court,* but to exclude the Gentiles. This process points out two things:

a.  The worshipers of God in the inner court (most favored status) are measured, counted and sealed first.
b.  The Gentiles are initially excluded from the count because they have not had the opportunity to hear the truth yet. Later, they will hear the three angel's messages, decide upon it, and be tested on their decision.

**5. Satan Appears**

The supreme deception of all ages is the appearing of Satan claiming to be Jesus. He comes before the close of probation to do three things:

1. Unify the false religious systems of the world and persecute all refusing to submit to him
2. Lead all people on earth to participate in his divine government
3. Receive the worship due God

Satan's appearing on earth is the fifth trumpet event. He is the angel king who reigns over the swarm of demons that come up out of the Abyss (Revelation 9:11). The people of earth will be astonished when they see him with their own eyes. (Revelation 17:8) He is the eighth king who will rule over the seven false religious systems. (Revelation 17:11) He will cause fire to come down from heaven, and deceive the world with his miracles. (Revelation 13:13) His work lasts for a short season (about a year before individual probation closes), and at the Second Coming, Satan is put back in the Abyss for 1,000 years. (Revelation 20:2,3)

Satan's demons will be allowed to torment those who have not received the seal of God. Thus, he infuriates the wicked and then blames God's unscathed people as being responsible!

Two major points:

a. Satan appears before probation's close to deceive the people of earth. There would be no point in his appearing after probation's close to deceive the people of earth - for all decisions have been made by probation's end.
b. Unification of earth's great religious systems and global powers is only possible through the supernatural efforts of Satan. He will use signs and wonders to confirm that he is God. Revelation 13:13 says, **"And he performed great and**

miraculous signs, even causing fire to come down from heaven to earth in full view of men."

## 6. The Seventh trumpet sounds

The sounding of the last trumpet confirms that probation has closed. This trumpet is directly associated with several things:

a. A loud proclamation is made in heaven: The earth becomes the kingdom of Jesus. (Revelation 11:15) At this point in time, Jesus stands up, lays aside His priestly garments, and puts on His kingly robes. That which was promised to Him now becomes His property. This is the moment described in Daniel 12:1 where Jesus (angel name: Michael) stands up and delivers His people from any further death. Also, a time of distress now commences that has not happened before!

b. The 24 elders get up from their thrones and fall before God acknowledging the *rightful* assumption of power by Jesus. (Revelation 11:17) The 24 elders have witnessed the judgment process as they sat on their thrones since 1798. (Revelation 4:4 & Daniel 7:9) When the judgment process began and Jesus was found worthy to receive the book sealed with seven seals in 1798, the 24 elders recognized the *worthiness* of Jesus and fell down and worshiped Him. (Revelation 5:14) At the close of the judgment process, they do the same thing again acknowledging His righteous claim over the peoples and the territories of earth.

c. The elders state, "It is time for your wrath to come," indicating that the time for the seven last plagues has come. (Revelation 11:18) The display of God's wrath, without mercy, is contained in the seven last plagues. (Revelation 15:1)

d. The time has come for avenging the dead. This phrase can be understood as "executing justice on behalf of those who were martyred for Jesus." (Revelation 6:9) The martyrs are those who died between the opening of the fifth seal and the sounding of the seventh trumpet.

e. The time has come to reward the faithfulness of your prophets, the saints and all those who fear you by stopping the martyrdom and delivering them from death. (Revelation 11:18) The first reward is the cessation of death. There will be no more martyrs after the close of probation. The second reward will be shelter from the wrath of the Almighty.

f.   The time has come to destroy those who destroy the earth. (Revelation 11:18)  The outpouring of God's wrath in the seven last plagues fully accomplishes this. At the seventh plague, the wicked remaining will either be killed by hail or the glory of Christ.

These items demonstrate the grand finale of probation's closing.  We also find in verse 19 the vacancy of the heavenly sanctuary, and John says that the Ark of the Covenant *was seen*. I believe this will be a visual experience for the whole world. The wicked will behold God's law which they refused to recognize — the law that condemns them to death. The righteous will behold the value of the gift of righteousness. Then, the wicked will experience life on earth without an intercessor. The power of God's law will be seen.

**Seventh trumpet**

Another supporting point is presented indicating the seventh trumpet is associated with the close of probation.  The reference is found in Revelation 10:7, **"But in the days when the seventh angel is about to sound his trumpet, the mystery of God will be accomplished, just as he announced to his servants the prophets."** What is the "mystery of God" that is accomplished just before the seventh angel sounds?  Answer: That sinful mortals may be found perfect in Christ through faith!

Paul said, **"I have become (the church's) servant by the commission God gave me to present to you the word of God in its fullness - the mystery that has been kept hidden for ages and generations, but is now disclosed to the saints. . . so that we may present everyone perfect in Christ."** (Colossians 1:25-27)

Certainly, those teaching and those receiving the three angel's messages recognize that eternal life is only possible through Christ's righteousness. The mystery that is fully accomplished by the seventh trumpet is God's ability to save to the utmost. Keep in mind that millions of Gentiles will receive the three angel's messages upon hearing it for the first time! We're not talking about the salvation of people who have been many years with Christ and have highly developed and noble characters. We're talking about men and women that have been held captive by the chains of sin and darkness. The mystery of God's love is accomplished in the salvation of wretched and unworthy people!

The close of probation fully demonstrates to all the heavenly host that God has done everything possible to save - even to the far ends of the earth. The purpose of the trumpets is to warn, alarm and awaken the world that Jesus is imminently coming. If the trumpets cannot awaken and bring salvation to sinful human beings, if the Holy Spirit cannot reach their hearts with the need for salvation, if the 144,000 cannot reach their minds with truth, then nothing more can be done for them. This point is most important, for God's wrath is about to be poured out without any mixture of mercy. The seven last plagues are punitive — punishment for open rebellion against the Almighty.

## 7. Individual probation closes

Probation for individuals closes after the three angel's messages have gone to every nation, kindred, tongue and people. Jesus, speaking about the close of probation, said, **"No one knows about that day or hour, not even the angels in heaven, nor the Son, but only the Father."** (Matthew 24:36) The KJV does not include the words "nor the Son," but the Sinaiticus manuscript (a fourth century manuscript) includes the phrase. A study of Revelation 14 seems to confirm the idea that Jesus does not personally close probation! Here's why: After the third angel's message has been given, two interesting events take place in heaven. First, John says, **"I looked, and there before me was a white cloud, and seated on the cloud was one like a son of man with a crown of gold on his head and sharp sickle in his hand. Then another angel came out of the temple and called in a loud voice to him who was sitting on the cloud, Take your sickle and reap, because the time to reap has come, for the harvest of the earth is ripe. So he that was seated on the cloud swung his sickle over the earth, and the earth was harvested."** (Revelation 14:14-16)

This scene marks the closing of the third angel's message. This is the close of probation. It is symbolized as a reaping because "the harvest of the earth is ripe." Jesus is told by an angel coming from the sanctuary to wave His sickle over the earth and "reap." Thus, the words of Jesus in Matthew that even the Son does not know the day or hour agrees with Revelation's account.

The text above also describes Jesus gathering the wheat before the grapes are gathered. This is an important point when considering what John saw next. **"Another angel came out of the temple in heaven, and he too had a sharp sickle. Still another angel, who had charge of the fire (on the Altar of Incense), came from the altar and called in a loud voice to him who had the sharp sickle, 'Take your sharp sickle and gather the clusters of grapes from the earth's vine, because its grapes are ripe.' The angel swung his sickle on the earth, gathered its grapes and threw them into the great winepress of God's wrath. They were trampled in the winepress outside the city, and blood flowed out of the press, rising as high as the horses' bridles for a distance of 1,600 stadia."** (Revelation 14:17-20)

Here the angel at the Altar of Incense, the one that threw down the censer, comes into focus again at the close of probation! He tells the angel with the sharp sickle to gather the grapes of earth and put them in the great winepress of God's wrath where they will be trampled to death. The amount of grapes is obviously vast given the amount of *blood* that John saw flow out of the winepress. This is the end of salvation. Those receiving the mark of the beast are represented as grapes. The grapes will be trampled (receive the full wrath of God) by the seven last plagues.

## 8.  Satan Unmasked

Through the 144,000, God sends a loud cry to earth: "Behold Jesus Comes." As described above, Satan visits the metropolitan areas of earth claiming to be THE LAMB. For this reason, he is described in Revelation as the lamb-like beast. His mission is twofold: Deceive the world into submission and secondly, see that all of God's people are exterminated.

By far, the majority of the world will receive Satan as Jesus. Satan, in the guise of Jesus, claims responsibility for the devastation of the seven trumpets. In order to establish his "so-called kingdom of righteousness" on earth, he must have the loyalty of every person; then there will be peace on earth. Given his beauty, power, signs, wonders and wonderful charm, the world will receive the beast as though he were Jesus. In this guise, Satan will lead the whole world to agree upon a universal death decree for those disloyal to his government.

He will tell the leadership of earth (both religious and political) that he sent the trumpet events upon places where evil was great. "Just like Sodom and Gomorrah, these people and places were beyond redemption," he will say. "They were destroyed because they were rebellious." He then charges the leaders of the world with the task of cleaning up evil. Use whatever force is necessary he demands, just get rid of all *refuseniks.*

As the trumpets cease and the seven last plagues begin, greater devastation and suffering is observed by the people of earth. They plead with their false Jesus to stay the judgments - and he more firmly insists on the loyalty of all people upon earth. He says that when the earth is free of all *refuseniks,* then he will cease to send judgments and eternal peace will begin.

But, Jesus unmasks the devil during the fifth plague by sending this plague directly upon him and his throne. The world will then realize that something is wrong - why would their "Jesus" send a terrible plague upon himself and his own organization? The light of truth finally dawns - the world recognizes the deception. "Jesus" is the Antichrist! God Himself has sent this plague upon Satan!

In their fury and anxiety to reclaim all that had been given Satan, the last war occurs. It is called Armageddon. All the wicked will be involved. (See article on Armageddon in this book.)

As the final battle begins, Jesus opens the sixth seal. Now, Jesus will be physically revealed — THE LAMB — the true Lamb of God will appear in clouds so bright that men and women will run for shelter! Soldiers will turn from their earthly struggle to hide from the angry face of Jesus. (Revelation 6:16) Evil cannot stand in the presence of God. Even those who have received the free gift of the righteousness of Christ cry out, "Who can stand?" The world has come to a temporary end for 1,000 years.

### 9. 1,290 days & 1,335 days

With the story essentially complete, two important time periods must be put in their respective places. Notice the words of Daniel: **"From the time that the daily sacrifice is abolished and the abomination that causes desolation is set up, there will be 1,290 days. Blessed is the one who waits for and reaches the end of the 1,335 days."** (Daniel 12:11,12)

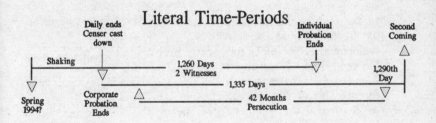

Literal Time-Periods

If the throwing down of the censer marks the end of the daily, then 1,290 days later, the people of God should witness some abominable act that brings utter desolation. This act is a universal death decree that will be set for the people of God. This evil act is an attempt to rid the earth of all God's people *at one time*. (Revelation 13:15)

But, a special blessing is promised for God's people as they wait in solitary places and dungeons. Apparently, the appearing of Jesus is about 45 days after the universal death decree. The total time for the Great Tribulation, from beginning to end is a maximum of 1,335 days (3.6 years). The earthquake associated with throwing down the censer marks the beginning date. The 1,335 day time-period is called a maximum because God will cut it short. Jesus said, **"If those days had not been cut short, no one would survive, but for the sake of the elect those days will be shortened."** (Matthew 24:22)

I find that God put these time-periods in Bible prophecy so that His people will have encouragement. Given the darkness and discouragement of those days, knowing the number of remaining days will be great consolation to "hang on."

## Summary

The throwing down of the censer does not indicate the close of individual probation. It does identify the close of the daily service and the end of Christ's work on behalf of earth (corporate probation). Six concepts are presented that support this conclusion:

1. In the Old Testament sanctuary services, the trumpets began on the first day of the seventh month. The Day of Atonement (close of Israel's yearly probation) took place on the tenth day. According to the Talmud, the trumpets sounded their warning each day warning the people to prepare for the Day of Atonement. Thus, in the Old Testament model we learn that the trumpets occur **before** the close of probation.

2. Since the censer is an instrument of atonement, the throwing down indicates an end of its use for atonement. The throwing down of the censer in heaven and the resulting earthquake on earth marks the end of the sealing of the 144,000 and the beginning of the seven trumpets. The earthquake marks the beginning point in time for counting 1,290 days. The 1,290 day time period of Daniel 12:11 is a last days application beginning with the termination of the daily. The end of the daily in heaven is identified on earth by the earthquake.

3. The seventh trumpet clearly points to a time when Jesus receives great power to reign over Earth. His work as mediator for individuals is concluded at this point, thus He stands up and receives His kingly robes. This trumpet further indicates that the Elders recognize the end of Christ's intercessory ministry as they declare the time has come for Him to avenge the saints of their suffering. They also say that time has come for Him to destroy those who destroy the earth.

4.    The opening of the Most Holy place of the heavenly sanctuary during the seventh trumpet reveals no mediator between God's law and a planet in rebellion. Thus, the sanctuary service of atonement is now finished.

5.    The close of probation is further described in Revelation 14. Two major points were presented on this section: First, Jesus (who is still seated) is told by the angel at the Altar of Incense to wave His sickle over the earth. This indicates someone other than Jesus ultimately decides when probation should close. Secondly, an angel harvests the grapes (evil people) of earth. These are put in the great winepress of God's wrath and these receive the seven last plagues.

6.    The mystery of God is finished by the time of the seventh trumpet. That mystery is how God can save sin-full people. That mystery is how God can love us so much and save us through the righteousness of Jesus. That mystery is the Plan of Salvation. That mystery is the eager, out-stretched reach of God's love to every nation, kindred, tongue and people.

The close of individual probation does not come without extensive warning — both in the Church and in the world. If we choose to reject His warnings and entreaties, then nothing more can be done for our salvation. When all people on earth have intelligently or willfully (not necessarily the same) made up their minds and have been sealed in their decision, Jesus declares the end by saying: **"Let him who does wrong continue to do wrong, let him who is vile continue to be vile, let him who does right continue to do right; and let him who is holy continue to be holy."** (Revelation 22:11)

# The 144,000 will soon appear

(Reprinted from the February, 1992, issue of *Day Star*)

## Part I

The subject of the 144,000 servants of God in Revelation often brings more heat than light. No group of people in the Bible has attracted more attention than these. Neither is it surprising that several denominations claim the 144,000 to be their own. For example, The Church of Christ, The Church of God, Mormons, Seventh-day Adventists, Jehovah's Witnesses and others teach that the 144,000 are *their* offspring. Further, there are internal disputes within these churches as to the identity of the 144,000. Some people say the number, 144,000, symbolizes another number, a larger number. Others say the 144,000 represent the numberless multitude that shall go through the great tribulation and be redeemed when the Lord appears. Even though the population of the world currently exceeds 5.6 billion, other people believe that only 144,000 people are going to be *alive* when Jesus comes. Still others suggest that the 144,000 are converted Jews who carry the gospel to the world during the great tribulation. So, who are they? What does the Bible say about the 144,000?

### Old Testament background on the 144,000

The subject of the 144,000 involves far more than the 13 texts that directly discuss them in Revelation 7 and 14. The prophetic roots of this subject are firmly laid in the Old Testament. Therefore, some Old Testament background becomes essential to understanding the identity and purpose of the 144,000.

Students of Bible history know that Abraham was the father of two great nations: the Arabs and the Jews. Ishmael became the father of 12 tribes (Genesis 17 & 25) and Jacob, the grandson of Abraham, also became the father of 12 tribes (Genesis 35). God loved Ishmael, but He would not allow the trusteeship of His covenant of faith to be passed down through Ishmael even though Abraham asked God to accept his son. **"And Abraham said to God, 'If only Ishmael might live under your blessing!' Then God said, 'Yes, but your wife Sarah will bear you a son, and you will call him Isaac. I will establish my covenant with him**

**as an everlasting covenant for his descendants after him.' "** (Genesis 17:18,19)

In firm but gentle tones, God told Abraham that the covenant of faith belongs to those who will live by faith! For this reason, God chose the lineage of Isaac to be the trustee of His covenant. The birth of Isaac demonstrates the importance of faith. Isaac was the product of faith whereas Ishmael was the result of human works. Because Ishmael came through human devising, God would not pass His covenant through Abraham to Ishmael even though he was the firstborn of Abraham.

As time passed, the 12 sons of Ishmael scattered throughout the East and became great leaders of tribal nations. The offspring of Isaac were different, they stayed together as one large family. See Genesis 25:27. Eventually Isaac died and Jacob became heir to the covenant. When Jacob was 130 years old, he and his family moved down into Egypt because of a famine.

### How 12 sons became 13 tribes

The sons of Jacob numbered 12 when he entered Egypt at the age of 130 years. Jacob lived in Egypt for 17 years, but just before Jacob died, he did something unusual. He blessed Joseph with a double portion of his blessing by displacing Joseph in the lineage of his 12 sons. Jacob adopted Joseph's two sons, Ephraim and Manasseh, as his own (Genesis 48:5). So, when the Exodus occurred, *the tribes (sons) of Jacob totaled 13!*

A few months after the Exodus, the Israelites met God at Mt. Sinai. And when Moses came down the mount, he saw the Israelites dancing around a golden calf. Moses was indignant with Aaron's apostasy and angrily asked if anyone in the camp was on the Lord's side. During the revelry that had attended the worship of the golden calf, only the tribe of Levi had not apostatized from the Lord. And when Moses called to see who was on the Lord's side, the Levites responded promptly. (They were sent through the camp to kill those who led the apostasy. They killed about 3,000 idolaters. Exodus 32:28) The Lord honored the loyalty of the Levites and He subsequently blessed the tribe of Levi with the responsibility of looking after His temple. See Exodus 32:29.

After two years of wilderness living, the Lord intended to take the Israelites right into Canaan. So, the Lord had Moses send out 12 spies (the tribe of Levi was excluded, Numbers 13:4-16) to view the Promised Land. While the spies were away, God told Moses: **"Take a census of the whole Israelite community by their clans and families, listing every man by name, one by one.... You must not count the tribe of Levi..."** (Numbers 1:2,49) At that time, the number of men 20 years and older and the names of the tribes were:

|     |           |               |
|-----|-----------|---------------|
| 1.  | Reuben:   | 46,500        |
| 2.  | Simeon:   | 59,300        |
| 3.  | Gad:      | 45,650        |
| 4.  | Judah:    | 74,600        |
| 5.  | Issachar: | 54,400        |
| 6.  | Zebulun:  | 57,400        |
| 7.  | Ephraim:  | 40,500        |
| 8.  | Manasseh: | 32,200        |
| 9.  | Benjamin: | 35,400        |
| 10. | Dan:      | 62,700        |
| 11. | Asher:    | 41,500        |
| 12. | Naphtali: | 53,400        |
| 13. | Levi:     | not included  |
|     | **Total:**| 603,550       |

**Intermediate summary**

Four things need to be highlighted here. First, notice in the list that there are really 13 tribes even though one is not counted. Secondly, notice that God required a census *before* entering the Promised Land. Thirdly, remember that the lineage of Isaac, not that of Ishmael, received the trusteeship of God's covenant of faith. Lastly, the division of 13 tribes is important because the 144,000 come from the 12 tribes of Israel.

## So close and yet so far

As a body, the Israelites did not have a faith experience in the Lord when they reached the door of Canaan. Upon their return from the beautiful land, the spies voted 10 to 2 that they should not proceed into the Promised Land. This made God angry and He sentenced His faithless people to death in the wilderness. **"The LORD said to Moses, 'How long will these people treat me with contempt? How long will they refuse to believe in me, in spite of all the miraculous signs I have performed among them? ...In this desert your bodies will fall—every one of you twenty years old or more who was counted in the census and who has grumbled against me.' "** (Numbers 14:11, 29)

Thus, an entire generation fell in the desert. Those who left Egypt did not reach their goal. But, the Lord did not lose patience. He poured out His love and affection to the next generation to see if they would trust Him enough to live by faith. Much could be said on these matters; however, the point has to be made that when the time came to enter the Promised Land after 38 years of wandering in the desert, God required a second census. See Numbers 26. (The second total was 601,730 men.)

## The biological tribes fail

Perhaps the saddest story ever written is the repeated failures of the nation of Israel. Certainly, no nation ever had greater potential and no nation ever fell so far from God's purpose. When the 70 weeks of probationary time ended in A.D. 33, God abandoned the nation of Israel as trustees of His covenant. This point is repeatedly affirmed in the Scriptures. (See *18 End-Time Bible Prophecies,* Appendix A.) Jesus pronounced final sentence upon Israel saying, **"Therefore I tell you that the kingdom of God will be taken away from you and given to a *people* who will produce its fruit."** (Matthew 21:43, italics added.)

Because the 13 tribes of Israel forfeited their calling, a new trusteeship was installed. Think of it this way: Plan A failed. Therefore, God implemented Plan B. As you know, Jesus chose a total of 13 disciples (Matthias was the 13th. See Acts 1.) to carry the gospel to the world. Some argue that Judas wasn't chosen; however, Jesus clearly considered him to be chosen even though He knew he was a devil. See John 6:70.

Under Plan B, God eliminated the matter of nationality. Now, there would be no difference between Jew and Gentile, male and female. Paul said, **"There is neither Jew nor Greek, slave nor free, male nor female, for you are all one in Christ Jesus. If you belong to Christ, then you are Abraham's seed, and heirs according to the promise.** " (Galatians 3:28,29) Savor the meaning of these verses. If you belong to Christ, you are Abraham's seed—an heir of the promise—the promise of a beautiful homeland and eternal life! The point here is that the trusteeship of the covenant was taken away from the nation of Israel and given to those who would live by faith. *Those who live by faith have become the spiritual nation of Israel.*

In fact, Paul clearly says, **"A man is not a Jew if he is only one outwardly, nor is circumcision merely outward and physical. No, a man is a Jew if he is one inwardly; and circumcision is circumcision of the heart, by the Spirit, not by the written code. Such a man's praise is not from men, but from God."** (Romans 2:28,29)

So, there was a transition. The opportunities granted to the biological descendants of Abraham became the opportunities of the spiritual descendants of Abraham. The privileges granted to the descendants of Abraham were transferred to those who would live by faith in Jesus Christ. If God could not fulfill His purposes through the biological nation of Israel, He would seek out those people in every nation who would respond to His call to live by faith and accomplish the task of saving human beings through them.

The laws and ceremonies that were required of Israel were abolished at the death of Jesus, but the purposes behind the ceremonial system were disclosed so that the Gentiles might understand the economy of salvation. This is a profound point. *Even though the sacrificial system has been abolished, the realities behind the sacrifices remain.*

For this reason, God's *purpose* for the 12 tribes remains intact today. The chosen people of God today are not biological descendants of Abraham, but followers of Jesus. These are the heirs of the covenant given to Abraham. Indeed, the promises offered to the descendants of Abraham have been improved and now they belong to the followers of Jesus which are reckoned by God as descendants of Abraham! Notice how this works: **"While Jesus was still talking to the crowd, his mother** and brothers stood outside, wanting to speak to him. {47} Someone told him, 'Your mother and brothers are standing outside, wanting to speak to you.' {48} He replied to him, 'Who is my mother, and who are my brothers?' {49} Pointing to his disciples, he said, 'Here are my mother and my brothers. {50} For whoever does the will of my Father in heaven is my brother and sister and mother.' " (Matthew 12:46-50) Jesus clearly says that those who do the will of the Father belong to His family.

### Twelve tribes today — not biological

The apostles used the term "twelve tribes of Israel" in a spiritual sense. Notice this text: **"James, a servant of God and of the Lord Jesus Christ, To the twelve tribes scattered among the nations: Greetings."** (James 1:1) To whom was James writing—the biological tribes of Israel who had rejected Jesus, or the followers of Jesus who had been scattered because of religious persecution? The contents of his book clearly show that it is addressed to those who have accepted Jesus. James said, **"My brothers, as believers in our glorious Lord Jesus Christ...."** (James 2:1) The point here is that James reckoned the twelve tribes as those believing in Jesus!

When Paul was captured and taken prisoner for preaching Jesus Christ, he stood before King Agrippa and said, **"And now it is because of my hope in what God has promised our fathers that I am on trial today. {7} This is the promise our twelve tribes are hoping to see fulfilled as they earnestly serve God day and night. O king, it is because of this hope that the Jews are accusing me."** (Acts 26:6,7) Look carefully at this verse and you will see that Paul spoke of "our fathers" in the spiritual sense; i.e., descendants of Abraham who lived by faith. He contrasts those who have been earnestly serving God, the twelve tribes, with the biological descendants of Abraham by calling them Jews! Look again at the verse.

But, if any question remains about God's method of determining lineage, look at the words of Jesus. Jesus clearly defined the principle of spiritual descendancy when He was upon Earth. Here's the story: **"They answered him, 'We are Abraham's descendants and have never been slaves of** anyone. How can you say that we shall be set free?' {34} Jesus replied, 'I tell you the truth, everyone who sins is a slave to sin. {35} Now a slave has no permanent place in the family, but a son belongs to it forever. {36} So if the Son sets you free, you will be free indeed. {37} I know you are Abraham's descendants. Yet you are ready to kill me, because you have no room for my word. {38} I am telling you what I have seen in the Father's presence, and you do what you have heard from your father.' {39} 'Abraham is our father,' they answered. 'If you were Abraham's children,' said Jesus, 'then you would do the things Abraham did. {40} As it is, you are determined to kill me, a man who has told you the truth that I heard from God. Abraham did not do such things. {41} You are doing the things your own father does.' 'We are not illegitimate children [as you are],' they protested. 'The only Father we have is God himself.' {42} Jesus said to them, 'If God were your Father, you would love me, for I came from God and now am here. I have not come on my own; but he sent me. {43} Why is my language not clear to you? Because you are unable to hear what I say. {44} You belong to your father, the devil, and you want to carry out your father's desire. He was a murderer from the beginning, not holding to the truth, for there is no truth in him. When he lies, he speaks his native language, for he is a liar and the father of lies.' " (John 8:33-44) The ultimate deception occurs when truth is believed to be a lie. Now, reread verses 39 and 44 and you will see how God reckons offspring.


## Twelve tribes will be recognized throughout eternity

"And he carried me away in the Spirit to a mountain great and high, and showed me the Holy City, Jerusalem, coming down out of heaven from God... it had a great, high wall with twelve gates, and with twelve angels at the gates. On the gates were written the names of the twelve tribes of Israel." (Revelation 21:10-12) Why does the New Jerusalem have the names of the twelve tribes of Israel on the gates? Because all who enter the Holy City will enter through the gate according to their tribe. Even more, there will be a census of the tribes and 12,000 from each tribe will lead their members to God's throne.

When the redeemed enter through the gates into the Holy City, each person will enter through the gate that marks his experience of faith.

In other words, there are twelve unique experiences in the Lord, and each person enters through the gate that identifies his faith experience. Just as the children of Israel were counted as 12 tribes, so the family of God will be divided into 12 tribes. Each tribe has a unique experience in faith and will be blessed accordingly. (See Genesis 49.)

**144,000 come from twelve tribes**
>  From the tribe of Judah 12,000 were sealed,
>  from the tribe of Reuben 12,000,
>  from the tribe of Gad 12,000,
>  from the tribe of Asher 12,000,
>  from the tribe of Naphtali 12,000,
>  from the tribe of Manasseh 12,000,
>  from the tribe of Simeon 12,000,
>  from the tribe of Levi 12,000,
>  from the tribe of Issachar 12,000,
>  from the tribe of Zebulun 12,000,
>  from the tribe of Joseph 12,000,
>  from the tribe of Benjamin 12,000.
>  Revelation 7:5-8:

Two items should be noted in Revelation's listing of the 12 tribes. First, the tribe of Levi *is included* and the tribe of Dan is left out. The tribe called Joseph in this list is probably a name substitution for the second son of Joseph, Ephraim, since all the descendants of Joseph were to fall under Ephraim or Manasseh. The omission of Dan has been the subject of much speculation. However, the reason Dan is omitted appears to be quite simple. The tribe of Dan was likely destroyed by repeated invasions from the North during centuries of Israel's apostasy. The tribe of Dan inhabited the northernmost territory of the promised land and would have been exposed to more violent and more frequent attacks than tribes geographically below them. That entire tribal nations were destroyed during war campaigns was not unusual. And living on the "front line" meant a higher number of casualties. Secondly, unlike both census accounts in the book of Numbers, the number taken *from* each tribe in Revelation is 12,000 before the four winds blow. This suggests that these *servants* are God's finest from each tribe. Also, 144,000 is a very small number when compared to the population of the world. (1 per 40,000 people.)

### John saw two distinct groups of people

John *saw* two different groups of people stand before the throne of God in Revelation. One group is numbered (144,000) the other group is numberless. Compare Revelation 14:1-5 and Revelation 7:9-14. The Bible clearly says that the people who go through the great tribulation and are victorious are *numberless!* Notice the distinction. One group, the elite *from* each tribe is numbered (144,000), the other group is so large that it is numberless.

### Five specifics about the 144,000

We find in Revelation a number of specific things about the 144,000. Here are five:

1.   The 144,000 are servants of God (Revelation 7:3). As a matter of fact, the 144,000 are servant-prophets of God! Notice this verse: **"But in the days when the seventh angel is about to sound his trumpet, the mystery of God will be accomplished, just as he announced to his servants the prophets."** (Revelation 10:7)

     The story of Revelation clearly distinguishes between the saints of Jesus and the prophets of Jesus during the time period of the great tribulation. Notice this verse: **"The nations were angry; and your wrath has come. The time has come for judging the dead, and for rewarding your servants the prophets and your saints and those who reverence your name, both small and great—and for destroying those who destroy the earth."** (Revelation 11:18) Did you notice that prophets and saints are distinguished in this verse? Notice this verse: **"In her (Babylon) was found the blood of prophets and of the saints, and of all who have been killed on the earth."** (Revelation 18:24) This verse clearly identifies that the great harlot, Babylon, is drunk with the blood of prophets *and* saints. Some people claim that Babylon is drunk from centuries of bloodshed of saints and prophets. Not so. Notice these verses: **"The third angel poured out his bowl on the rivers and springs of water, and they became blood. {5} Then I heard the angel in charge of the waters say: 'You are just in these judgments, you who are and who were, the Holy One, because you have so judged; {6} for they have shed the blood of your saints and prophets, and you have given them blood to drink as they deserve.' "** (Revelation 16:4-6) These verses say that the recipients of the third plague are deserving of this reward for *they were the murderers of saints and prophets during the great tribulation.* So who are the prophets during the great tribulation? The servant-prophets of God—the 144,000.

2.    The 144,000 are selected and sealed just before the four winds blow (Revelation 7:1-4). God chooses those who shall make up the 144,000 before the four winds blow. He places the seal of ownership upon the foreheads of these servants. (2 Corinthians 1:22) Later, John says that the seal is the name of the Father and the Lamb. **"Then I looked, and there before me was the Lamb, standing on Mount Zion, and with him 144,000 who had his name and his Father's name written on their foreheads."** (Revelation 14:1) The seal of the Father is placed upon 12,000 people within each faith-experience. These mature examples of living faith will be empowered by the Holy Spirit to proclaim the final gospel call to the world. The 144,000 will be pure in heart and character. They have overcome besetting sins through a strong contest with self and gained the victory through faith in Jesus.

3.    The 144,000 are firstfruits (Revelation 14:4). Firstfruits is an Old Testament term that deals with the first and best of the annual harvest (Deuteronomy 26). And, the firstfruits became the property of the high priest. Thus, the 144,000 will be firstfruits of the harvest of Earth and they will be the property of Jesus, man's High Priest. They will attend Him throughout eternity, wherever He goes.

4.    The 144,000 will sing a song that no one else can sing (Revelation 14:3). This means they go through an experience that the rest

of the saints don't go through. Actually, this song is about the privilege of entering into the suffering of Jesus.

The suffering of Jesus may be understood from this perspective. He came to earth with a mission and He suffered in proportion to the accomplishment of that mission. In like manner, the 144,000 receive a difficult mission and they suffer enormously with the burden and responsibility of fulfilling that mission which will be done under most difficult circumstances.

5.      The 144,000 are pure in heart. No lie was found in their mouths (Revelation 14:5). This means the 144,000 faithfully and fully represent the truth of Jesus regardless of consequence. They will face the kings and rulers of earth. They will face angry mobs. They will be the most rejected of all people on earth, yet they will fearlessly and fully tell the whole truth and not compromise their message for popularity or acceptance.

## Summary

The 144,000 are those who know how to live by faith. As trustees of the covenant of faith, they will receive the fullest outpouring of the Holy Spirit during the last days. Daniel 12:3 says, **"Those who are wise (margin, "teachers") will shine like the brightness of the heavens, and those who lead many to righteousness, like the stars for ever and ever."**  These people are the personal representatives of Jesus at His second coming just as John the Baptist was a representative of Jesus at His first coming. They will powerfully proclaim the three angel's messages of Revelation 14 and the world will hear their message. The 144,000 will present five doctrines: the worship of God, the sanctuary of God, the salvation of God, the second coming of God and the nature and condition of man in life and death. As a result of their powerful ministry, a numberless multitude will receive Jesus as Lord and Savior and be saved when He comes.

One last thing. The number 144,000 is a literal number. If it were symbolic, wouldn't the Bible clearly show us the meaning of the symbol? In fact, there is no such thing as a symbolic number in the Bible. Why would God use one number to represent another number? The point here is that God takes a census before the saints enter the promised land and

12,000 from each tribe, the firstfruits of the harvest, will lead the redeemed into God's eternal rest — first on earth, then in heaven.

But, the most beautiful thing about this whole subject is this: the 144,000 are ordinary people who have developed extraordinary faith. These will come to the place on earth where they live only to serve Jesus for that will be their job throughout eternity.

## Part II

**Elijah-type people**

**"See, I will send you the prophet Elijah before that great and dreadful day of the LORD comes. {6} He will turn the hearts of the fathers to their children, and the hearts of the children to their fathers; or else I will come and strike the land with a curse."** (Malachi 4:5,6)

This prophecy was given about 350 years before the birth of Jesus and Jewish leaders during the time of Christ were not sure of its meaning. They did know two things, however. First, they knew that Elijah had been taken to heaven in a fiery chariot (2 Kings 2). Secondly, they well knew that the great and dreadful day of the Lord was coming (Joel 2, Obadiah 1, Isaiah 13 and Ezekiel 30). But the Jews saw the great and dreadful day of the Lord as a two-part installment. The *great part* would be their exaltation and the *dreadful part* would be the destruction of their enemies. Such was the Jewish mindset on Malachi 4 when John the Baptist came preaching.

A large number of people went out to the wilderness to hear John because he spoke with unusual clarity and power. His message of the coming Messiah brought hope to his hearers. With compelling power, John called men and women to repentance so that they might be members of the coming kingdom of God. A number of scribes and Pharisees, wishing to "get in on the ground floor" of the new kingdom, came to John for baptism. But John saw their outward pretense and he exposed the contents of their hearts with harsh rebuke: **"...You brood of vipers! Who warned you to flee from the coming wrath?"** (Matthew 3:7)

At that time, the nation of Israel was in serious trouble because Rome had just deposed Archelaus, the son of wicked Herod, and many of

Israel's finest had died in the revolt. The iron hand of Rome bore heavy upon the neck of Israel. The painful grip of Rome was magnified by mutual hatred. The Jews hated the Romans as much as the Romans hated the Jews. And, as a tiny tribal nation within the vast Roman empire, the Jews desperately needed a Savior.

The appearing of John the Baptist not only seemed prophetic, it raised hope that God had sent the deliverer. The Bible says, **"The people were waiting expectantly and were all wondering in their hearts if John might possibly be the Christ."** (Luke 3:15) This particular moment in time was filled with expectancy because many people believed the fulfillment of Daniel 9 was due. This prophecy, 200 years older than Malachi's prophecy, predicted that Messiah would appear during the first year of the 70th week. (Daniel 9:25) Because John was proclaiming "the kingdom of God is at hand," and it was the 484th year since the decree of Artaxerxes to rebuild Jerusalem, many suspicioned that John might be the Messiah.

So, the *Religious Affairs Secretary* in Jerusalem sent a deputation of priests out to the wilderness to investigate this mysterious man and his message. Note their words: **"Now this was John's testimony when the Jews of Jerusalem sent priests and Levites to ask him who he was. {20} He did not fail to confess, but confessed freely, 'I am not the Christ.' {21} They asked him, 'Then who are you? Are you Elijah?' He said, 'I am not.' 'Are you the Prophet [predicted by Moses]?' He answered, 'No.' {22} Finally they said, 'Who are you? Give us an answer to take back to those who sent us. What do you say about yourself?' {23} John replied in the words of Isaiah the prophet, 'I am the voice of one calling in the desert, Make straight the way for the Lord.' "** (John 1:19-23) Did you notice that after he told them he was not the Messiah, they asked him if he was Elijah? Their inquiry was prompted by the prophecy of Malachi. If this man was Elijah they thought, then Messiah could not be far behind.

### Why must Elijah appear?

Teachers of Israel talked openly and frequently about the coming of Elijah, although Elijah's identity was the subject of many discussions.

How would people recognize the true Elijah if he appeared? How could he be positively identified?

After Peter, James and John beheld the transfiguration of Jesus on the mount, they had positive proof that Jesus was the Messiah, the Son of God and Jesus forbade them to disclose this information until He was resurrected. But, this wonderful revelation exposed a prophetic problem. They wondered why Elijah had not first appeared according to the prophecy of Malachi. They knew that John the Baptist was not Elijah. So, trying to reconcile the transfiguration experience of Jesus with the prophecy of Malachi, they asked obliquely, **"...'Why then do the teachers of the law say that Elijah must come first?' Jesus replied, 'To be sure, Elijah comes and will restore all things. But I tell you, Elijah has already come, and they did not recognize him, but have done to him everything they wished. In the same way the Son of Man is going to suffer at their hands.' "** (Matthew 17:10-12)

These verses contain more than most people realize. First, Jesus affirms the surety of Malachi's prophecy saying, "To be sure, Elijah comes and will restore all things." This phrase indicates that the prophecy of Malachi will be fulfilled. Then, Jesus draws a parallel from the prophecy for their time. He said, "Elijah has already come and they did not recognize him."

**Note:** The fulfillment of Malachi 4:5,6 is inseparably connected to "the great day of the Lord." Many people stumble over this fact as they try to demonstrate a fulfillment of this prophecy by saying that John the Baptist fulfilled this prophecy. If the reader can accept the following two statements, there is a simple explanation about Jesus' use of this prophecy. First, if Israel had met the redemptive conditions outlined in the 70 weeks prophecy, the plan of salvation would have been worked out much differently than what we know today. Many of the Old Testament prophecies of Isaiah, Jeremiah, Joel, Amos, Ezekiel and others would have been fulfilled as predicted. The point here is that the great day of the Lord would have happened sometime after the birth of Jesus had Israel met the conditions set forth by God in the 70 weeks prophecy of Daniel 9. Secondly, because God's original plan for Israel was not implemented, many prophecies that applied to Plan A were modified and will be fulfilled under Plan B. In other words, the appearing of

Elijah, as found in Malachi 4, is connected to the great day of the Lord which was supposed to happen soon after the first advent. However, God scrapped Plan A because Israel failed to meet the conditions placed upon them, but the prophecy of Malachi 4 will be fulfilled before the second advent of Jesus because Jesus renewed the promise of fulfillment in Revelation 7.

Now, notice what Jesus says about John the Baptist on another occasion. **"As John's disciples were leaving, Jesus began to speak to the crowd about John: 'What did you go out into the desert to see? A reed swayed by the wind? {8} If not, what did you go out to see? A man dressed in fine clothes? No, those who wear fine clothes are in kings' palaces. {9} Then what did you go out to see? A prophet? Yes, I tell you, and more than a prophet. {10} This is the one about whom it is written: 'I will send my messenger ahead of you, who will prepare your way before you.' {11} I tell you the truth: Among those born of women there has not risen anyone greater than John the Baptist; yet he who is least in the kingdom of heaven is greater than he. {12} From the days of John the Baptist until now, the kingdom of heaven has been forcefully advancing, and forceful men lay hold of it. {13} For all the Prophets and the Law (the Scriptures) prophesied until (of) John. {14} And if you are willing to accept it, he is the Elijah who was to come.' "** (Matthew 11:7-14)

In this discourse, Jesus quotes from Malachi 3:1 (see verse 10 above). Malachi predicted that God would send a messenger to announce the appearing of Jesus and John the Baptist was that messenger and Jesus clearly says so. Then, Jesus goes on to apply the fulfillment of Elijah to John. But, Jesus said, "if you are willing to accept it, he (John) is the Elijah who was to come." Why did Jesus say "IF" you are willing to accept it?

The great day of the Lord mentioned in Malachi 4 was not going to happen during the days of Israel. Jesus knew this. In fact, we now know that the great day of the Lord would not happen for another 2,000 years. Therefore, Jesus said, *if you can accept this principle, John the Baptist is a representative of what the prophecy offers.*

### The Spirit and power of Elijah

Notice what was said of John the Baptist before his birth. "But the angel said to him: 'Do not be afraid, Zechariah; your prayer has been heard. Your wife Elizabeth will bear you a son, and you are to give him the name John. {14} He will be a joy and delight to you, and many will rejoice because of his birth, {15} for he will be great in the sight of the Lord. He is never to take wine or other fermented drink, and he will be filled with the Holy Spirit even from birth. {16} Many of the people of Israel will he bring back to the Lord their God. {17} And he will go on before the Lord, in the spirit and power of Elijah, to turn the hearts of the fathers to their children and the disobedient to the wisdom of the righteous—to make ready a people prepared for the Lord.' " (Luke 1:13-17)

So, John was granted the spirit and power of Elijah that he might *turn* the hearts of fathers to their children and the disobedient to the wisdom of the righteous—to make ready a people for the coming of the Lord. John turned the hearts of the fathers to their children through repentance. By compelling fathers to consider their God-given responsibilities as head of the house, John revealed the seriousness of spiritual neglect. The nation of Israel had become corrupt because the fathers of Israel had become negligent. John told his listeners that God holds men responsible for the spiritual training of their offspring. The laxity of fathers as spiritual role models, the neglect of maintaining the family altar, the careless behavior of fathers granting the church and/or the school the responsibility of training their children; these and other aspects of John's message were powerfully preached. Conviction followed and many fathers repented of their sins.

John did not neglect to speak to the youth, either. They listened to his call. After all, John was a young man himself—about 30 years of age. As young people listened, they were surprised at the boldness and penetration of John's message. John's message struck the hearts of many youth with precision greater than that of a cruise missile. He minced no words as he pointed out that most youth were totally unfit to belong to the coming kingdom. Their inner rebellion against their parents and self-centered ways made them worthless to the cause of God. He declared that God had a controversy with the youth because their interests centered on pleasure and themselves. John called, "where are those who will serve God? Where are those who will seek righteousness so that they may be found worthy to live within the coming kingdom of God?"

### Malachi 4 and Revelation 7

The promise of Elijah before the great and dreadful day of the Lord still awaits fulfillment. Revelation reveals the identity of Elijah for our day! It also explains what those who go forth in the spirit and power of Elijah will do. This is the *next* prophetic event. Revelation reveals that there will be 144,000 servants of God having the spirit and power of Elijah. Revelation tells us that God is holding back the four winds of His wrath until the Elijah people are prepared and ready to do their work.

Revelation also tells us that the Elijah messengers will be effective for 1,260 days. Revelation tells us that some of the Elijah people will be martyrs for God during the time of their ministry just as John the Baptist became a martyr for the cause of Christ. And lastly, Revelation tells us that the Elijah messengers will turn the hearts of millions of people to the worship of God. Therefore, a numberless multitude will be ready to meet the King of kings when He arrives.

If we place the events on a chart, the following order of events can be outlined. Here are three important steps:

1.   Four angels hold back the four winds (destructive judgments of God) until 144,000 servants are selected and sealed.
2.   The 144,000 will proclaim their message within the Church before the trumpets (the four winds) occur. This will cause the shaking of Adventism and separate remnant(1) from those who are indifferent, spiritually careless and foolish.

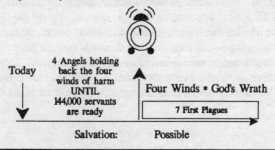

3.  The trumpets of Revelation will sound and God's people in Babylon, remnant(2), will be called out by the ministry of the 144,000.

## Perspective

There are 5,600,000,000 people currently on Earth. Revelation says that 144,000 will be selected as servant-prophets of God. This is a ratio of 1 prophet per 40,000 people. Notice:

| Location | Population | Servants |
|---|---|---|
| Dayton, Ohio | 1,000,000 | 25 |
| State of Ohio | 14,000,000 | 350 |
| U.S.A | 260,000,000 | 6,500 |
| China | 1,100,000,000 | 27,500 |

## Summary:

The 144,000 are people upon whom the Lord will pour out His Spirit with great power. For reasons beyond the scope of this article, I suspect they will begin to appear on or about 1994, but time will tell. Joel 2:28-32 says, **"And afterward, I will pour out my Spirit on all people. Your sons and daughters will prophesy, your old men will dream dreams, your young men will see visions. {29} Even on my servants, both men and women, I will pour out my Spirit in those days. {30} I will show wonders in the heavens and on the earth, blood and fire and billows of smoke. {31} The sun will be turned to darkness and the moon to blood before the coming of the great and dreadful day of the LORD. {32} And everyone who calls on the name of the LORD will be saved...."** The 144,000 servants, both men and women, will prepare the way of the Lord in the Spirit and power of Elijah. John the Baptist was to the first advent of Jesus what these people will be to the second. And, many will receive the same fate. The 144,000 will reap a great harvest of souls for the kingdom—a multitude like the sands of the sea! If only 20 percent of the world's 5.6 billion are saved (and I hope the percentage will be larger than this), the resulting number would be more than 1,120,000,000 people! Truly a numberless multitude. Hallelujah! Amen!

# Jesus in the Most Holy Place in A.D. 64?
(Reprinted from the January, 1993, issue of *Day Star* under the
title "The fallibility of prophets.")

**Q.** It is widely believed that the book of Hebrews was written about
A.D. 62-65. The author of Hebrews clearly says that after Jesus ascended
to heaven, He began to function as *high priest* behind the veil; that is,
in the very presence of God. (Hebrews 6:19,20; 9:24) As I read the
book of Hebrews, the author leaves no room for dispute on the timing
of this matter. I question why you ignore this testimony and insist that
Jesus began to function as high priest in 1798 (*Day Star,* October, 1992)
and began cleansing the heavenly temple in 1844.

**LW.** Your observations are correct and I fully agree with you that the
author of Hebrews was convinced that when Jesus ascended to heaven,
He immediately entered heaven's Most Holy Place (holiest place KJV)
— behind the veil, in the very presence of the Father to serve as our
high priest. In fact, the book of Hebrews is the *only book* in the Bible
that explicitly places Jesus in heaven's Most Holy Place serving as our
high priest! So, your question is full of significance and my response
involves several matters.

First, the author of Hebrews uses explicit language and declarations to
emphasize the ministry of Jesus in heaven while he waits for the second
advent. Remember, Jesus had been absent from earth some 30 years
when Hebrews was written and the believers in those days anticipated
an imminent return of their Lord. For this reason the author of Hebrews
(Paul, I believe) thought he was living at or very close to the end of
time. Notice these three references (emphasis mine) about his view of
chronology:

**Hebrews 1:1-2** "In the past God spoke to our forefathers through the
prophets at many times and in various ways, {2} but *in these last days*
he has spoken to us by his Son...." **Hebrews 9:26** "...But *now* he [Jesus]
has appeared once for all *at the end of the ages* to do away with sin by
the sacrifice of himself." **Hebrews 10:37** "For in just *a very little while,*
'He who is coming will come and will not delay.' "

These three texts reveal something of the author's perspective. In the first text, he begins by claiming that he lives "in the last days." In the second text, he declares that the present time is "the end of the ages" and in the third text, he points out that in "a very little while" Jesus will return. I mention these three texts because fairness requires that we examine the author's claims concerning the ministry of Jesus from his perspective in A.D. 64.

After reading through the book of Hebrews a few times, most people conclude that the author was fully convinced that Jesus had entered into heaven's Most Holy Place — there to intercede for man *in the very presence of the Father.* (Hebrews 7:25; 9:24-26) The office of Jesus, the location of Jesus and the ministry of Jesus in heaven is clearly integrated within the book of Hebrews because the author well knew that the only person who could enter into the Most Holy Place and stand in the very presence of God in the earthly sanctuary was the High Priest. Notice the sense of timing in the verbs and the location of Christ's ministry in each of the following verses (italics mine):

**Hebrews 2:9** "But we see Jesus, who was made a little lower than the angels, *now crowned* with glory and honor because he suffered death, so that by the grace of God he might taste death for everyone."

**Hebrews 6:19-20** "We have this hope as an anchor for the soul, firm and secure. It enters the *inner sanctuary behind the curtain,* {20} where Jesus, who went before us, *has entered* on our behalf. He *has become* a high priest forever, in the order of Melchizedek."

**Hebrews 8:1** "The point of what we are saying is this: *We do have* such a high priest, *who sat down* at the right hand of the throne of the Majesty in heaven."

**Hebrews 9:11-12** "When Christ *came as high priest* of the good things that are already here, he went through the greater and more perfect tabernacle that is not man-made, that is to say, not a part of this creation. {12} He did not enter by means of the blood of goats and calves; but *he entered the Most Holy Place once for all* by his own blood, having obtained eternal redemption."

**Hebrews 9:15** "For this reason Christ *is* the mediator of a new covenant, that those who *are called* may receive the promised eternal inheritance—now that he has died as a ransom to set them free from the sins committed under the first covenant."

**Hebrews 9:24** "For Christ did not enter a man-made sanctuary that was only a copy of the true one; he entered heaven itself, *now to appear* for us in God's presence."

**Hebrews 9:26** "Then Christ would have had to suffer many times since the creation of the world. But *now* he has appeared once for all *at the end of the ages* to do away with sin by the sacrifice of himself."

After considering these texts, we can make no mistake about the author's sense of timing, location and function of Jesus. As far as he was concerned, Jesus was already in the Most Holy Place serving as our high priest. Later, I'll address why some people claim that the NIV translation (used above) is faulty.

For now, synthesize three important matters: First, Jesus was *designated* as man's High Priest (intercessor before God) the day sin entered the world. (See Psalm 2:7; Galatians 3:22; 2 Timothy 1:9; Revelation 13:8.) Then, after living victoriously over sin for 33 years, and suffering death on the cross, Jesus became qualified to serve as man's High Priest. (Hebrews 5:8-10) Secondly, a new covenant (having new terms) was put into effect after the resurrection of Jesus. The new covenant is based on different statutes and Jesus became the mediator of it. (Hebrews 8:6) Therefore, the commandments and statutes of the old covenant were abolished. (Ephesians 2:11-15) This includes the statutes given to Moses concerning the office of high priest. (Hebrews 7:12-18) And lastly, the author of Hebrews wants his readers to understand that this new information about the role of Jesus, His ministry and the new covenant was true because the Holy Spirit had recently revealed what had been kept a mystery for ages past. (Hebrews 9:8, Ephesians 3:1-6)

**Q.** So far, it appears that you agree with my understanding on the ministry of Jesus as revealed in Hebrews. So, why do you insist that Jesus entered the Most Holy Place in 1798 — and in 1844, He began a pre-advent judgment of human beings?

**LW.** The author of Hebrews is wrong about the timing of Christ's ministry.

**Q.** What did you say?

**LW.** The author of Hebrews thought that Christ's ministry in the Most Holy Place in heaven had already begun when in actuality, it had not.

**Q.** Do you realize what you are saying? How can a prophet of God be wrong? If the author of Hebrews is wrong about the timing of Christ's ministry, and another Bible writer is wrong on something else, how can we have confidence in the Bible? How can we tell what is right and wrong? Don't you believe the Bible is the infallible and inerrant Word of God?

**LW.** Oh yes, I believe the Bible is true! And, the Bible is the unfailing Word of God when properly understood. Absolutely! But, it is not inerrant because prophets can and do make mistakes. (See 1 Kings 13; Acts 21:11-14 and Galatians 2:11.) Prophets are, after all, ordinary human beings. But, you need to more fully understand the nature of inspiration. If God were to reveal something to you in a vision this very day, would that make *everything* you say and write hereafter about God 100% accurate and inerrant? And, what if God didn't tell you everything that He intended to reveal because He often reveals more information on a subject long after a prophet's life is over. (Ephesians 1:4, 3:5; Colossians 1:25) For this reason Paul appeals to the fact that the mystery of God was revealed in his day! So, how could anyone become an infallible and inerrant source of knowledge and wisdom about the ways and plans of an infinite God after a few visions?

**Q.** I see the problem. Are you saying that God reveals truth in segments over time?

**LW.** Yes. Therefore, a prophet can reach a faulty conclusion because all that God has to say or reveal about a certain subject is unfinished.

**Q.** But, if I were an inspired person, my report about my visions would be true and trustworthy—wouldn't they?

**LW.** O.K. Let's assume your report, like the writer of Hebrews, was given to best of your ability. Let's also assume, like the writer of Hebrews that you *apply the scenes within your vision* to the context of your day and time because God didn't tell you that Jesus was going to wait for nearly 2,000 years to return to earth. In other words, I am saying the author of Hebrews tried to *apply* his vision and understanding of Christ's ministry according to his knowledge of remaining time. We have already noticed his convictions about living in the last days and the nearness of the second advent. However, God had not finished revealing everything that He intended to have put in the Bible by A.D. 63. For example, the vision given to John on the isle of Patmos (recorded in the book of Revelation) occurred about 30 years after the book of Hebrews was written and we also know that the book of Daniel was sealed up until the end of time. The sealing up of Daniel necessarily means that God didn't want some things known until the time of the end should arrive.

My point is that most prophets *assume* that their visions apply to their day and time. And indeed, Bible history confirms that prophets often make this mistake. This is not a moral wrong. The Almighty knows what He is doing, and He knows what His prophets are doing. Rather, this is the process that God uses to reveal larger purposes. Some visions apply to time—periods much later than those of the prophet. For example, the books of Hebrews, Daniel and Revelation deal with time-periods far beyond the lifetime of any Bible prophet.

**Q.** In other words, you're saying that the author of Hebrews is truthfully reporting on his visions. But, when he writes the book, he applies the contents of his visions to his day in the first century A.D. because he doesn't know that 19 centuries were still to come?

**LW.** That is the point. No prophets of the Bible, as inspired as they were, knew that the year 1993 would ever be reached. When John was given the visions of Revelation, he had no idea that 19 centuries were still to come. And to avoid saying that prophets can and do make mistakes about timing, I have heard preachers say some rather foolish things. For example, some say that the "last days" began at the cross or the ascension of Jesus. If this were true, then we have had more than 715,500 *last days* since Jesus ascended to heaven. Such a statement is non-sense to me. If another 715,500 days were to pass before the second advent, they must be called last days also. I have also heard preachers say that the issue of timing in the Bible is unimportant because Jesus can return at any time. This is not true at all! God has clearly laid out a number of events in Bible prophecy that shall take place before Jesus comes. For instance, the gospel will be presented to every man, woman and child on earth before Jesus comes. (Matthew 24:14) You can be assured that heaven and earth will pass away before God's Word fails.

**Q.** If your assertion is true, that a number of Bible prophets have misapplied the timing of their visions, there should be other instances of this mistake. Right?

**LW.** Yes. Here is a short list. However, as you investigate each statement, consider the date when the prophet made his comment:

Paul wrote in the first century: **1 Corinthians 7:29** "What I mean, brothers, is that the time is short. From now on those who have wives should live as if they had none."

Peter wrote in the first century: **1 Peter 4:7** "The end of all things is near. Therefore be clear minded and self-controlled so that you can pray."

James wrote in the first century: **James 5:8** "You too, be patient and stand firm, because the Lord's coming is near."

John wrote near the end of the first century: **1 John 2:18** "Dear children, this is the last hour; and as you have heard that the antichrist is coming, even now many antichrists have come. This is how we know it is the last hour."

Obadiah wrote during the seventh century B.C.: **Obadiah 1:15** "The day of the Lord is near for all nations. As you have done, it will be done to you; your deeds will return upon your own head."

Joel wrote during the seventh century B.C.: **Joel 2:1** "Blow the trumpet in Zion; sound the alarm on my holy hill. Let all who live in the land tremble, for the day of the Lord is coming. It is close at hand—"

Zephaniah wrote during the seventh century B.C.: **Zephaniah 1:14** "The great day of the Lord is near— near and coming quickly. Listen! The cry on the day of the Lord will be bitter, the shouting of the warrior there."

**Q.** So, you're saying that several Bible prophets have been wrong about the amount of remaining time. This appears contrary to everything I've heard or believed about Bible writers. I mean, if you can't trust the writers of the Bible, who can you trust?

**LW.** Just a minute! Do thy faith no harm! We must make a sharp distinction. There is an important difference between moral issues concerning right and wrong and chronological matters concerning the amount of remaining time before Jesus comes. When it comes to behavior, moral righteousness is eternal and there is consistent harmony from all the prophets on the meaning and necessity of righteousness.

But, we are discussing the issue of *remaining time*. Many prophets and all the apostles thought they were living at the end of the ages. And God never told any prophet or apostle the amount of time that would pass before Jesus returned. Since God has been silent on this matter, the prophets assumed that they were living at the end. Time has proven that such was their assumption — not the "Word of the Lord."

For example, if Peter, Paul, James and John had known about the 1,260 years allocated for the suffering of God's people in Revelation 12:6,14 (also mentioned in Daniel 7:25) they would have known that more than a millennium of time was still to come before Jesus would return to earth.

**Q.** Are you suggesting that God wanted the disciples to think they were living in the last days when in reality He knew they weren't?

**LW.** We cannot accuse God of misleading people, for God does not tempt people so that they are mislead. God says what He means and means all that He says. And, He says what He means in words that are explicit in our language. Notice what Jesus said to His disciples: **"I have much more to say to you, more than you can now bear."** (John 16:12) Later, when asked about the establishment of His kingdom, "He said to them: **'It is not for you to know the times or dates the Father has set by his own authority.' "** (Acts 1:7)

The first verse reveals that Jesus allows people to use His silence as they see fit. The second verse indicates that the Father *has set* times and dates and those times and dates for the salvation of man were not for their knowledge. If Jesus had told His disciples that He would not return to earth for about 2,000 years, He would have dealt the disciples a terrible blow. If your wife had said, "Yes, I'll marry you in 50 years," what would this have done to your affections the day you asked her to marry you? So, this is why Jesus said that He had much more to say, more than they could bear to hear.

**Q.** What about the words of Jesus in Revelation 22:12?

**LW.** The word "soon" is used eight times in Revelation. The phrase "the time is near" is also used twice. And Jesus is clearly quoted in Revelation 22:12 as saying that His coming is soon. How do these words harmonize with the fact that 19 centuries have passed since they were given? What does "soon" or "near" mean?

The only solution I can offer to your question is this: Jesus didn't know the length of time that would pass between this vision (given about 95 A.D.) and His second coming. I say this on the basis of Scripture. Carefully notice what Jesus said: **"No one knows about that day or hour, not even the angels in heaven, *nor the Son*, but only the Father."** (Matthew 24:36, emphasis mine.)

I suspect the actual timing of Christ's return has been kept hidden from Jesus by the Father. While this comment invokes another subject of discussion, my guess is that the day Jesus became the Lamb of God, He put on a "blindfold," as it were, and became subject to the plan of salvation — a plan with hidden dates, times and details known only by the Father. (Similar to the plan when Abraham and Isaac went to the top of Mt. Moriah. The son did not know what was to occur until the time came.) In short, since the day Jesus offered Himself to the Father for us, He had to put complete faith in the Father. In John 17:4, Jesus said to the Father, **"I have brought you glory on earth by completing the work you gave me to do."**

**Q.** So, your answer to my first question is that the author of Hebrews was simply wrong about the timing of Christ's ministry in heaven's Most Holy Place? In other words, what he saw was true, but when he applied it to his day, he made a mistake?

**LW.** Yes. The author of Hebrews did not understand the timing of Daniel 7:13,14 or Daniel 8:14 nor could he have known about the timing of related events in Revelation. (Revelation had not been given when Hebrews was written.) So, the visions given to the author of Hebrews about the ministry of Jesus as our High Priest are, without doubt, true. But, his assumption about the timing of Christ's ministry in the Most Holy Place is simply wrong because God had not revealed all the facts about Christ's ministry in A.D. 63, specifically the timing of that ministry.

**Q.** Isn't the word "wrong" too strong to use on a prophet of God?

**LW.** Notice what Paul said of Peter: **"When Peter came to Antioch, I opposed him to his face, because he was clearly in the wrong."** (Galatians 2:11)

**Q.** So, how can we know the timing of events surrounding the ministry of Jesus in the Most Holy Place in heaven?

**LW.** The timing and order of events is the purpose of apocalyptic prophecy. Apocalyptic prophecy lays out the chronology of salvation's events. Apocalyptic prophecy aligns all the pieces so that we can tell *when* all events transpire. Think of apocalyptic prophecy as the skeleton to which all events must be properly connected. And, when all the pieces are properly aligned, the harmony of the sum of the parts provides a system of checks and balances so that we can accurately know God's timing—both past and future.

**Q.** Is this why the book of Daniel was sealed up until the time of the end?

**LW.** Yes. The book of Daniel is unsealed at the end of time because the last generation needs to know the timing of a number of things. They need to know how all of salvation's pieces align because God wants His people to know in advance what He is about to do. And, as a result, God's people now have the opportunity to understand the order and timing of events that will occur during the Great Tribulation.

**Q.** Are you aware that some claim that the book of Hebrews is not dealing with the ministry of Jesus in the Most Holy Place, but rather, in the Holy Place?

**LW.** Yes. I understand the controversy in Hebrews stems over the translation of the Greek word *hagion*. In the KJV, the word *hagion* is translated "holiest" (as in the Most Holy Place) three times, translated "holy place" two times, translated "sanctuary" four times and translated "holy places" one time. In the NIV, *hagion* is translated "Most Holy Place" six times, translated "holy place" once, and translated "sanctuary" three times. Given the divergent choice of words used by different translators, we have to ask a primary question: "What was the author's intent behind the word *hagion* in Hebrews?"

It is possible that one could do an exhaustive word study on the use of *hagion* in the first century A.D. and still miss the author's intent. So, I don't take this controversy too seriously for three reasons. First, the core message to the Hebrews was that Jesus Christ had become their high priest. This assertion opposed the millennial teaching of the Jews that the one serving in Jerusalem's Most Holy Place was *their* high priest. The author of Hebrews clearly says that believers in Jesus have an advocate with God because Jesus can go into the very presence of God on our behalf and obtain all that is needed! This is the primary truth found in the book of Hebrews. Secondly, the Hebrews well knew that only the high priest could enter the Most Holy Place, and then, only once a year when he presented an annual sacrifice. (Exodus 30:10; Hebrews 10:3) However, other priests conducted regular services in the front room of the sanctuary, the Holy Place. So what is the point of a high priest serving in the front room, the Holy Place, when "lesser" priests were able to do that? In other words, the supporting truth behind the high priesthood of Jesus is the fact that He *alone* can enter into the very presence of God — a place off limits to everyone else!

And lastly, the high priest could only enter the Most Holy Place *once* a year on the Day of Atonement. (Leviticus 16:2) Because the services in the earthly tabernacle were a model of the services in the true tabernacle in heaven, we should understand that Jesus would present His sacrifice for the world before the Father only once, at the appointed time. (Hebrews 9:24-26; 10:12) And that day occurred at the coronation of Jesus in 1798. According to the prophecies in Daniel 7-9 and Revelation 4-6, forty-six years later, in 1844, Jesus began to cleanse the heavenly temple.

**Q.** So, if I understand your position correctly on the ministry of Jesus, you're saying that Jesus did not begin to function as high priest until 1798. Then, in 1844, He began to cleanse heaven's sanctuary— a pre-advent judgment process.

**LW.** Yes.

**Q.** So, what did Jesus do in heaven between His ascension and 1798?

**LW.** Jesus returned to heaven and served before the Father as our priest until the appointed time should come when the services of a high priest would be needed. A priest is one chosen by God to serve in divine matters. So, Jesus fulfilled the responsibilities of priest until the time came for His promotion. When I say that Jesus served as our priest, I not referring to the *position* of Jesus, I am referring to *services* of Jesus. In other words, Jesus has held the position, "Son of God," ever since the day sin began. But, the only services needed in heaven's sanctuary was that of priest. However, when the time came for the services of high priest, Jesus alone was found worthy of that honor. (Revelation 6:9-13; Hebrews 7:20-28)

In 1798, the appointed time came. Jesus was found worthy to serve as our high priest because He was the only one who had lived as a man without sinning and He is the only one to ever experience the second death. These two points have to be enlarged to be properly appreciated. First, in God's system of justice, the Son had to experience the power of sin *as a human being does* before He could properly weigh the fate of human beings in heaven's court. (Daniel 7:13,14; Revelation 5:9) Secondly, no creature in God's universe is sentenced to a punishment that God Himself has not already suffered. Such is God's fairness.

**Q.** How do you calculate the timing of Christ's ministry as our High Priest in heaven's sanctuary?

**LW.** As I said before, apocalyptic prophecy provides the answer. Think of apocalyptic prophecy as a skeleton upon which the chronology of all events hang. This skeleton provides the framework upon which all events are chronologically aligned. And none of the Bible prophets understood this framework because knowledge of the framework was sealed up until the end of time.

Notice what the angel twice told Daniel about his book: **"But you, Daniel, close up and seal the words of the scroll until the time of the end. Many will go here and there to increase knowledge."** (Daniel 12:4) And again, **"He replied, 'Go your way, Daniel, because the words are closed up and sealed until the time of the end.' "** (Daniel 12:9)

These two verses clearly say that the book of Daniel was sealed up until the time of the end. So, none of the Bible prophets could know about the apocalyptic framework that was sealed up in Daniel because none of the Bible prophets live today.

**Q.** You're saying the book of Daniel is now unsealed?

**LW.** Yes. I believe the rules of interpretation necessary to understand the apocalyptic prophecies of Daniel *and* Revelation are now known.

Q. So, your view of inspiration is that God reveals information to His prophets. Then, His prophets are free to explain the information in their own words and apply it to their time — as they desire. However, a correct understanding of the timing within any vision from God has to ultimately harmonize with the "prophetic skeleton" of events outlined in Daniel and Revelation.

LW. Yes.

Q. Then, what prophecy says that Jesus begins to serve as High Priest in heaven's sanctuary in 1798?

LW. There is no text that says that Jesus began to officiate as our High Priest in heaven's sanctuary in 1798. This matter involves several large themes. So, I'll try to be brief. Notice these four texts:

First, notice that God appointed a specific day for the annual cleansing of the earthly sanctuary: **"The Lord said to Moses: 'Tell your brother Aaron not to come whenever he chooses into the Most Holy Place behind the curtain in front of the atonement cover on the ark, or else he will die, because I appear in the cloud over the atonement cover.' {29} This is to be a lasting ordinance for you: On the tenth day of the seventh month you must deny yourselves and not do any work—whether native-born or an alien living among you— {30} because on this day atonement will be made for you, to cleanse you. Then, before the Lord, you will be clean from all your sins."** (Leviticus 16:2,29,30)

Secondly, I find in Hebrews that the earthly sanctuary was a model of the heavenly one. The implication is obvious. Services in the earthly temple were a shadow of things in the heavenly temple. This means that earthly services were representations of heavenly services. **"They [earthly priests] serve at a sanctuary that is a copy and shadow of what is in heaven. This is why Moses was warned when he was about to build the tabernacle: 'See to it that you make everything according to the pattern shown you on the mountain.' "** (Hebrews 8:5)

Thirdly, Paul says that God appointed a specific time when He will judge the world by Jesus: **"For he [the Father] has set a day when he will judge the world with justice by the man he has appointed. He** has given proof of this to all men by raising him from the dead." (Acts 17:31) Jesus confirmed this point saying, "Moreover, the Father judges no one, but has entrusted all judgment to the Son." (John 5:22)

Lastly, Daniel tells us when the cleansing of the *heavenly* sanctuary occurs: "He said to me, 'It will take 2,300 evenings and mornings; *then* the sanctuary will be reconsecrated.' " (Daniel 8:14) I cannot in the space provided discuss why the sanctuary mentioned in Daniel 8:14 is in heaven, nor can I explain here why the 2,300 evenings and mornings represent 2,300 years. (These matters are covered in detail in my book, *The Revelation of Jesus.*)

But, in response to your question, the Bible clearly says that God has appointed a day when Jesus will judge the world. From the earthly sanctuary services we find that the cleansing of the sanctuary only happened on the annual Day of Atonement. We know from Hebrews 9:25,26 that the heavenly sanctuary only needs cleansing once and from Daniel 9:24 and Daniel 8:14, the time for that cleansing is 2,300 years after the decree to restore and rebuild Jerusalem. The decree was issued in the Spring of 457 B.C. and 2,300 years later reaches to 1844. (This brief summary does not prove the point. See my books, *The Revelation of Jesus* and *18 End-Time Bible Prophecies.*)

But, perhaps the most important concept we can assemble from these texts is that the services of a high priest were specifically required on the Day of Atonement. No other person could go behind the veil and appear in the very presence of God. (Leviticus 16, 21; Hebrews 9) This salient point is the central thrust in the book of Hebrews. The author intimately connects Jesus with the cleansing of heaven's sanctuary because human beings need an advocate "behind the veil," seated at the right hand of God. Our advocate is there to see that the needs of God in heaven and people on earth are met. "Therefore, since we have a great high priest who has gone through the heavens, Jesus the Son of God, let us hold firmly to the faith we profess." (Hebrews 4:14)

Q. What is the point about Jesus being a High Priest like Melchizedek?

LW. The point is that even in the days of Abraham, before there was a Jew or a Jewish nation, there was one greater than Abraham. This is proven by the fact that Abraham gave his tithes to Melchizedek and Melchizedek *blessed* Abraham. Since the Jews had to admit there was one greater than Abraham, the author of Hebrews draws an important parallel. There is a high priest greater than those descending through Aaron and His appearing proves that the covenant delivered to Moses at Mt. Sinai is now obsolete. (Hebrews 5:10; 7:18,21; 9:10)

This is a matter worthy of much deeper study. Notice this text: **"So Christ also did not take upon himself the glory of becoming a high priest. But God said to him, 'You are my Son; today I have become your Father.' And he says in another place, 'You are a priest forever, in the order of Melchizedek.' "** (Hebrews 5:5,6) The quote for Hebrews 5:5 is taken from Psalm 2:7. Notice the context: **" 'I have installed my King on Zion, my holy hill.' {7} I will proclaim the decree of the Lord: He said to me, 'You are my Son; today I have become your Father. {8} Ask of me, and I will make the nations your inheritance, the ends of the earth your possession. {9} You will rule them with an iron scepter; you will dash them to pieces like pottery.' {10} Therefore, you kings, be wise; be warned, you rulers of the earth."** (Psalms 2:6-10)

Who made the utterance recorded in Psalms 2? The Father. When did this utterance take place? The day Jesus offered Himself a substitute for man. When Jesus went before the Father to secure salvation for Adam and Eve, Jesus offered to become subject to all the terms and conditions set forth in the plan which had been prepared long before sin arose. After Jesus and the Father agreed that the plan should be implemented, the Father spoke to Jesus saying, "You are my Son; *today* I have become your Father." And at Christ's baptism, the Father affirmed His covenant with the Son by saying, **"This is my Son, whom I love, with Him I am well pleased."** (Matthew 3:17)

The significance of this is very beautiful. Jesus is as much God as is the Father. Jesus has the same powers and abilities as the Father. Jesus is both equal and co-eternal in every way with the Father. Yet, the day Jesus committed Himself as man's substitute for the wrath of God, Jesus became *subject* to the plan of salvation just as a son is born subject to his father. As Isaac (the son) was submissive to Abraham (the father), so Jesus became a *submissive son to the Father and the plan to save man.* When Jesus submitted to the terms and conditions of the plan of salvation, He was given a covenant containing three things that would be fulfilled as necessary to complete the salvation of man and the vindication of God:

1.  Jesus was placed in the office of priest—the office of one appointed to represent man in matters pertaining to God. Consequently, it was Jesus Himself who dealt with the patriarchs and the Jews. From day one, Jesus has stood between guilty man and God carrying out the plan of salvation. (1 John 2:1,2) He was also designated to eventually serve as high priest if He accomplished all that was given to Him to do.

2.  After gaining victory over sin and shedding His blood upon the cross, Jesus returned to heaven to serve as man's intercessor on the basis of His shed blood — a better covenant. Notice that His work didn't change, what changed was the basis of the work. Then, when the appointed time came, the time for cleansing heaven's sanctuary, He was selected as high priest because no one else in the whole universe was found worthy. (Revelation 5) Notice this text: **"Although he was a son, he learned obedience from what he suffered {9} and, once made perfect, he became the source of eternal salvation for all who obey him {10} and was designated by God to be high priest in the order of Melchizedek."** (Hebrews 5:8-10)

    Being designated is not the fulfillment of the promise. (A man or a woman may be designated for marriage, but they remain unmarried until the day of the wedding.) So, Jesus was designated as high priest on the basis of his perfect compliance to the plan of salvation while on earth. The implementation of Christ's position as high priest is chronologically pin-pointed in Daniel 7:13,14 and Revelation 5. This is one reason why the issue of Christ's worthiness is so important in Revelation 5.

3.  Lastly, after Jesus has finally completed all that the plan of salvation requires (at the end of the millennium), He shall be fully revealed for all that He is. He is God. But one thing overwhelms me more than anything else. After Jesus has settled the matter of sin and has been fully revealed, He will return His great authority to the Father so that He might live among His people as one of them. See 1 Corinthians 15:22-28. Can you grasp such love for man?

# The coming wrath of God, the 1,335 days and the shaking

(Reprinted from the July, 1993, issue of *Day Star.*)

**Q.** Daniel 12:11,12 says that the 1,290 days and the 1,335 days begin with the abolishing of the daily sacrifice. What is the daily sacrifice that Daniel speaks of?

**LW.** In a sentence, the abolishing of the daily sacrifice in Daniel 12:11 refers to the termination of Christ's corporate mediation in heaven on behalf of the world. In short, Jesus has been interceding between the wrath of God and this planet since the day Adam and Eve sinned. When that *daily* intercession comes to an end, we can start counting the days (1,290 to be exact) when the abomination that causes desolation will be set up.

**Q.** What do you mean "corporate mediation?" Isn't there one close of probation?

**LW.** Yes, there is one close of probation for individuals. However, there is also a limit to God's patience with this world in a corporate sense. For example, when I say that Israel rejected Jesus, I speak of Israel *corporately* because there were some individuals in Israel that received Jesus. In a similar way, the plan of salvation deals with man corporately and it deals with men and women individually. God's purpose for mankind is longer than one generation, so He deals with us corporately. So, one must understand the sharp distinction between God's corporate actions and God's dealings with individuals. For example, John 3:16 is a corporate text: **"For God so loved the world...."** Compare this with 1 John 5:12 which is directed to individuals: **"He who has the Son has life...."** The first text says that God loved the world — the whole world. The second text says that he who receives the Son will have life. The larger significance between God's corporate work and His work for individuals will be seen in a moment.

**Q.** What is the abomination that causes desolation?

**LW.** The universal death decree for God's people.

**Q.** How did you arrive at that meaning?

**LW.** It is clear from Revelation 13:15 that a time is coming when a decree will be enforced upon people in every nation. Those who refuse to obey the decree to obey the image of the beast (the coming one-world church/state) are to be killed. It is also clear from the Bible that the term, "abomination that causes desolation," refers to an evil act (an abomination) that causes the destruction of God's people.

Notice the following two texts. Both refer to the *same event* while using different words: **"So when you see standing in the holy place 'the abomination that causes desolation,' spoken of through the prophet Daniel—let the reader understand—"** (Matthew 24:15) **"When you see Jerusalem being surrounded by armies, you will know that its desolation is near."** (Luke 21:20) Matthew quotes Jesus using a Hebrew phrase and Luke quotes the same speech of Jesus using the Greek equivalent. The net result is that we can clearly understand the idea behind Jesus' words. The coming armies that Jesus spoke of (which Daniel predicted) were the armies of Rome. In A.D. 70, the armies of Rome fully desolated Jerusalem just as Daniel predicted. (Daniel 9:26,27; 11:31) So, "the abomination that caused desolation" in A.D. 70 was the destruction of Jerusalem by Rome.

But, Daniel 12:11 is not talking about the destruction of Jerusalem. Daniel 12:11 says that the abomination that causes desolation is SET UP at the END of the 1,290 days and the 1,290 days begin with the abolishing of the daily.

Some have tried to terminate the 1,290 days with the fall of the little horn power in 1798, but Daniel says *the abomination* that causes desolation is "set up" — not brought down. This point is emphasized because some people believe the collapse of the little horn in 1798 is the abomination mentioned in Daniel 12:11. But, the 1,290 and the 1,335 time-periods have nothing to do with the little horn power of Daniel 7. Rather, the 1,290 and the 1,335 time-periods have to do with the horn power of

Daniel 8 which appears at the end of the world. (See Daniel 8:11,17,19,23; and chapter 8 in my book, *The Revelation of Jesus*.) Further, the 1,290 and 1,335 days are literal time-periods, because they occur after the expiration of the Jubilee calendar which expires in the Spring of 1994.

But, the most **important component** within Daniel 12:11 is the event that marks the commencement of these two time-periods. Both the 1,290 and the 1,335 days begin with **the cessation of the daily.** Since there has been no daily *on earth* since A.D. 70, where should we look for the cessation of the true daily? Answer: In heaven.

**Q.** What is the daily?

**LW.** The term comes from the *daily* sanctuary services which were conducted every evening and morning by priests. (Exodus 29:38,39) The daily services in the wilderness sanctuary were a shadow of Christ's ministry in heaven that began the day that Adam and Eve sinned. The daily services in the earthly sanctuary reveal that Jesus intercedes before God each day and because His intercession is approved, the wrath of God upon mankind has been delayed. The *daily* offering mediates between God and the whole world—not God and one individual. On the other hand, the sin offering conducted at the altar of burnt offering mediates between God and a sinner. Both sacrifices, the daily and the sin offering, figure prominently in the cleansing of heaven's temple.

**Q.** What do you mean?

**LW.** Daniel, using the future perfect tense in Daniel 8:14, says that the cleansing of heaven's sanctuary begins after 2,300 evenings and mornings expire. (The 2,300 evenings and mornings are to be interpreted as day/years because they occur during the operation of the Jubilee calendar.) The vision of Daniel 8 is called, "The vision of the evenings and mornings" (Daniel 8:26) because it affirms the continual operation of daily services in heaven for 2,300 evenings and mornings! In fact, the daily continues in heaven long after 1844. The daily does not end until Jesus ceases to mediate on behalf of the whole earth. Remember, the daily services in the wilderness sanctuary were not for the benefit of any one individual, the daily was conducted for the benefit of the whole camp of Israel. And, to the surprise of many, you must understand that there can be no cleansing of heaven's temple if there is no daily in heaven!

**Q.** You're saying there could be no cleansing of heaven's temple without the daily also taking place in heaven?

**LW.** Yes. The sanctuary service in the wilderness clearly teaches that there are two types of sacrifices: one for the camp of Israel (corporate offering), the other for individuals. The corporate offering was called the daily and its benefits were not directed at any one individual. Each day, blood from a perfect one-year-old lamb was deposited on the horns of the *altar of incense,* morning and evening. This blood "record" provided for continual or daily atonement for the whole camp of Israel. On the other hand, blood from a sinner's goat or lamb was deposited to the horns of the *altar of burnt offering* when a sinner brought his sacrifice for his sin to the sanctuary. The point here is that the *altar of incense* provided atonement for the whole camp of Israel, the *altar of burnt offering* provided atonement for individuals.

**Q.** OK, let's assume the termination of the daily in heaven is still future. What marks the cessation of the daily in heaven so that people on earth can know when to begin counting the days?

**LW.** There will be a global earthquake, flashes of lightning, rumblings deep in the earth and peals of thunder all over the world.

**Q.** Are you speaking of the casting down of the censer in Revelation 8:5 that occurs just before the seven trumpets sound?

**LW.** Yes.

**Q.** If the casting down of the censer in Revelation 8:5 points to the close of *individual* salvation, and the trumpets follow, this means they would have to sound after the close of salvation, wouldn't they?

**LW.** Many correctly understand that the act of casting down the censer in Revelation 8:5 indicates the cessation of atonement at the altar of incense. However, the service at the altar of incense described in Revelation 8:5 is neither a routine worship service nor is it the close of salvation for individuals. Rather, the casting down of the censer at the altar of incense marks *the end of the daily*. Here's how:

Following the pattern of the wilderness sanctuary, there are two altars in heaven's temple. John saw both altars. (See Revelation 8:3 and 6:9.) The latter reference implies the altar of burnt offering because the blood of sacrifices was kept beneath the altar. See Exodus 29:12. The casting down of the censer at the altar of incense marks the end of atonement services, and the only service conducted at that altar was the daily. So, according to Revelation 8, after the daily comes to an end, the trumpets begin to sound and the purpose of the first four trumpets is to awaken the people of the world to the terms and conditions of salvation.

On the Day of Atonement in ancient Israel, the cleansing of the temple involved three articles of furniture in this order: the ark, the altar of incense and lastly, the altar of burnt offering. The order of atonement is mentioned twice in Leviticus 16:20-33. My point is that Jesus follows this same order in cleansing heaven's temple. First He makes atonement before the ark, then for the altar of incense and lastly, for the altar of burnt offering.

**Q.** Wait a minute! You're saying that three items in the temple had to be cleansed in a particular order?

**LW.** Yes. God prescribed a specific order for the cleansing of the sanctuary. Three articles of furniture were cleansed of guilt and restored to a holy state. Each atonement by the high priest shadows a specific event conducted by Jesus in heaven's temple. For example, the atonement made before the ark represents the first step in the cleansing of heaven's sanctuary. In 1798, heaven's court was called and seated. The Father then conducted a search throughout the universe for someone worthy to take the book sealed with seven seals. (Revelation 5:1-6) Only Jesus was found worthy. He alone could make atonement for God's law. His was the only life in all the universe that was born under the condemnation of law, was tempted in every possible way, and yet, never sinned. His perfect life and sacrifice confirmed the holiness and virtue of God's law. He *alone* was found worthy to restore God's law to its rightful honor. He alone could reconcile an evil world to the Father and He alone could spare the faith-full from the coming wrath of God which the law requires. (Romans 4:15; 5:9,10) The point here is that Jesus fully restored the holiness of the law of God before beginning the services of the investigative judgment.

**Q.** What you mean by atonement?

**LW.** Atonement is nothing less than restitution — full and complete. For example, suppose I stole $10 from you. What do you think would be required for restitution or atonement in God's sight? Answer: $10 plus $2. (See Leviticus 6:2-5.)

**Q.** I don't understand. How was God's law violated so that it needed atonement?

**LW.** By sin. (See Leviticus 16:16.) The devil claimed for 4,000 years that it was not possible for any human to keep God's law. The proof of his claim was secure, that is, until Jesus came and lived on earth. And, no one since Jesus has perfectly kept the law of God.

So, Jesus is the only One who has demonstrated that God's law can be kept. Thus, Jesus was found worthy to serve as man's High Priest at the appointed time of cleansing the temple in heaven, and even more, Jesus could verify the holiness of God's law on the basis of His perfect life.

**Q.** What did animal sacrifices have to do with man's atonement?

**LW.** God, who is higher than the highest, who is greater than the greatest, who is the undisputed Eternal and Immortal King of all the universe, has a number of universal laws that apply to all of His creation. One of His laws says: Obey the King of Heaven and Earth and live, disobey the King of Heaven and Earth and receive the wrath of the King: death.

Since God grants the power of choice to all His subjects, it is each creature's privilege to decide if he will live or die. Understand that God's immutable law is not concerned with how one disobeys or under what influences one might disobey. This law is simple. It is universal. Paul wrote, **"The sting of death is sin, and the power of sin is the law."** (1 Corinthians 15:56)

To teach man about the properties of law, sin and salvation, God went to some extraordinary lengths. Notice this text: **"For the life of a creature is in the blood, and I have given it to you to make atonement for yourselves on the altar; it is the blood that makes atonement for one's life."** (Leviticus 17:11) In other words, God required man to put animals to death in order to teach man about His postponed wrath upon sinners. Sinful men were supposed to understand that the killing of animals as sacrifices was a "teaching device" revealing the consequences that God's law required. (Indeed, those who came to understand salvation by faith also came to understand the true meaning of animal sacrifices. See Hebrews 11 and Psalm 51.) Because animal sacrifices were used, God explained that the life of the creature was in the blood because the wrath of God demands the life (the blood) of the offender.

We cannot afford to misunderstand this sublime point. In the simplest of terms, atonement is nothing less than complete restitution plus 20%. Sin (the violation of law) requires death and God's wrath, even though postponed, does not relent until the sinner (law-breaker) is put to death. Then, atonement is made. The penalty of sin is death. The terms are elegantly simple: "Disobey and die."

In the Garden of Eden, even before the creation of Eve, Adam was fully warned of God's law and its consequences. **"But of the tree of the knowledge of good and evil, thou shalt not eat of it: for in the day that thou eatest thereof, thou shalt surely die."** (Genesis 2:17 KJV) According to this verse, the penalty to Adam for violation would be immediate and fatal "within the day." *The execution of justice is God's wrath expressed.* Because Adam and Eve were destined to receive the wrath of God the very day they sinned, Jesus moved quickly the moment they sinned. Because of their disobedience, they were to be "justifiably" killed. But Jesus stepped between the execution of God's wrath and the guilty pair. Jesus interceded on behalf of man and stayed the wrath of God by offering Himself to the Father as man's substitute. Jesus and the Father entered into a plan to save man and they agreed to the following terms:

1. Jesus could mediate for a time between God and man, so that man could be saved if Jesus was willing to receive the full wrath of God which is the second death.

2. Jesus would come to earth at a specific time. He would be born of a woman — born subject to the wrath that comes through law. He would live a sinless life and die in the hands of the Father as the *Lamb of God* upon Calvary. By doing this, Jesus would validate the holiness of God's law which Lucifer had brought into question and man had violated.

3. In turn, the Father agreed to impute the sinless life of Jesus to all sinners who would put their faith in Jesus as their Savior. Further, the guilt of those sinners who receive Christ would be transferred to the horns of the altar of burnt offering in heaven until the time came for the cleansing of that altar. Thus, sinners could be "saved" down through the ages even though the plan of salvation remained unfinished until the temple is fully cleansed and the sins in the temple are put upon the head of the scapegoat.

4. Near the end of probationary time, the process of cleansing the temple would begin. First, the ark (the law of God) would be cleansed of any guilt or question. The sinless life and second death suffered by Jesus, and consequently the worthiness of Jesus, would dismiss any question about the holiness of God's law. Secondly, at an appointed time, the altar of incense would be cleansed and its daily services terminated. Lastly, the altar of burnt offering would be cleansed after everyone on earth had made his decision for or against God's offer of salvation.

5.    Then, the guilt of those saints who had transferred their sins to
the altar of burnt offering would be placed upon the head of the
scapegoat and the scapegoat would receive the penalty of all sins
placed upon its head. (Leviticus 16:22)

The Bible says that the Father so loved the world that He accepted the
unmerited offer of Jesus on behalf of mankind. Thus, Jesus because
man's mediator or intercessor *the day Adam and Eve sinned.* Paul is
clear on this point, **"For there is one God and one mediator between
God and men, the man Christ Jesus."** (1 Timothy 2:5) But, there is
another important point here. Jesus is the mediator for all of earth, all
human beings, saved or unsaved. Ever since the day Adam and Eve
sinned, Jesus has been holding back the wrath of God for the whole
world so that individuals can come to a saving knowledge of God's
salvation!

So, to answer your question again, God used animal sacrifices and religious
ceremonies as a model to explain the properties of how salvation was
to be implemented. The death of every animal at man's hand was to be
a lesson pointing forward to God's coming wrath upon sinners, including
His own Son. In each sacrifice, man was to take note of his guilty position
as a sinner and as such, a recipient of God's coming wrath. But, most
of all, God wanted man to understand that He had provided a perfect
Lamb to receive His wrath and human beings could escape His postponed
wrath by receiving His Son! God wants everyone to do just what Jesus
did: Submit to the terms and conditions of the everlasting covenant and
be saved!

Q. I've been told that Genesis 2:17 means that Adam and Eve would
begin dying the day they sinned. In other words, because of being separated
from God by sin, Adam and Eve would eventually die. This is totally
different than their being *executed* by God.

LW. The issue you raise is very important. There is a distinct difference
between the penalty for sin and the consequences of sin. That's why two
goats were required to cleanse the sanctuary. The penalty for sin and
the requirements for atonement concerns the presence and operation of

law. However, the *consequences* of sin are the outcome of sin's effect. If you kill someone, the penalty and atonement for murder *according to law* is one thing, but the consequences of that deed are something else. But, your question boils down to a much more significant question than you have asked. It is this: "Does God directly or indirectly kill people? I find in the Bible that God kills people both ways.

Q. Where?

LW. First, here is some evidence that the Lord kills people directly. Carefully notice what the Lord told Moses: **"On that same night I will pass through Egypt and strike down every firstborn--both men and animals--and I will bring judgment on all the gods of Egypt. I am the Lord. When the Lord goes through the land to strike down the Egyptians, he will see the blood on the top and sides of the doorframe and will pass over that doorway, and he will not permit the destroyer to enter your houses and strike you down."** (Exodus 12:12,23)

Some people claim the destroyer in verse 23 is not the Lord. This is contrary to contextual evidence. The Lord is the destroyer. He is the One passing through the land killing the firstborn, both men and animals (verse 12). Also consider that the Lord is the One who *spares* the firstborn if He finds blood on the doorposts! To say that the Lord conspired with the devil to kill the firstborn of Egypt is to say that God *uses* the devil to fulfill the demands of His law, which requires death for disobedience.

The Lord is righteous in everything He does. Notice what the Bible says about God, **"He is the Rock, his works are perfect, and all his ways are just. A faithful God who does no wrong, upright and just is he. ...There is no god besides me. I put to death and I bring to life, I have wounded and I will heal, and no one can deliver out of my hand."** (Deuteronomy 32:4,39) The Bible is clear. The Lord is a sovereign God. He has power over life. He has power over death.

Now, here's a text showing that God kills indirectly: **"Son of man, if a country sins against me by being unfaithful and I stretch out my hand against it to cut off its food supply and send famine upon it and kill its men and their animals, {14} even if these three men—Noah, Daniel**

and Job—were in it, they could save only themselves by their
righteousness, declares the Sovereign Lord." (Ezekiel 14:13-14) In this
case, God sends famine and people die as a result of having no food.
Even though the end-result is death, the method of famine is indirect
but the responsibility for death in this case still belongs to God. In a
similar way, notice how God reckoned responsibility for the death of
Uriah the Hittite. Remember, David had Joab send Uriah to the front
line of battle so that he might be killed and the king could have Uriah's
wife? Nathan, the prophet, was sent to David and he said, **"Why did
you despise the word of the Lord by doing what is evil in his eyes?
You struck down Uriah the Hittite with the sword and took his wife
to be your own. You killed him with the sword of the Ammonites."** (2
Samuel 12:9) So, as far as God was concerned, David killed Uriah with
the sword of the Ammonites!

**Q.** OK, God kills directly and indirectly. Can the devil do likewise?

**LW.** I find no text in the Bible where the devil has killed anyone directly.
However, there is evidence that he can kill indirectly. Here are a couple
of examples: **"Do not be like Cain, who belonged to the evil one and
murdered his brother. And why did he murder him? Because his own
actions were evil and his brother's were righteous."** (1 John 3:12) Clearly,
the devil had an influence upon Cain and under the influence of the
devil, Cain killed Abel.

Another example showing that the devil kills indirectly is found in Job
1. Remember, Job lost his sons, daughters and servants in calamitous
events connected with his great test. So, it seems clear that as far as
God allows, the devil kills people through sword, lightning and wind and
other calamities. But, as for the devil, I have not found where the devil
can directly kill people.

**Q.** So, you're convinced that the next event in heaven's process of cleansing
the temple is the cessation of the daily? And, this event will be marked
in heaven by the casting down of the censer at the altar of incense and
the trumpets will then begin?

**LW.** Yes.

**Q.** When the censer is cast down, there will be physical phenomena on earth: peals of thunder, rumblings, flashes of lightning and an earthquake?

**LW.** Yes.

**Q.** But, the casting down of the censer is not the close of salvation?

**LW.** No, not for individuals. The casting down of the censer means that God's patience with this evil and rebellious world has reached its limit. When we discuss the shaking, I'll explain the close of probation for individuals more completely.

**Q.** Then, what difference does it make if the daily comes to an end?

**LW.** Simply this: With Jesus taken out of the way, the wrath of God begins to break out upon the earth. Jesus has been standing between the wrath of God and a guilty world for almost 6,000 years. And when the daily ends, God's wrath begins. Paul knew of this coming wrath. He warned, **"Put to death, therefore, whatever belongs to your earthly nature: sexual immorality, impurity, lust, evil desires and greed, which is idolatry. {6} Because of these, the wrath of God is coming."** (Colossians 3:5,6)

Understand that after the daily ends, during the trumpets, there is mercy. In fact, the offer of God's mercy will be broadcasted by 144,000 servants all over the world at that time. The world will have a chance to hear of God's gracious call. The mystery of God is not completed until the seventh trumpet sounds. (Revelation 10:7) The mystery of God is that He is willing to save sinners, even more, He has made salvation free to all.

During the trumpets, as the people of the world hear the gospel, they will be required to make a decision. Each person's decision will be tested and then they will be sealed in their choice. The judgment of the living is simple. The living will be pressed hard by circumstances to decide for or against God's salvation. Then, when the last decision has been made, probation closes. There are no more decisions to be made. The services at the altar of burnt offering are finished. The last item in heaven's temple is cleansed and he that is righteous will remain righteous forever and he that is wicked will be destroyed soon.

Q. So, probation for individuals closes all through the seven trumpets. Some will be sealed earlier and some will be sealed later. All but the 144,000 will be sealed during that time-period?

LW. Yes.

Q. How long do you believe the seven trumpets will last?

LW. As far as I can tell, about 1,080 days. But, this is only a guess. (See apocalyptic chart in the back of *The Revelation of Jesus*, 2nd edition.)

Q. How long do you believe the seven last plagues will last?

LW. Again, my best guess is 255 days. The total time-period of the trumpets and plagues is a maximum of 1,335 days.

Q. Given the length of the seven first plagues (the seven trumpets) and seven last plagues, when is the universal death decree set up?

LW. If we subtract the 1,290 days from the 1,335, we find the universal death decree is 45 days before the Second Coming.

Q. Do you think we can closely calculate the date of the Second Coming?

LW. No. Jesus clearly says that those days "will be shortened." (Matthew 24:21,22) This means that the actual time-period of the Great Tribulation is less than 1,335 days and no one knows the amount of reduction in time.

**Q.** When do you expect the daily to come to an end?

**LW.** My guess is during the fall of 1994.

**Q.** Why then?

**LW.** Because it appears that the Jubilee calendar expires with 70 cycles in the Spring of 1994. At that time, or soon after, I anticipate the empowerment of the 144,000 and they will begin to proclaim the return of Jesus with great power and authority. This will cause a mighty shaking among those claiming to be the people of God. After the shaking has done its work in the church, the censer will be cast down.

**Q.** We'll discuss the shaking in a moment, but when the daily ends, the trumpets begin?

**LW.** Yes.

**Q.** When the seventh trumpet sounds, probation is over?

**LW.** Yes.

**Q.** Are there other texts in the Bible that speaks of Jesus ending the daily and the consequences that follow?

**LW.** Yes. **"For the secret power of lawlessness is already at work; but the one who now holds it back [*Jesus*] will continue to do so till he [*Jesus*] is taken *out of the way*. And then the lawless one [man of sin] will be revealed, whom the Lord Jesus will overthrow with the breath of his mouth and destroy by the splendor of his coming."** (2 Thessalonians 2:7,8; italics mine)

**Q.** Are you saying that Satan cannot be revealed until the daily ends?

**LW.** That is what the Bible says. Satan cannot physically appear on earth until Jesus steps out of the way and the wrath of God is allowed to begin. The devil is not allowed to appear until most of the world has heard the gospel and decided against it. Paul says of the wicked, "...They perish because they refused to love the truth and so be saved. For this reason God sends them a powerful delusion so that they will believe the lie." (2 Thessalonians 2:10,11) In other words, God allows the devil to physically appear before the people of the world claiming to be God (the powerful delusion) because they refused to love the truth and so be saved. Therefore, God sends a powerful delusion which forces everyone into a decision so the Great Tribulation can come to an end.

## The shaking discussed

**Q.** Changing the subject, I have a few questions about the shaking. First, what is the shaking that you speak of and when does it happen?

**LW.** The shaking occurs during a short time-period just before the seven trumpets begin. During this time, the professed followers of Jesus will be tested for the purpose of separating the faith-full from the faith-less. I understand that the shaking will occur a few months before the daily is abolished — perhaps beginning as early as the Spring of 1994, but time will tell for sure.

**Q.** It seems that Christians are being tossed to-and-fro today with every kind of doctrine. Is this part of the shaking?

**LW.** Indirectly, yes. But, the shaking that I am speaking of has not begun as yet. One might think of the shaking as having two phases. First, there is the rotting or decaying phase. Then, there is the collapsing phase. The coming event that I am referring to is the collapsing phase.

There is a lot of spiritual rot and decay in the church today. Christians have drifted far away from Bible study. This is proven by the fact that all kinds of doctrines are blowing about and many are confused. They don't know what or whom to believe because they don't know what the Bible teaches. This problem is compounded by the fact that truth doesn't stand still. God's truth is marching forward and if one decides to stand where his grandparents stood, he will be left behind in darkness.

The uncertain condition in the church today over the content of truth comes from the ministry of negligent pastors. Many have led their congregations to believe that the positions of the forefathers are adequate, or that tradition is truth, or that members should look to their church leaders to define what is truth. The end result is that today's generation of laity, especially the youth, have drifted far away from a Bible based Christianity. And if the laity do not understand the Bible for themselves, how can they determine the value of greater light or truth?

For this reason we find church leaders scrambling to keep the laity in tow. Pastors are growing increasingly negative at those expositors that challenge the "traditions of the forefathers," but their efforts at keeping the sheep in the fold will be proven futile in the end because sheep without knowledge are easily scattered. One lone wolf can scatter a herd of a thousand sheep.

**Q.** What will cause the shaking and what will be the result?

**LW.** The collapsing phase of the shaking will be caused by the Holy Spirit resting upon individuals. These will present the truth from the Bible in the plainest and clearest terms. The coming crisis will be a great dispute over the truth in the Bible. The 144,000 will powerfully proclaim the timeliness and relevancy of Bible prophecy and our individual need of preparation to meet God. And people and leaders alike will not be able to bear the testimony that comes straight from the Bible.

I have observed a small sample of this already. A number of pastors complain about my teaching without ever turning to the Bible to tell their people what the Bible actually says! For example, I recently challenged a dissenting pastor, "Open your Bible and explain Revelation, verse by verse, to your members and see how many will accept your exposition. Lead your members into becoming good Bible students by showing them HOW to study the Bible and you will have nothing to fear from me or anyone else who teaches new ideas." According to members, that pastor has yet to open his Bible and explain Revelation. Why is this?

Bible prophecy is integral to mission and philosophy. Bible prophecy tells us WHAT God is going to do, HOW He is going to do it, and WHY He must do it. And, Bible prophecy is indispensable on or about the time of fulfillment. For this reason, God is going to select and empower the 144,000 soon and they will powerfully reveal the forthcoming plans and actions of Jesus. The 144,000, like Noah of old, will clearly tell the church what Jesus is about to do. However, the testimony of Jesus will be found in opposition to the established plans, mission and purposes of men. Thus, a great dispute will result.

This coming moment will be most distressing. The controversy will be twofold. First, each person will have to decide for himself what the Bible actually says. And his decision will determine his subsequent course of action. Secondly, each person will have to decide if the human instrument proclaiming Bible truth is truly sent by God. This will be a tough test and history shows that religious people often fail in recognizing the servants of God. (Matthew 23:37)

Also, don't overlook this agonizing point. Under the power of the Holy Spirit, secret sins will be made public just like the sins of Ananias and Sapphira in Acts 5. This will prove to be highly embarrassing for many professed Christians. But, God will have a pure people. Thus, a number of supporting people will join with the 144,000 *before* the seven trumpets begin. I call this group of supporting people "remnant one." During the time-period of the seven trumpets, "remnant two" will be gathered out of Babylon through the ministry of the 144,000 and the support of remnant one.

**Q.** Does the Bible speak about the shaking?

**LW.** Yes. Here are some texts that deal with the shaking. Keep in mind that the shaking has to do with purifying God's people: See Amos 9:9; Haggai 2:6; Hebrews 12:26; Zechariah 13:7-9; and Revelation 10:11-11:1. (The reader should refer to Prophecy 10 in my book, *18 End-Time Bible Prophecies* to appreciate the last reference.)

**Q.** Since the shaking happens before the seven trumpets, does God give His people a fair chance? I mean, it seems that the trumpets would be far more convincing than the appearing of the 144,000. Is the church judged first?

**LW.** The shaking of the church occurs before the trumpets begin. The professed remnant of God will hear the testimony of Jesus directly through the 144,000. The powerful, Spirit-filled preaching and teaching of the 144,000 will move the people in the church to either accept or reject present truth. This is the key. All middle ground will be eliminated. The church will be split into two camps so that when the censer is cast down, the judgment of the living will begin and the first to be judged will be those who have had an opportunity to know what is truth. Some will be sealed with God's seal of approval, and many will be sealed without God's seal of approval. The church will be sealed first because they have already made up their minds! So, the church, those at the "inner altar" in Revelation 11:1, are judged first (1 Peter 4:17) because they claimed to be God's people.

**Q.** How long does the shaking last?

**LW.** I believe about six months. This length of time appears to fit within the total picture of last-day events which includes other time-periods such as the 1,290 days, the 1,335 days, the 42 months of persecution and the 1,260 days of the Two Witnesses.

**Q.** How will one recognize that the shaking has begun?

**LW.** The outpouring of the Holy Spirit will occur in a very marked way — signs and wonders will be seen. I cannot be more specific than that, but if we are watching for it, we shall not miss it!

**Q.** What can I do to get prepared?

**LW.** Study, pray and share your hope without ceasing.

# Questions on Armageddon

(Reprinted from the March, 1993, issue of *Day Star*.)

**Q.** Your view of Armageddon puzzles me. In your book, *18 End-Time Bible Prophecies*, you say that Armageddon begins about 45 days before the second coming, around the time of the universal death decree for the saints (pp. 149-161). However, you say the saints who are alive at that time will be delivered from death by the voice of Jesus. Further, you claim that the devil himself announces the coming of Jesus to the wicked and then he moves the world to attempt the destruction of Christ at His second appearing. Your teaching provokes a number of questions. Are you saying that Armageddon *is not* the next world war?

**LW.** Armageddon is not the next world war.

**Q.** Will Armageddon be fought in the Middle East?

**LW.** Not exclusively. Armageddon will be a world-wide war, not a Middle East war. Because it is world-wide, people in the Middle East will be involved.

**Q.** Do you believe the Bible predicts another world war is going to happen prior to Armageddon?

**LW.** Yes.

**Q.** What war are you speaking about?

**LW.** I believe the Bible predicts a *global* war is going to happen within the next three or four years. But, this war will not be like WWI or WWII. The coming war will be a civil war. It won't be East against West, or one group of nations aligned against another group of nations. Rather, the coming war will take place *within* each nation. This coming war is predicted in the sixth trumpet. (Revelation 9:13-21)

**Q.** When you say civil war, do you mean that each nation of the world will be fighting within itself?

**LW.** Yes.

**Q.** What will each nation be fighting over?

**LW.** The establishment of a new world order which is called the image of the beast in Revelation 13:14.

**Q.** Your comment runs contrary to the current attitude of the United Nations. There is more talk and interest in world order than ever before. So, why will the establishment of a new world order cause global war?

**LW.** True, there is much talk and interest about a new world order at the United Nations. The leaders of our world clearly realize the need for world order because international trade is now the backbone of each nation's economy. But, the leaders of the world do not anticipate the first five trumpets of Revelation. They do not know about the Great Tribulation that God is soon to send upon the earth. They do not realize the nearness of time, consequently, they do not know about the properties of the world order that will soon occur. In short, an unanticipated world order is coming that will be vastly different than world leaders anticipate today.

**Q.** You said, "The coming world order is the image of the beast." What are you talking about?

**LW.** There are two beasts in Revelation 13. The first beast is a composite beast. It has seven heads and ten horns. The second beast of Revelation 13 is a lamb-like beast. The first beast represents a confused coalition of the world's religious systems which is yet to be formed in response to the devastation of the first four trumpets.

About two years after the coalition forms, the second beast will appear on earth. The lamb-like beast of Revelation 13 represents the physical appearing of the devil claiming to be the Lamb of God. However, the lamb-like beast is simply the devil in sheep's clothing.

My point is that after the devil is physically upon the earth, and after he has convinced billions that he is the living God, he will move to consolidate the seven religious systems (the seven heads) of the world into a one-world-religion. (The reader should understand that the devil will demand a one-world religion since diversity of opinion about God will be resolved by simply asking the devil who is here "in the flesh.")

The coming one-world-religion is called the image of the beast in Revelation 13 because an image is simply a "likeness" of something. The devil will lift some doctrine from each of the world's religions, merge the doctrines together and form a new false religion that will be *forced* upon all the inhabitants of earth. This one-world-religion is called an image to the beast because the devil's one-world-religion will teach the same *falsehoods* about God as did Babylon.

**Q.** When is the image set up?

**LW.** During the sixth trumpet war.

**Q.** Explain the sixth trumpet war.

**LW.** To understand the sixth trumpet war — or the battle of Armageddon which occurs during the sixth plague, one has to *first* understand the seven trumpets of Revelation. In short, the seven trumpets of Revelation are seven global events that signal the end of the world and the second coming of Jesus. These events are designed by God to awaken 5.6 billion people to the realization that Jesus Christ is Lord and King over all people. The authority and salvation of Jesus will be fully revealed through the events associated with the trumpets.

**Q.** What are the seven trumpets?

**LW.** The seven trumpets (Revelation 8, 9 and 11) are:

1. Meteoric showers of burning hail — great unquenchable fires will be ignited all over the world.
2. A great asteroid will impact the sea — a large number of ships will sink and there will be enormous loss of sea life — the affected ocean will fill up with red algae.
3. A great asteroid will impact a continent — resulting ground waves break sewer systems and merge toxic waste with drinking water and millions will die from drinking contaminated water.
4. The ring of fire will erupt — billions of tons of ejecta will be blown into the atmosphere by violent volcanic eruptions — sunlight will be blocked from reaching earth — crops will perish for lack of sunlight.
5. The devil will physically appear before the people of earth claiming to be God — he will do many mighty miracles to prove his claims — billions will receive him as God.
6. The devil will demand the establishment of a global church-state — he will be given the honor of deity — those refusing to obey the devil will be put to death.
7. A great earthquake will occur marking the end of God's mercy. The offer of salvation comes to an end. Then, seven last plagues fall upon those who have received the mark (the number 666 or the name of the devil).

**Q.** So, you're saying the devil is going to physically appear before the people of earth claiming to be God during the fifth trumpet?

**LW.** Yes.

**Q.** When do you expect the seven trumpets to begin?

**LW.** Perhaps in the Fall of 1994.

**Q.** When do you expect the devil to physically appear?

**LW.** Late 1996 if the trumpets begin in 1994. Keep in mind this is only a guess. The Bible doesn't give a date for these events. However, the Bible does tell us *the order* of events.

**Q.** Put the trumpet events together in a brief scenario so I can see how they relate to each other.

**LW.** I believe the first four trumpets occur in quick succession. Perhaps during a period of just 30 to 60 days in late 1994. The first four trumpets are designed by God to inflict a fatal blow to the earth. As the infrastructures of each nation collapse and our man-made securities fail, some people will be literally scared to death. The enormity of destruction and death occurring as a result of the first four trumpets is beyond description. And, the months and years of suffering that follow will be exceedingly terrible.

**Q.** How long does the tribulation last?

**LW.** I believe the Great Tribulation (including the seven trumpets and the seven last plagues) will be less than 1,335 days in length. (See Daniel 12:12 and Matthew 24:22.)

**Q.** Why does God send the trumpets?

**LW.** God sends the trumpets to get earth's *full* attention. These events are not random, neither are they without cause. Indeed, sin always requires atonement (restitution) and our corporate guilt as a world filled with sin, requires a divine response. While we may not individually see ourselves as having done anything horrible enough to warrant the outpouring of God's wrath, we must understand that as a citizen of earth, we all share in earth's corporate guilt. (Isaiah 24:1-6)

**Q.** So the first four trumpets inflict a mortal wound upon our planet and the survival of civilization becomes questionable?

**LW.** Yes.

**Q.** Then, what happens?

**LW.** During the months that follow, Jesus sends the 144,000 throughout the earth proclaiming His salvation. The 144,000 explain why Jesus has sent the trumpets and they deliver the gospel of salvation to every nation, kindred, tongue and people.

But, most of the people will not listen to God's prophets. In fact, the nations will set up and enforce laws to appease God in ways that are obviously contrary to God's law — specifically, the fourth commandment! So, a period of religious controversy will begin and it will grow in intensity. And, the more powerful the presentation of God's truth by the 144,000, the more stubborn will be the hearts of wicked men and women. Hatred and persecution will break out everywhere.

After a period of time passes (I believe about two years), most of the people of earth will have heard and rejected the gospel presented by the 144,000. Then God responds to this planet in rebellion. *God turns the world over to the devil.* In effect, God will say to the world, "Since you have refused to hearken to my servants and receive salvation, I will release to you the prince of this world — the ruler of darkness. In refusing Me, you have chosen him. Therefore, all inhabitants of the earth, except those who shall receive my salvation, will obey him or die."
The devil will physically appear before the people of earth in the great cities at various times. The devil will claim to be God, and he will openly prove his masquerade by means of miracles that he has power to do — even causing fire to come down from heaven in full view. Billions of people will believe his lies because they refused to love the truth when presented by God's servants, the 144,000. (2 Thessalonians 2:11,12)

**Q.** How long does the devil travel around earth claiming to be God?

**LW.** The Bible says the torment of the fifth trumpet is five months long. Given the events that follow the fifth trumpet, I believe the total time between the commencement of the fifth trumpet and the Second Coming to be less than 600 days.

**Q.** What will be the devil's agenda?

**LW.** To establish a global throne so that he might receive the worship, submission and adoration of all peoples upon earth.

**Q.** How will he accomplish this?

**LW.** At first, he will appear to be a kind and benevolent benefactor of mankind. He will say the most wonderful things. He will perform marvelous miracles of healing and benefit. And since the earth will be in shambles as a result of the first four trumpets, he will easily pass as the anticipated Savior — king of earth, and ruler of the seventh millennium.

Incidentally, the torment under the fifth trumpet will be horrible. In effect, the devil's angels will inflict great suffering on the wicked. The devil, masquerading as God, will claim that the suffering is caused by "spells" cast by the 144,000. (The 144,000 will have miracle-working powers. Revelation 11:6) The end result is that great hostility will be generated against the true prophets of God. Many of the 144,000 will be killed.

After the devil has deceived billions of people into believing that he is Almighty God, he will change behavior. He will then become demanding. He will demand the creation of a universal city (community) and the world will install him as high priest and king. This is how the sixth trumpet war begins.

The devil will send out an order to his followers that they should overtake their community, city, state, nation or province for his sake and in his name. Actually, the devil's order is a demand for homogeny, one faith, one Lord, and one day of worship for all mankind. All who refuse to comply with the universal day of worship are to be put to death.

The day that shall be established as the universal day of worship will be contrary to the Law of God. The Bible doesn't say which day will be selected. Perhaps, the devil will exalt Sunday as the universal day of worship since the Christian population is larger than the Moslem. (Moslems worship on Friday.) Jews, Moslems, Hindus and all inhabitants will be required to comply with the universal day of worship or be killed.

But, the day of worship will separate people. Those who submit to the universal day of worship established by the devil will come forward and receive a visible mark on their body. This act seals the eternal destiny of each recipient. For fear of starvation and the want of life's necessities, billions of people will choose to wear an ugly mark on their face or right hand. This visible mark is necessary so that only the "participants" in the new world order can buy and sell.

Back to my story, the devil's objective is nothing less than global control. And his victory comes after total anarchy has destroyed the fabric of every nation. If I might borrow from Saddam Hussein, this war will be the "mother of all battles."

**Q.** When do you expect this war?

**LW.** In 1996 or 1997.

**Q.** How long do you think it will last?

**LW.** A little less than a year.

**Q.** What will be the outcome of the war?

**LW.** First, the number killed in this war will be greater than any war ever recorded. Secondly, as a result of the war, the devil will gain complete control of the world — even every nation. Thirdly, all survivors will either wear the mark, the name or the number 666 to show allegiance to the devil's one-world order. Of course, I am excluding those faithful to Jesus. The world will be one giant concentration camp. Those in the camp will be wearing tattoos just like prisoners did during WWII. Those outside the camp will be cut off from means of support. This will be a terrible time — worse than anything I can describe.

**Q.** This is a horror story.

**LW.** I know. But, in this terrible ordeal, there is good news. The good news is that Jesus is on His way. And during this time of tribulation, the world will behold spectacular manifestations of God's grace and mercy toward those who reach out to take His extended hand of mercy. "The just shall live by faith."

Incidentally, the Great Tribulation will demonstrate the properties of living by faith in God. And throughout the endless ages of eternity, those who come out of the Great Tribulation will tell of God's salvation that comes only by faith!

**Q.** Are you saying that the mark of the beast is set up during the sixth trumpet war?

**LW.** Yes. The sixth trumpet war is the means by which the devil gains control of the world. As he gains control, he will set up his one-world-religion and institute the wearing of the mark. The mark will be a plainly visible, non-transferable tattoo showing allegiance to the new world order. Those who receive the mark will willingly abandon their religious beliefs and join in the one-world-religion so that they might buy and sell. Incidentally, the one-world-religion is also described in Revelation 17 as a great whore.

**Q.** Why a great whore?

**LW.** Because the one-world-religion is a coalition of people willing to commit prostitution. They will abandon their old religion to join a new one.

**Q.** I don't understand. What makes this prostitution?

**LW.** A whore is one who willingly exchanges virtue for something of temporal value. At the time when the mark of the beast is implemented, those who receive the mark will willingly abandon their religious values and receive the well known evil number, 666, or the name of the devil, in order to survive. This is spiritual prostitution.

**Q.** How does the sixth trumpet war relate to Armageddon?

**LW.** The sixth trumpet war begins with the "letting loose" of the angels bound at the river Euphrates. And, Armageddon begins with the "drying up" of the river Euphrates.

**Q.** It's interesting that the river Euphrates is involved with the sixth trumpet and the sixth plague. What is the connection?

**LW.** Before I answer your question, please notice the following text: **"The sixth angel sounded his trumpet, and I heard a voice coming from the horns of the golden altar that is before God. {14} It said to the sixth angel who had the trumpet, 'Release the four angels who are bound at the great river Euphrates.' {15} And the four angels who had been kept ready for this very hour and day and month and year were released to kill a third of mankind. {16} The number of the mounted troops was two hundred million. I heard their number."** (Revelation 9:13-16)

To appreciate the meaning of this text, one needs to first know three things from the Old Testament. First, the Promised Land that God intended Israel to occupy reached from the Nile in the South to the Euphrates in the North. (Genesis 15:18; Deuteronomy 1:7, 11:24) In other words, the reader needs to associate the direction "North" and Euphrates together to understand what Revelation is predicting. Secondly, the reader should know that the great river Euphrates occasionally overflows its banks and inundates a large area. This, of course, brings widespread death and destruction to those who dwell close to the river. Lastly, destruction is represented as coming from the "North" in Bible times. For example, during the days of Jeremiah, the impending destruction upon Jerusalem by the Babylonians was prophesied as "destruction from the North." (Jeremiah 1:14, 4:6, 25:9) Also, the destruction of Egypt and Babylon was prophesied as "destruction coming from the North." (Jeremiah 46:24, 50:9) So, the releasing of four angels bound at the river Euphrates to kill a third of mankind is a description of great destruction, a great war that comes from the North — the direction of destruction.

Notice how the language of a flood is used in this text: **"Because this people has rejected the gently flowing waters of Shiloah and rejoices over Rezin and the son of Remaliah, {7} therefore the Lord is about to bring against them the mighty floodwaters of the River [Euphrates]**

-- the king of Assyria with all his pomp. It will overflow all its channels, run over all its banks {8} and sweep on into Judah, swirling over it, passing through it and reaching up to the neck. Its outspread wings will cover the breadth of your land, O Immanuel!" (Isaiah 8:6-8) Compare the analogy of a flood in Isaiah with Hosea: "Judah's leaders are like those who move boundary stones. I will pour out my wrath on them like a flood of water." (Hosea 5:10) Lastly, notice the language of this text describing the end of Israel: "After the sixty-two 'sevens,' the Anointed One will be cut off and will have nothing. The people of the ruler who will come will destroy the city and the sanctuary. The end will come like a flood: War will continue until the end, and desolations have been decreed." (Daniel 9:26)

The point here is that war or devastation is often described as a flood in the Bible because of the utter destruction that attends both. The fact that Euphrates is mentioned in connection with the sixth trumpet war suggests that the coming destruction will be great (great rivers produce great destruction). The releasing of the angels, which are bound in the North, to kill a third of mankind, is nothing less than horrific war. Even the number of troops is an impressive 200,000,000. When you consider that the whole world has less than eight million people serving in the military right now, you can see that this war will be most significant.

**Q.** Do you believe that a third of 5.6 billion people will be killed in the sixth trumpet war?

**LW.** It's possible. However, for reasons that we don't have time to discuss, I believe the text means that a third of the troops involved in this war are killed. So, a third of 200 million would be about 67 million.

**Q.** What role does the Euphrates play in the battle of Armageddon?

**LW.** Notice the text: "The sixth angel poured out his bowl on the great river Euphrates, and its water was dried up to prepare the way for the kings from the East." (Revelation 16:12)

When the sixth plague is poured out, the Euphrates is dried up. If the flooding of the Euphrates represents war and its horrible consequences;

then, the drying up of the Euphrates suggests the cessation of war and the collapse of an empire built upon the spoils of war.

In fact, the Bible offers a splendid parallel of this event. Ancient Babylon "sat" upon the river Euphrates. The river flowed through the city making her invincible. With a never ending source of water, no would-be-conqueror could set siege and hope to starve the inhabitants into submission. Further, the walls of Babylon were so great and heavily armed that no army could overcome them. In short, ancient Babylon was to be the invincible city for all time. Then came Cyrus.

Cyrus, king of Persia, diverted the great river Euphrates. As the water level fell during the darkness of night, his soldiers entered the city of Babylon by crawling under the steel doors that directed the river through the city. Once inside, the soldiers quickly opened the main gates of the city and the rest is history. (Daniel 5:30,31)

The point is that during the sixth plague, God is going to "dry up" the authority of the image of Babylon. The image and the great whore are the same thing. In other words, the devil's world order will begin to break apart. The Bible says, **"The beast and the ten horns you saw will hate the prostitute. They will bring her to ruin and leave her naked; they will eat her flesh and burn her with fire."** (Revelation 17:16) This text says that the seven heads and ten horns will come to hate the one-world-religion. They will abandon it and destroy it. This event produces a complete collapse of Babylon.

(Note: During the fifth plague, the devil is unmasked. At that point in time, the inhabitants of earth will behold the truth about the one they call God. (The reader is encouraged to read Prophecy 14 in my book, *18 End-Time Bible Prophecies,* to better associate the details of this discussion with the events of the seven last plagues.)

Q. Who are the kings from the East mentioned in Revelation 16:12?

LW. The Father and Jesus. Most people don't know that when Jesus comes, the Father also comes! Jesus said, " 'Yes, it is as you say,' Jesus replied. **'But I say to all of you: In the future you will see the Son of**

Man sitting at the right hand of the Mighty One and coming on the clouds of heaven.' " (Matthew 26:64) See also Revelation 6:17.

**Q.** I've always heard that Armageddon refers to the plain of Megiddo in the Middle East and this is where the battle of Armageddon starts or takes place. Is this true?

**LW.** No. There is a small plain called Megiddo. But, the Greek term transliterated from Revelation does not refer to a small plain in Megiddo. Rather, the Greek word *harmegeddon* means the mountain of Megiddo. Notice the text: **"Then they gathered the kings together to the place that in Hebrew is called Armageddon."** (Revelation 16:16)

The reference to the place of Armageddon is like the reference to the river Euphrates. Both are analogous. As stated before, the literal river Euphrates does not dry up during the sixth plague. Rather, God drys up the support that the one-world-religion had received. Babylon begins to break apart.

As the devil beholds the collapse of his empire right before his eyes, notice what he does: **"Then I saw three evil spirits that looked like frogs; they came out of the mouth of the dragon, out of the mouth of the beast and out of the mouth of the false prophet."** (Revelation 16:13) These evil spirits are not frogs. They are demons that shall be quickly dispatched to the kings of the earth to prevent the collapse of Babylon. Notice what the Bible says about the three evil spirits: **"They are spirits of demons performing miraculous signs, and they go out to the kings of the whole world, to gather them for the battle on the great day of God Almighty."** (Revelation 16:14)

John says the three evil spirits *looked* like frogs. What does John mean? Are we to understand that three evil creatures will hop about on the ground like frogs? No.

Consider this text: **"Then the Lord said to Moses, 'Go to Pharaoh and say to him, 'This is what the Lord says: Let my people go, so that they may worship me. {2} If you refuse to let them go, I will plague your whole country with frogs. {3} The Nile will teem with frogs. They will come up into your palace and your bedroom and onto your bed, into**

---

the houses of your officials and on your people, and into your ovens and kneading troughs." (Exodus 8:1-3) The point here is that the frogs in Egypt covered the *whole* land and they were so distressing that Pharaoh was willing to let Israel go because they were everywhere!

In a similar way, evil demons will go through the earth. They will perform miraculous signs to convince the people not to abandon Babylon. In fact, they will convince the kings to implement the universal death decree upon the saints and then urge the kings of earth to prepare for war against the coming Jesus.

The kings comply. They agree to the universal death decree for the saints. At the moment the decree becomes effective, Jesus speaks from heaven declaring the safety of the saints. **"Behold, I come like a thief! Blessed is he who stays awake and keeps his clothes with him, so that he may not go naked and be shamefully exposed."** (Revelation 16:15)

**Q.** So, how does the place, Armageddon, fit in?

**LW.** The demons will influence the kings of the earth to remain loyal to the devil. They appeal to the kings as ambassadors from his highness, the devil himself, to kill the saints and to war against Jesus, for they are told that Jesus is soon to appear. Thus, the kings are brought to a place, a circumstantial place, a place of open conflict with Almighty God. This is the meaning of Armageddon: the mountain or place of contest with God.

I believe the word Megiddo keys to the foolish death of king Josiah. He was warned by God not to fight against Egypt, but he refused to listen and perished in the battle at Megiddo. (2 Chronicles 35:20-24; 2 Kings 23:29)

In the same manner, the kings of earth will violate the will of God and go out to fight. In doing so, they meet their destruction on the day that Jesus appears.

Read for yourself the outcome of the battle: **"I saw heaven standing open and there before me was a white horse, whose rider is called Faithful and True. With justice he judges and makes war. {12} His eyes are like blazing fire, and on his head are many crowns. He has** a name written on him that no one knows but he himself. {13} He is dressed in a robe dipped in blood, and his name is the Word of God. {14} The armies of heaven were following him, riding on white horses and dressed in fine linen, white and clean. {15} Out of his mouth comes a sharp sword with which to strike down the nations. 'He will rule them with an iron scepter.' He treads the winepress of the fury of the wrath of God Almighty. {16} On his robe and on his thigh he has this name written: KING OF KINGS AND LORD OF LORDS. {17} And I saw an angel standing in the sun, who cried in a loud voice to all the birds flying in midair, 'Come, gather together for the great supper of God, {18} so that you may eat the flesh of kings, generals, and mighty men, of horses and their riders, and the flesh of all people, free and slave, small and great.' {19} Then I saw the beast and the kings of the earth and their armies gathered together to make war against the rider on the horse and his army. {20} But the beast was captured, and with him the false prophet who had performed the miraculous signs on his behalf. With these signs he had deluded those who had received the mark of the beast and worshiped his image. The two of them were thrown alive into the fiery lake of burning sulfur." (Revelation 19:11-20)

Q. If the devil is thrown into a lake of fire at the second coming, who is put into the Abyss for 1,000 years?

LW. The false prophet is the physical devil that is thrown into the lake of fire at the second coming. In other words, the body of the devil is burned up along with the bodies of people that made up his administration. But, the devil is not destroyed. This confuses a lot of people. Think of it this way: The devil does not have a visible body right now, yet he lives. But, a time is soon coming when he can have a visible body. At the second coming, the visible body is destroyed, yet the devil will continue to live, and in fact, be put in the spirit world of the Abyss for 1,000 years.

Q. So, the body of the devil will be destroyed. Who is the beast that shall also be burned up?

**LW.** The people that make up the administration of Babylon will be burned up; namely, the seven heads and the ten kings.

**Q.** So, there is a lake of fire at the second coming?

**LW.** Yes.

**Q.** Does it burn throughout the millennium?

**LW.** Yes.

**Q.** What makes you think so?

**LW.** The Bible says that at the end of the millennium, the devil will be finally thrown into the *same* lake of burning sulfur where his apparition had been thrown! **"And the devil, who deceived them, was thrown into the lake of burning sulfur, where the beast and the false prophet had been thrown. They will be tormented day and night for ever and ever."** (Revelation 20:10)

**Q.** Will there be no sea in the new earth?

**LW.** There will be lots of water in the new earth! You are no doubt questioning John's comment saying, "and there was no more sea." (Revelation 21:1) However, I don't believe that John was talking about oceans of water, I believe John was talking about the enormous lake of fire that consumes the earth. A fire that hot would boil like water or magma from a volcano. We also find that from the throne of God, the river of life flows down the middle of the great city in four directions. (Revelation 22:1,2 and Ezekiel 47)

**Q.** One last question: Why is the devil called the false prophet?

**LW.** A prophet is a spokesperson. A true prophet speaks for God. A false prophet either speaks for the devil or himself. The physical devil that shall appear on earth is given the title, False Prophet, because he claims to be God, but he speaks for himself. This stands in direct contrast to the 144,000 who speak for God as true prophets during this time of earth's history.

But, the impact of the devil's title is this: When Jesus appears in the clouds of glory, the world will behold a great scene: They will see the great liar (false prophet) for what he is and they will see those who tried to warn them about him (the 144,000 true prophets).

**The mark of the beast is an actual mark!**

The coming mark of the beast will be a visible mark that people will either wear on their forehead or on their hand as the Hebrews did in Egypt. (See Exodus 13:9-16.) The Bible says the mark will either be the number 666 or the name which the devil assumes when on earth in person. No doubt this sounds like an absurd thing to say in 1993; however, one needs to understand the context of the mark of the beast and even more, the beast that demands the mark!

In response to the first four trumpets, legislators will quickly pass laws to appease God. Friday laws will be implemented in Moslem countries, Saturday laws will be implemented in Israel, and Sunday laws will be implemented in Catholic and Protestant countries. Simply said, governments will enact "righteous laws" based on the views of their religious majority.

The pope will seize the opportunity and move to unite the religions of the world in a global common cause, but confusion will mark his efforts because of the world's diverse religious conscience and culture. The Moslem cannot conscientiously worship the God of the Catholic, nor can the Protestant conscientiously worship the gods of the Hindu.

Time passes. Suffering continues. "Righteous laws" become more extensive in all nations. Respect for God's authority becomes a hotly debated topic. Intolerance escalates. Penalties for disobedience will drastically increase.

Then, the devil physically appears claiming to be the Lamb of God (thus, the *lamblike* beast). Millions, even billions will receive him as God. After a few months, he calls for world unity, one faith, one Lord, and one day of worship for all mankind. This call will ignite the sixth trumpet war. As the devil gains control of the world, he consolidates Babylon. This consolidation is called "the image" in Revelation 13 and a whore in Revelation 17. All refusing to comply with the one-world-religion and its universal day of worship are to be put to death.

The day that shall be established as the universal day of worship will stand in opposition to the fourth commandment which requires the observance of the seventh day. The Bible doesn't say which day the devil will select as the day of worship. Perhaps, in appreciation for the efforts of the papacy, the devil will exalt Sunday as the universal day of worship. This isn't far fetched if one considers the fact that Catholics and Protestants will constitute the single largest block of worshipers in the one-world-religion. Thus, Jews, Moslems, Hindus and all others will have to comply with the authorized day of worship.

The establishment of the universal day of worship will fully separate people. And those who submit to the universal day of worship established by the devil will come forward and receive a visible mark (tattoo) upon their forehead or right hand. This act seals their eternal destiny. For fear of starvation and the want of life's necessities, billions will wear a horribly ugly mark upon their bodies so they can buy and sell. The issue will be survival.

Reflect on this for a moment: God will see to it that everyone knows at that time that 666 is an evil number. Everyone will know that the receipt of the mark is wrong, but billions will choose to receive it anyway. Lastly, the evil mark is obviously defacing and ugly and even this will not stop people from receiving it. The test will be simple: receive the mark so food and necessities can be obtained or refuse the mark and forfeit the necessities of life.

The absence of the evil mark will visibly expose God's people and their faith in the Almighty.

# Questions on Christ's righteousness

(Reprinted from the April, 1993, issue of *Day Star* under the title of Questions on perfection and the observance of feast days.)

**Q.** I recently viewed your # 109 video seminar series and you said a few things that were too good to be true. Near the end of the seminar, you said that a time is coming when God is going to impart His righteousness to every person willing to receive salvation. What do you mean by this? Assuming I want to receive salvation during the time-period of the trumpets, will I receive this righteousness from God as a gift because I reached perfection or because I could not make myself perfect?

**LW.** Notice these verses: **"For in the gospel a righteousness from God is revealed, a righteousness that is by faith from first to last, just as it is written: 'The righteous will live by faith.' But now a righteousness from God, apart from law, has been made known, to which the Law and the Prophets testify. {22} This righteousness from God comes through faith in Jesus Christ to all who believe...."** (Romans 1:17; 3:21,22)

Paul reveals two key points: First, the gospel reveals a righteousness that has nothing to do with man's behavior (righteousness apart from law). (To prove his point, Paul adds that the Old Testament, the Law and Prophets, speaks of this righteousness.) Secondly, Paul says that God's righteousness is not produced by man nor is God's righteousness found within man because God's righteousness comes *from* God to man by faith.

The subject of righteousness by faith can be very confusing and frustrating. In many ways, the study of God's righteousness is much like the study of prophecy. If we do not define the elements very well, and if we do not correctly identify the relationships between the elements, we can get very confused.

So, for this discussion, I'd like to make a sharp distinction between man's righteousness and God's righteousness. Yes, there are two types of righteousness. Each is distinct, both are important, and they are unlike each other. Man's righteousness is produced by man's obedience. Man's righteousness comes from obedience to law(s). Man's righteousness is

---

produced by obedience. *The more closely man conforms to the requirements of law, the more perfect man becomes in the eyes of the law since there is less for the law to condemn.* (Keep this definition of man's righteousness in mind during this discussion.)

God's righteousness, on the other hand, is totally different from man's righteousness. God's righteousness is His character. The qualities that make up God's character go far beyond our highest understanding. His ways are not our ways. *God's righteousness is His character of complete selflessness.* He has all power, all knowledge and is omnipresent, yet everything God does is for the benefit of His creation. God's righteousness is not defined by His laws. Rather, God's laws reflect His righteous character. (Keep these matters in mind during our discussion.)

Jesus came to earth to reveal God's righteousness (God's character). And Jesus revealed God's righteousness through His life of complete selflessness. Jesus said, **"For I have come down from heaven not to do my will but to do the will of him who sent me...."** (John 6:38) **"...I do nothing on my own but speak just what the Father has taught me."** (John 8:28) **"But the world must learn that I love the Father and that I do exactly what my Father has commanded me."** (John 14:31) Jesus was completely devoted to the service of His Father. Not once did Jesus violate the will of the Father, thus He *never* fell short of the glory of God.

So, there are two distinct types of righteousness: One is human (defined by law), the other is God's character of selflessness which was revealed by Jesus.

Q. If there are two types of righteousness, there must be two types of sin?

LW. That's right. There is a sin that leads to death and a sin that does not lead to death. **"If anyone sees his brother commit a sin that does not lead to death, he should pray and God will give him life. I refer to those whose sin does not lead to death. There is a sin that leads to death. I am not saying that he should pray about that."** (1 John 5:16)

**Q.** Explain these two sins.

**LW.** If a man violates a law, he commits sin, for sin is transgression of law. And, sin is larger than just the commission of a wrong deed. Sin also includes omission — a failure to fulfill the intent of law. But, there is a sin that is not fatal to eternal life. For example, the thief on the cross was there for the violation of law, but his sin did not prevent him from receiving eternal life.

On the other hand, there is one sin that leads to death. This sin is rebellion against the Holy Spirit. I'll address this more fully in a moment.

**Q.** So, if there are two types of righteousness, man's righteousness and God's righteousness, aren't both necessary for salvation?

**LW.** No. Only God's righteousness is necessary for salvation. Period. This is the good news of the everlasting gospel: God will grant His righteousness to all who choose it.

This is not to say that man's righteousness is of no value. On the contrary, man's righteousness is beneficial. But, man's righteousness is no substitute or extension of God's righteousness.

Don't misunderstand this critical point. Man's righteousness is beneficial for man — not God. God commands that man obey His laws. God gave laws to us for our well being. And, we should make every effort to live by the principles that God has revealed in His laws.

But, this issue confuses many people because they think that man's righteousness contributes to life eternal and this is not true at all. This confusion is the source of many faulty ideas about God, His laws, and His salvation.

Paul makes it very clear that man's righteousness will not, indeed cannot, satisfy the requirements for eternal life! **"For it is by grace you have been saved, through faith—and this not from yourselves, it is the gift of God— {9} not by works, so that no one can boast."** (Ephesians 2:8-9)

Make no mistake about it. The gospel doesn't waver on this point. We can't save ourselves by obedience (man's righteousness)! No one can be saved by merits of obedience. If this were possible, Jesus would not have died on the cross. And, let's press the matter a little further, no one will receive God's righteousness because they were obedient to His laws!

It's easy to get mixed up on this topic — especially if one grew up in a home where religious obedience was demanded. The Pharisees in Christ's day were convinced that obedience was the key to salvation. Those blind leaders of Israel were known for their careful compliance with hundreds of religious laws. They taught that perfect obedience was the key to life eternal — and their legalism shut out the hope of life eternal for everyone. But, their extraordinary commitment to obedience made them blind to their need for God's righteousness. They became bigots, self-centered hypocrites and blind guides in trying to establish their own righteousness. They lost sight of mercy, justice and love — the principles underlying God's moral law. And, Jesus rebuked them saying, **"Woe to you, teachers of the law and Pharisees, you hypocrites! You give a tenth of your spices—mint, dill and cummin. But you have neglected the more important matters of the law—justice, mercy and faithfulness. You should have practiced the latter, without neglecting the former."** (Matthew 23:23) Here, Jesus plainly shows that man's righteousness is important (saying it's proper to give God the tenth), but it is a greater wrong to neglect justice, mercy and faithfulness. Again, it must be said that *God does not grant salvation on the basis of man's righteousness.* Jesus told the disciples, **"For I tell you that unless your righteousness surpasses that of the Pharisees and the teachers of the law, you will certainly not enter the kingdom of heaven."** (Matthew 5:20) These words astonished the disciples, for they regarded the Pharisees as "holy men."

On another occasion, Jesus demonstrated that man's righteousness is no substitute for God's righteousness. A rich young ruler came to Jesus asking what he must do to have a place in the coming kingdom of heaven. Jesus, knowing the heart of the young man, engaged the young man's attention by appealing to his sense of self-righteousness. Jesus said, "You know the commandments." The young man eagerly assured Jesus, "I've kept them since I was a boy." Then, Jesus said, "You still lack one thing. Go sell *everything* you have and give the money to the poor and then follow me." The young man was stunned by this qualification for salvation. And he turned away, sorrowfully.

As the disciples watched, they were baffled about the properties of salvation. What they thought necessary for salvation and what Jesus taught about salvation was not the same! Jesus knew their thoughts were baffled as the rich young ruler walked away. He turned to them and said, " 'Indeed, **it is easier for a camel to go through the eye of a needle than for a rich man to enter the kingdom of God.' {26} Those who heard this asked, 'Who then can be saved?' {27} Jesus replied, 'What is impossible with men is possible with God.' "** (Luke 18:25-27) Notice again that last sentence: "What is impossible with men is possible with God."

So, the way to life eternal is not through man's righteousness — as useful and important as it is. Obedience to law has never saved anyone, nor can it. The way to eternal life is not based on man's righteousness. It is based on God's righteousness altogether! And God will grant His righteousness to anyone who becomes willing to live a selfless life. In a sentence, this is the gospel!

**Q.** So, both types of righteousness are required by God?

**LW.** Yes. One brings salvation, the other, nobility of character.

**Q.** Is perfection possible?

**LW.** Perfection of what? If you play a song on the piano that has 10,000 notes and you hit one wrong note, was the song perfect? In a similar way, our lives are a continuum just like a song. Everyday we are adding the next measure, and if I were to live the next thirty years without committing one sin, my life would still be imperfect. Because I have sinned, I am imperfect.

Don't misunderstand. By God's indwelling power, today's measure can be perfect. I can do all things through faith in God. I can overcome any temptation through God's power. God's laws are not beyond us. They can be kept if His power dwells within. However, obedience only produces man-made righteousness. This righteousness will never be perfect as God is perfect. Paul said, **"Therefore no one will be declared righteous in his sight by observing the law; rather, through the law we become conscious of sin."** (Romans 3:20)

**Q.** Are you saying, "Once a sinner, always a sinner?"

**LW.** Yes. Once a vase is broken, it forever remains imperfect.

**Q.** Is this why Adam and Eve were cast out of the Garden of Eden?

**LW.** Yes. God could not even allow forgiven sinners to live forever.

**Q.** If the only way to heaven is through God's righteousness, how is this righteousness obtained?

**LW.** God's righteousness is given to human beings as a gift when we become willing to love God supremely and our neighbor as ourself. God's gift of righteousness is contingent upon this one condition. This is where the rich young ruler failed. This is where the Pharisees failed. Neither was motivated by selfless love for God and man. Their ambitions were selfish from the start. They were interested in establishing their own righteousness and in saving themselves. And when people are only interested in their own salvation, something is wrong. Those who receive the gift of God's righteousness become more concerned about the salvation of others than about their own!

Self-righteousness lives at the center of human nature. If you don't believe me, conduct this experiment: Condemn someone for something insignificant and watch them justify their deed! It's natural for human nature to justify itself, regardless of the seriousness of its behavior. (This is a mystery: Prisons are full of self-justifying people.)

This is the heart of the matter concerning righteousness. Human nature wants to justify self by depending upon human effort. God, on the other hand, knows that our nature is corrupt. Sinners are self-centered. So, God Himself provided an atonement for us because man could not atone for his sin. Jesus became the Lamb of God — notice, Jesus was not the *Lamb of man*. God needed a perfect man to make atonement for man, and He provided that perfect man: His only Son. Once man was atoned for, God then proceeded to grant His righteousness to man through faith as a free gift.

**Q.** Was the gift of God's righteousness withheld until man was atoned for?

**LW.** For reasons beyond the scope of this discussion, no one was "saved" until the judgment of man began in 1844. In other words, no decision for eternal life or death was made upon anyone until the judgment began.

My comment, "Once man was atoned for, God then proceeded to grant His righteousness to man as a gift through faith," means that the penalty for sin had to be paid before God could actually save man.

**Q.** Enoch, Elijah and Moses and others were taken to heaven before 1844. How could they be saved before the penalty for sin was paid?

**LW.** They were saved on the "credit card" concept. God purchased them for Himself on the basis that He would make the necessary payment at the appointed time. I use the term "a credit card purchase" because this speaks of a process that Americans are well acquainted with.

**Q.** Was the atonement for man finished at the cross?

**LW.** No. The sanctuary service in the Old Testament clearly shows that the slaying of the lamb was necessary, but the priest had to apply the blood of the lamb after it was slain. Indeed, the priests had to apply the blood of sacrifices each day of the year until time came for the High Priest to cleanse the sanctuary. So, the atonement process for man is not finished until the sanctuary in heaven is cleansed.

**Q.** I'd like to go back to receiving the gift of salvation. Are you saying that the gift of salvation is bestowed when we surrender all that we have to the service of God and man?

**LW.** Yes. God grants His righteousness at that point.

**Q.** What makes a selfless attitude so hard to have?

**LW.** Paul said that he was "sold as a slave to sin." (Romans 7:14) He meant that he had no control over his birth as a sinner, just as a slave has no control over his sale. Because our grandparents Adam and Eve sinned, we inherited the curse of sin. We are therefore born with selfish tendencies whether we like it or not. Since we come from the womb with a self-seeking, self-justifying, and self-centered nature, and since the devil preys upon our selfish nature, it is *impossible* to have an attitude of selflessness unless God lives within us. If there is any desire for selfless service, it comes by the ministry of the Holy Spirit, for nothing good dwells within us. (Romans 7:18) This is why rebellion against the Holy Spirit is fatal, the unpardonable sin. If we shut out God's prompting to a life of selfless service, how can we receive the gift of God's righteousness?

**Q.** What is living by faith like?

**LW.** It's like standing in a small closet with the door closed and the light off. You can't see forward, backward or to either side. And when you look up, it's just as dark. To the natural eye, that's what living by faith looks like.

But, man's extremity is God's opportunity. So, when we commit ourselves to Jesus, we have to learn to walk by faith. This can only happen through trials. We have to learn to lean on His everlasting arms — and stop trusting in our own. So watch for tests of faith. God allows situations to develop so that the walls will close in. He does this to reveal His interest in us. He puts us where we can't see our way out so faith and patience can be developed. And faith in God is this: You *know* that He will come through at just the right time.

It is this repetitive experience that reveals the reality of God. Nothing on earth compares with the experience of witnessing God's mighty hand move on my behalf. Imagine this: God Himself delivered me! Here again is the core of salvation that comes by faith: As long as we are willing to go where God sends, to be all that we can for the glory of God, and to do all that God asks us to do, we have the assurance of God's attention and of course, the gift of His righteousness *through faith* and the hope of eternal life is ours. Period.

**Q.** Is there a way that I may test myself to see if I am completely willing to serve God and man?

**LW.** Yes. This is the primary purpose of the Ten Commandments. The Ten Commandments test us on two levels. First, they test our external behavior to see if we are living a selfless life. For example, the eighth commandment says that it is wrong to steal. So, if I take nothing that does not belong to me, I am in compliance with the law externally. However, the law doesn't stop there even though society benefits from my external behavior.

God asks that I internalize the intent of His Law. God wants me to get to the place in my life where I don't steal because I love my neighbor. This is the higher purpose of law. Paul said, **"Love does no harm to its neighbor. Therefore love is the fulfillment of the law."** (Romans 13:10) So, God gave us His law to test us externally and internally to see if we are giving selfless service.

**Q.** OK, let's assume you've chosen a life of service to God and man and a brother comes up to you insisting that God requires something more of you in order to be saved. What would you say?

**LW.** This often occurs to me. However, there are three steps that I try to follow. First, I am fully convinced that man's great need is God's righteousness which is granted, not on the basis of obedience to law, but on the basis of selfless service to God and man. Secondly, I listen to my brother to hear if his claim will open up a better means of service to God and man. I try to understand the underlying principle of my brother's claim to see if it is a disguised attempt to displace God's righteousness with man's righteousness or if it is a better means of loving service. Lastly, I look at the fruit of my brother's ministry to God and man to see how effective his work has been. While I may not be able to understand his claim at first, I can inspect his fruit.

I rely on the words of Jesus. **"But when he, the Spirit of truth, comes, he will guide you into all truth. He will not speak on his own; he will speak only what he hears, and he will tell you what is yet to come."** (John 16:13) *And, the ultimate test of having a saving relationship with Jesus is the ability to hear the Master's voice.* Jesus said, **"My sheep listen** to my voice; I know them, and they follow me." (John 10:27) If I hear the voice of Jesus speaking through my brother saying there is a better way to serve God and man, the Holy Spirit will confirm it in my heart.

One comment has to be made. The Apostle Paul understood a sublime point about the Christian experience. This point is that God allows everyone to believe whatever they wish to believe! God will allow you to believe that the sun is blue if you want to. Because God is generous, there is considerable room for diversity in the Christian walk. So, beware of those who would make the upward way the even more narrow way of seeking man's righteousness. Paul asked, "...For why should my freedom be judged by another's conscience?" (1 Corinthians 10:29) In Paul's day there was considerable dispute about the observance of feast days. I find that Paul saw the subject as having no religious value, but he saw that people would become bitter over disputes that were meaningless. So, he wrote, "One man considers one day more sacred than another; another man considers every day alike. Each one should be fully convinced in his own mind. You, then, why do you judge your brother? Or why do you look down on your brother? For we will all stand before God's judgment seat." (Romans 14:5,10)

**Q.** I want to ask more about the observance of feast days, but for now, how does justification, sanctification and glorification fit into the big picture of salvation?

**LW.** Justification is that all essential wedding garment that God provides. (Matthew 22:1-14) God freely offers His righteousness to all who are willing to serve Him and their neighbor in love, because this is a reflection of His selfless character. For example, I find Mother Theresa to be a shining 20th century example of selfless service to God and man. So, justification is the all-important process where God freely grants His righteousness to sinners. God's righteousness is THE essential element for salvation. Paul wrote, "For if, when we were God's enemies, we were reconciled to him through the death of his Son, how much more, having been reconciled, shall we be saved through his life!" (Romans 5:10) In other words, God grants to human beings the righteousness that Jesus revealed during His life on earth! This is most interesting. We were reconciled to God by Jesus through His death, but *we are saved through* *the life of Jesus.* Jesus' death made salvation possible for everyone. But, when I surrender myself to service for God, I am granted the righteousness which Christ revealed! And what human can improve the wedding garment of Christ's righteousness with one stitch of human works?

Now, sanctification is like practicing the piano. One may master a difficult song, but there are millions of songs. In fact, one may master a difficult song and then lose that accomplishment by concentrating on other songs! Sanctification is a life-work that produces man's righteousness — and this righteousness is evidenced by nobility of character. A selfless life of service, if accompanied by the knowledge that it cannot produce salvation, brings glory to God. Peter said, **"Live such good lives among the pagans that, though they accuse you of doing wrong, they may see your good deeds and glorify God on the day he visits us."** (1 Peter 2:12) Jesus said, **"...Let your light shine before men, that they may see your good deeds and praise your Father in heaven."** (Matthew 5:16) But, ten thousand good deeds cannot purchase eternal life. Ten thousand acts of obedience cannot produce eternal life, either. Man's righteousness is beneficial to man — not to God. Man's deeds can bring glory to God if the man doesn't forget that his good deeds are like filthy rags in God's sight. (Isaiah 64:6)

As I said earlier, the Ten Commandments play an important role in the process of sanctification. They serve as the standard whereby we can test ourselves to see if sanctification is taking place. For example, there is no room for covetousness in a heart of selflessness. Paul said, **"...Is the law sin? Certainly not! Indeed I would not have known what sin was except through the law. For I would not have known what coveting really was if the law had not said, 'Do not covet.'"** (Romans 7:7) James refers to the Word of God (law) as though it were a mirror, showing our true condition. He said, **"Do not merely listen to the word, and so deceive yourselves. Do what it says. {23} Anyone who listens to the word but does not do what it says is like a man who looks at his face in a mirror {24} and, after looking at himself, goes away and immediately forgets what he looks like."** (James 1:22-24) So, the Law of God defines holiness, and our pursuit of holiness is called sanctification. But, the righteousness that is necessary for salvation is not gained through sanctification.

Lastly, glorification is the physical receipt of God's righteousness. Justification occurs by faith. Sanctification occurs through commitment and glorification occurs at God's appointed time. My next comment may sound strange at first, so consider the whole idea before you get too nervous.

I find that glorification has been man's hope from the very beginning. Adam and Eve, Abraham, Moses and millions of pilgrims that followed, have looked forward to entering God's presence. (See Hebrews 11.) But, glorification is a scheduled event. I mean, glorification happens at a point in time, and those who died before that time arrived, died without receiving what they hoped for. **"All these people were still living by faith when they died. They did not receive the things promised; they only saw them and welcomed them from a distance. And they admitted that they were aliens and strangers on earth."** (Hebrews 11:13) When Paul wrote to the believers in Galatia, he looked forward to receiving God's righteous saying, **"But by faith we eagerly await through the Spirit the righteousness for which we hope."** (Galatians 5:5) John knew that glorification was forthcoming. He wrote, **"Dear friends, now we are children of God, *and what we will be has not yet been made known.* But we know that when he appears, we shall be like him, for we shall see him as he is."** (1 John 3:2, emphasis mine.)

Now, there is a distinct difference between God's imputed righteousness and God's imparted righteousness. The word, "imputed," means that God reckons a person as righteous even though the person is a sinner. The word, "imparted," means that God will actually bestow His righteousness upon a person. I mention these terms because God has been imputing His righteousness to all who looked to Him in faith for salvation ever since Adam and Eve sinned. However, when the time of glorification comes, God will *impart* His righteousness to all who look to Him through faith for salvation! God is going to bestow His character of righteousness upon every sinner willing to live by faith. This is the mystery of God. (Colossians 1:26,27; Revelation 10:7)

The time of glorification occurs during the 1,260 days of the Two Witnesses. This is the time of the Latter Rain, or outpouring of the Holy Spirit. This time period is unique in all of history, for during these 1,260 days, God will test and seal the living in their eternal destiny. In other words, there has never been a time when Christ's intercession on behalf of sinful man has not existed. But, that day is coming soon. It is identified in the Bible as the seventh trumpet and just before the seventh trumpet sounds, all who live by faith will have received the righteousness of God.

Prior to the sounding of the trumpets, God will empower His servants, 144,000 of them. **"And afterward, I will pour out my Spirit on all people. Your sons and daughters will prophesy, your old men will dream dreams, your young men will see visions. {29} Even on my servants, both men and women, I will pour out my Spirit in those days."** (Joel 2:28-29) These will proclaim the mystery of God. That mystery is that God will bestow His righteousness upon anyone who yields his life to Him — no matter how horrible or lawless their past. **"But in the days when the seventh angel is about to sound his trumpet, the mystery of God will be accomplished, just as he announced to his servants the prophets."** (Revelation 10:7) And Joel says, **"And everyone who calls on the name of the LORD will be saved; for on Mount Zion and in Jerusalem there will be deliverance, as the LORD has said, among the survivors whom the LORD calls."** (Joel 2:32)

Q. I thought glorification occurred at the second coming.

LW. The second phase of glorification, the glorification of the bodies of the redeemed (both the dead and living) occurs at that time. Mortal bodies of flesh will be transformed into imperishable bodies at that time.

Q. So, the glorification of man's nature occurs *before* the second coming?

LW. Yes. During the time period of the sealing.

Q. Now, we're getting to my original question. Are you saying that God is going to bestow His righteousness upon imperfect human beings during the out-pouring of the Holy Spirit?

LW. Yes. Every human being is a sinner, and thus imperfect like a broken vase. And, at the time of glorification, some will be more spiritually mature than others. But, during the time period of the Latter Rain, or the out-pouring of the Holy Spirit, God will freely bestow His righteousness to everyone who turns to Him in faith for salvation. This transformation will be no less dramatic than when Jesus cast out demons and healed the sick in His days on earth. Through the mercy and power of God, millions will be set free from their prisons of sin. They will turn from selfishness to selflessness. Just like Mary Magdalene, many will be fully delivered from a life of sin and demonic possession. The grace of God will abound!

**Q.** When did you say the Latter Rain occurs?

**LW.** During the 1,260 days of the Two Witnesses.

**Q.** So, many will be set free from sin and given the righteousness of God during the 1,260 day testimony of the Two Witnesses? That's an exciting thought. But, how does this fit in with the test of worship concerning the mark of the beast? If I am following your train of thought, isn't the mark of the beast a test of obedience, a test involving man's righteousness?

**LW.** The Two Witnesses are the Bible and Holy Spirit. These two agencies of truth will be carried throughout the earth by the 144,000. Understand, God condemns no one for believing a lie. Rather, God condemns people when they refuse to believe the truth. That's why God will empower His Two Witnesses. God wants the world to know about His free gift of righteousness and of the end of sin.

The mark of the beast is a series of terrible man-made laws demanding worship contrary to God's law. The mark will be implemented during the sixth trumpet. And at that time, those refusing to obey the laws of the devil will be captured and sentenced to death. (Revelation 13:7,15)

Notice the properties of the coming test. The Bible predicts that the devil will set up evil laws requiring all people on earth to disobey God's laws. This coming test will fully distinguish between those who obey God out of selfish motives from those who obey God out of selflessness. To the selfish heart, the preservation of one's life is priority number one. To the selfless heart, the giving of one's life for God or man is an honor. Jesus said, **"Greater love has no one than this, that one lay down his life for his friends."** (John 15:13) The imposition of heavy penalties for civil disobedience will fully reveal the selfish heart from the selfless heart.

Many will intelligently obey evil laws in order to save their lives. This stands in direct contrast to those who live by faith. The faith-full obey God's laws because they love God and man — regardless of personal consequence.

All means of earthly support will be cut off from the saints at that time. Those who keep the commandments of God will not be able to buy or sell. So, the coming test will reveal who has faith to obey God's law and who doesn't.

As I said earlier, God has given laws to man. And, He commands that men obey His laws — not for the purpose of salvation, but for man's benefit. In other words, *obeying the Law of God during the test of the mark of the beast will not merit salvation*. In fact, God has so designed the final test that no one can obey His law unless they *first* know how to live by faith!

The coming test will also reveal another aspect of our character. We shall discover the difference between "apparent" submission to God and "complete" submission to God. Let me explain.

Whenever a person surrenders his heart in service to God and man, to GO-BE-DO, that person may honestly believe that he has placed *everything* on the altar of service. This is "apparent" submission because he doesn't know what area in his life is not in submission. However, God knows that we, like Peter, don't know our own hearts very well. Jeremiah said, **"The heart is deceitful above all things and beyond cure. Who can understand it?"** (Jeremiah 17:9) So, God sends little tests of faith, day by day, to prepare us for larger tests. I've often said that the first rung on the ladder of faith is not 12 feet up. It's just an uncomfortable, but reachable step. But, when the mark of the beast comes, that test will reveal those in "complete" submission to God.

**Q.** If I understand correctly, you're saying that God is going to test our faith through obedience to His law?

**LW.** Yes. Our love for God will be tested just like the three Hebrews in Daniel 3. They refused to violate God's law and worship the golden image set up by King Nebuchadnezzar.

**Q.** You said that obedience to God's law does not merit salvation?

**LW.** That's correct. **"For we maintain that a man is justified by faith apart from observing the law."** (Romans 3:28)

**Q.** You're saying that God has designed the coming test so that we can't pass unless we know how to live by faith?

**LW.** That's correct.

**Q.** Then, there is a direct relationship between faith and obedience?

**LW.** Absolutely. **"You see that a person is justified by what he does and not by faith alone."** (James 2:24) **"Do we, then, nullify the law by this faith? Not at all! Rather, we uphold the law."** (Romans 3:31)

**Q.** So, faith in God's righteousness is the only means to life eternal. And obedience is...

**LW.** Obedience to God's law is required for all human beings. The observance of the Ten Commandments is binding upon all men — not as a means of salvation, but as rules from our Creator governing life on this planet. Let me say it another way. The observance of IRS tax code is binding upon all Americans — not as a means of establishing citizenship in this country, but as one of the rules governing citizens of this country.

Q. I would like to ask a few questions about the observance of feast days and the will of God.

LW. OK.

Q. Matthew 7:21 says, "Not everyone who says to me, 'Lord, Lord,' will enter the kingdom of heaven, but only he who does the will of my Father who is in heaven." Obviously, the will of the Father is important. What is the will of the Father?

LW. The will of the Father is two-fold. First, the Father is not willing that anyone should perish. He wants everyone to repent of sin and to love one another. (2 Peter 3:9, John 14:23) Secondly, the Father wants everyone to enter into the process of sanctification. (1 Thessalonians 4:3) Paul points out our obligation saying, "Therefore, brothers, we have an obligation—but it is not to the sinful nature, to live according to it. {13} For if you live according to the sinful nature, you will die; but if by the Spirit you put to death the misdeeds of the body, you will live." (Romans 8:12-13)

Jesus said, "If you love me, you will obey what I command." (John 14:15) Again, Jesus said, "You are my friends if you do what I command." (John 15:14) And, John adds these thoughts, "Do not love the world or anything in the world. If anyone loves the world, the love of the Father is not in him. {16} For everything in the world—the cravings of sinful man, the lust of his eyes and the boasting of what he has and does—comes not from the Father but from the world. {17} The world and its desires pass away, but the man who does the will of God lives forever." (1 John 2:15-17)

Q. Do you believe that it is the will of God that we observe all the statutes and laws recorded in the Bible, specifically the feast days mentioned in the Old Testament?

LW. No. I find that there are only ten moral laws binding upon human beings today. I could share many texts to support my findings, but in the context of this discussion, I've explained why I believe that obedience to law cannot produce salvation.

**Q.** A number of people insist that God requires the observance of feast days.

**LW.** I know. But, they also insist that God's requirements during feast day observances are null and void. In other words, I have not found anyone who believes that we should observe the Passover feast doing the things God required at the Passover feast. How can one insist on the observance of Passover and not observe the statutes and commands concerning the observance of Passover; namely, the slaying of the Passover Lamb? These people say, "But Jesus, the Lamb, has been slain. There is no need to slay the Passover Lamb." But I ask, "what does this have to do with the requirements given in Exodus 12 and Leviticus 23? The commandments and statutes concerning the feast of Passover (and other feasts) say nothing about Jesus or about the termination of sacrifices." Some respond further by saying that there is an important difference between the command to observe the Passover feast and the command to slay the Passover Lamb. Such a claim is foolishness. There is no support for such a claim in all the Bible.

Even more, if one believes in the observance of feast days, it seems that he must also insist on the observance of circumcision because the laws given through Moses were not a "pick and choose" menu. The laws of Moses either stand intact or they lie abolished. I find that they were abolished at the cross. Besides, the observance of the laws of Moses had nothing to do with salvation anyway.

**Q.** What do you mean?

**LW.** Think about this. If God requires obedience to any law as a prerequisite for salvation at any time in history, then salvation is not a gift — nor would salvation come by faith. Salvation would come through human obedience and this is contrary to the everlasting gospel. It's that simple.

In Old Testament times, God did not require Israel to obey His commandments, statutes or laws for the purpose of salvation at all! Paul clearly points out, **"...It is impossible for the blood of bulls and goats to take away sins."** (Hebrews 10:4) In other words, the religious system given to Israel was never a means to salvation. Rather, it was God's will that Israel observe certain laws until Christ died, but the observance of those commandments, laws, statutes or judgments did not, could not, and cannot produce salvation. My claim, of course, stands in contradiction to the position of the legal opinion of the Pharisees.

**Q.** You appear to distinguish between the Ten Commandments and the laws of Moses.

**LW.** Yes, there is a great difference between God's Ten Commandment law and the laws of Moses. Moral law, the Ten Commandments, is universal and eternal. The laws of Moses were parochial and temporary. God presented both laws to Israel and they never sorted out the relationship that existed between those laws, nor did Israel sort out the relationship between man's obedience and God's righteousness that comes by faith.

**Q.** Were the laws of Moses nailed to the cross because they were limited and temporary from their beginning?

**LW.** Yes. The laws of Moses were temporary from the day they were given. They were not an extension to the moral law, the Ten Commandments. The religious statutes given through Moses defined a model of the plan of salvation. But, the model did not, indeed could not, offer salvation.

**Q.** So, you do not observe feast days. Do you observe the seventh-day Sabbath?

**LW.** God cancelled the observance of feast days at the cross. However, He did not make void the seventh-day Sabbath which the fourth commandment requires. This is not a paradoxical position if one understands the difference between God's eternal law (moral law) and the laws of Moses (educational law). But, as I've said before, the observance of any law, including the seventh-day Sabbath of the Ten Commandments, does not affect my claim and hope for salvation. Rather, the observance of law brings benefit into my life. The law reveals areas of my life that constantly need improvement. The moral law continually tests me to see if I am giving selfless service to God (first four commandments) and selfless service to man (last six commandments).

Q. Most Christians see little difference between observing the seventh-day and observing a feast day. They believe that all the laws in the Old Testament were nailed to the cross.

LW. I know they say that, but they really don't believe it. For example, if the fourth commandment (the seventh-day Sabbath) was nailed to the cross, so was the eighth commandment (Thou shalt not steal). Whatever policy we apply to one of the Ten Commandments, we have to apply to the other nine. James said, **"For whoever keeps the whole law and yet stumbles at just one point is guilty of breaking all of it."** (James 2:10)

The observance of the seventh-day sabbath is commanded in the moral code given by God, the Ten Commandments. The Ten Commandments and the laws of Moses could be compared to Federal laws and the rules of Monopoly, the Parker Brothers game. Federal laws affect day to day living, the rules of Monopoly are only important or useful when playing the game. The Ten Commandments are ten moral rules that are perpetual and therefore, eternal. God wrote the Ten Commandments with His own finger on enduring stone. God Himself spoke the Ten Commandments from Mt. Sinai because they are that important to Him. And when the time of glorification comes, God is going to change our nature so that we will be in full harmony with His laws of righteousness! (Hebrews 8:7-12)

On the other hand, the laws of Moses were not moral. They were given to Israel for educational purposes—revealing the plan of salvation. The laws of Moses were indirectly conveyed to Israel through a man. They were probably written on animal skins. They were temporary like the material they were written on. And, all the laws of Moses were made null and void at the cross because the ministry of Jesus on earth revealed everything the laws of Moses pointed to; namely, the righteousness of God. (Quoting Paul here: "a righteousness, apart from law, which was revealed in the Law and Prophets").

**Q.** In the law of Moses, God forbade the eating of unclean flesh. Do you observe this law?

**LW.** About 1,000 years before Moses, God made a sharp distinction between clean and unclean meat. (Genesis 7:2,3) God made this distinction for the benefit of man's health — not for man's salvation. God renewed the benefits of health by commanding the Israelites not to eat unclean flesh. (Leviticus 11) However, the matter of eating clean or unclean flesh was and is not a moral issue. In fact, even though God permitted the Jews to eat flesh, I find a meatless healthstyle is even better. Again I say, compliance with the principles of God's law (including health laws) is beneficial—not for the sake of meriting God's righteousness, but for earthly benefit while in this body.

**Q.** Do you discourage people from observing feast days?

**LW.** Yes, if they claim it is a prerequisite to salvation. In fact, I know several sincere people who observe feast days and I'm sure they love the Lord. However, they don't understand the gift of God's righteousness as I do. They hold that the gift of God's righteousness is granted through perfect obedience. To me, this motive is completely contrary to the teaching of Scripture and it negates God's grace. On the other hand, I understand that obedience is necessary. And the better we understand the underlying principles of God's laws, and the more we apply them in our lives, the better the quality of life! But, this is only talk about earthly benefits.

**Q.** Have you been criticized by people because you disagree with them on the obligatory nature of feast days?

**LW.** Oh yes. I'm criticized by some since I refuse to accept the sacredness of feast day observances. But, red flags always go up whenever I hear someone telling me that I must obey any law or statute in order to be right with God. (Romans 5:10) For some, the observance of feast days may be a matter of conscience; therefore, I say let them keep peace with their conscience. But the observance of feast days is not a moral issue. Period.

It's true that many believers in Christ are still at the crossroads described in Acts 15. Many still have the same problem with understanding the gift of salvation as the early believers did. However, I am fully confident that God will make known His truth to every human in due time and in one way or another, those who live by faith will accomplish all that God wants. Soon, we shall see the truth about God. Even more, those who are faith-full will see God!

**Q.** This subject is expansive. Do you think God winks at our ignorance?

**LW.** I'm certainly ignorant. I know less about God than the ant knows about man. But, I find that God judges us on the basis of what we believe to be true and what we do with the ideas we hold to be truth. So, His judgment of you and His judgment of me is not identical. He is such a marvelous God!

## P.S.

As I consider the diversity of 5.6 billion people around the world, I am impressed that four universal laws govern religion. These laws operate upon human beings and produce the following effects:

**Law # 1:** Religion, by its very nature, almost always narrows the mind to new thoughts. For this reason, 90% of the world's population stays within the religious system it was born into. Moslems tend to stay Moslems, Jews tend to stay Jews, Catholics tend to stay Catholic, etc. This law allows people to justify the mistreatment others, even the killing others, in the name of God.

**Law # 2:** Religion, by its very nature, limits the investigation of ideas that might expose a faulty belief. For this reason: Moslems and Catholics have not cancelled a doctrinal position held in error for more than a 1000 years. The same is also true for contemporary denominations.

**Law # 3:** Religion, by its very nature, encompasses a body of knowledge that is larger than most of its members can understand. For this reason, most laity do not question the origin or foundation of their beliefs; rather, they turn to those regarded as authority and accept whatever they say (more or less). Religious leaders, knowing this, establish their own publishing houses.

**Law # 4**: No one can live without religion. Every person is born with an inherited need for the elements of religion. And, in some form, they are manifested in each person. The basic elements of religion are:

1. Admiration of someone or something greater
2. Submission to someone or something greater
3. Association with others loving the same someone or something

Religion, by its very nature, has compelling power for good and bad. But, religion has blinded billions of people to the properties of divine love. People end up worshiping religion instead of God. So, in these last days, God will not only reveal His love and truth through the preaching of the 144,000, He will demonstrate His love through His people in the days ahead. The saints will love their enemies as God loved us while we were still enemies. (John 13:35; Romans 5:10) Love is the ultimate distinction between truth and error. Hatred does not come from God. The coming demonstration of love will be powerful and compelling, but the power of love will only harden the heart if it doesn't win it.

To reach every person with the beauty of His gospel, God will soon break up the elaborate infrastructures of all religious systems on earth. Everyone is going to hear a gospel that runs contrary to their religion. What will cause 5.6 billion people to give due consideration to such a gospel? The trumpets of Revelation will arouse the interest of all people so that they can hear of the simplicity and beauty of the free offer of *Christ's* righteousness. So, keep an eye on 1994-1998. Keep your focus on Jesus. Promised events will soon begin.

# Supplemental Bible Study Helps

## Video & Audio Tapes

We record each seminar. Please call for information on the latest seminars.

## Books

1. *The Revelation of Jesus* This volume of 346 pages serves as a primary textbook for our seminars. The book not only addresses coming events, it presents a historical setting for understanding how the prophecies operate. It also contains several diagrams and charts on Daniel and Revelation.

2. **Day Star Newsletter** Our monthly newsletter usually contains Bible studies on topics that relate to current issues and/or the prophetic stories found in Daniel and Revelation. Some remaining back issues are available.

3. *18 End-Time Bible Prophecies* This book is a verse by verse explanation of the 18 apocalyptic prophecies found in Daniel and Revelation. It is written in a parallel format with text from the Bible. 282 pages.

4. *Warning! Revelation is about to be fulfilled* This 200 page book contains a summary of coming events. Read today what newspapers will print tomorrow. More than 125,000 are now in print. Editions of this book are also available in Spanish and large print.

**To order materials call or write:**

**Wake Up America Seminars, Inc.**
**P.O. Box 273**
**Bellbrook, Ohio 45305**
**(513) 848-3322**

Call between 9:00 am and 4:00 pm Eastern Time, Monday - Thursday for prices, availability and quantity discounts. Visa, Mastercard and Discover accepted.